Len Deighton

BLITZKRIEG

From the Rise of Hitler to the Fall of Dunkirk

With a Foreword by
General WALTHER K. NEHRING, aD
formerly Heinz Guderian's Chief of Staff

Alfred A. Knopf New York

THIS IS A BORZOI BOOK
PUBLISHED BY ALFRED A. KNOPF, INC.

Manufactured in the United States of America

"How good bad reasons and bad music sound when we march against an enemy."

—NIETZSCHE

Contents

Illustrations

PLATES

FIGURES

TABLES

Acknowledgments

My primary thanks must go to A. J. P. Taylor, who gave me the encouragement to begin this work. Thanks also to Walther Nehring, who was in 1940 chief of staff to Heinz Guderian. He has given me great help through all the many years it has taken to complete this account.

The Imperial War Museum in London, in particular the Department of Printed Books and Department of Documents, has given me the enormous friendly help for which they are well known. In Germany Hubert Meyer loaned me precious maps, notes, and photographs, and was most helpful. I also record my thanks to the many German societies and associations which helped me find men with memories of the battles, in particular Kyffhäuserbund and Kameradschaftsbund 6.Pz.Div. Individual thanks go to Willy Siegmueller and Wilhelm Damm for the loan of printed material otherwise unobtainable.

In Holland, Major Adrian van Vliet, of the Dutch Army Historical Department, gave me a great deal of his time and helped me with translations too. In the United States, General T. Timothy read a draft of my text and made many helpful suggestions.

I would also like to record my gratitude for the enormous amount of work done at Jonathan Cape Ltd by Tony Colwell not only over the text but in arranging all the illustrated material for the book. In this respect Denis Bishop must be thanked for the drawings as well as the great technical knowledge he contributed to the project. For permission to reproduce the photographs in the book I acknowledge the Army Historical Section of the Dutch archives LAS/BLS Koninklijke Landmacht (Plates 30 and 33); Bilderdienst Süddeutscher Verlag (3, 14, 15, 16, 21, 22, 24, 28, 29, 60); Bundesarchiv (18, 25, 36); E.C.P.

Armées, France (49 and 56); the Imperial War Museum, London (31, 32, 35, 46, 53, 55, 59); Keystone Press Agency (4, 9, 10, 11, 19, 24, 27, 34, 52, 57); the Mansell Collection (45 and 62); Military Archive and Research Services, London (58); Popperfoto (1, 2, 6, 7, 8, 12, 20, 26, 44, 48, 51); the Radio Times Hulton Picture Library (5, 13, 54, 61); the Robert Hunt Picture Library (43, 47, 50); and the John Topham Picture Library (17 and 38). Not the least of my thanks go to "Georgie" Remer for copy editing a complete text.

My thanks as usual must also go to Ray Hawkey for giving me a wealth of good ideas, to Ellenor Handley for typing and retyping various drafts of the book, and to Anton Felton for working behind the scenes.

—Len Deighton

Author's Note

Certain German military terms are used throughout this book to help distinguish German forces from those of the Allies, for which English usage is employed. Although German words are explained in the text, it may be helpful for readers to have an easy reference to the following commonly used German abbreviations:

Flak	Fliegerabwehrkanone (Antiaircraft artillery)
Kwk	Kampfwagenkanone (Tank gun)
OKH	Oberkommando des Heeres (High Command of the Army)
OKW	Oberkommando des Wehrmacht (High Command of all Armed Forces—army, navy, and air force)
Pak	Panzerabwehrkanone (Antitank gun)
Pz	Panzer (Armor, armor plate)
PzKw	Panzerkampfwagen (Tank)
7.Pz.Div	Panzerdivision (7th Armored Division)

Foreword

by General Walther K. Nehring, aD

In the 1920s, when the construction of rotor-driven ships was still being debated, the German Ministry of Defense arranged a trial run on the coastal waters at Stettin, for the benefit of officers and officials with an interest in technical developments. Among those who watched the trials was Heinz Guderian, then a major on the General Staff, 2nd (Stettin) Division. I was serving with the Defense Ministry at the time, and traveled down to the trials from Berlin.

Guderian and I had never met before. I still clearly recall that first impression he made on me. With his vital interest in technical matters, he stood out from the rest and would freely approach any officer whom he thought might share his ideas. It was in this way that I came to know him.

Then, in 1932, I was attached as First General Staff Officer to the Inspectorate of Motorized Forces, commanded by Major-General Oswald Lutz, whose chief of staff was none other than Guderian, by now OTL/Colonel. I served under him and under the subsequent chief of staff, Oberst Friedrich Paulus, right up to the end of September 1936, and was therefore at the very center of the whole development of the new panzer force.*

During those years I got to know my three superiors extremely well and was able to study them closely. Lutz was a man with great technical know-how, the father of motorized army units, while Guderian was the creator of the Panzerforce. As a man Guderian was a perfect complement to the older and more judicious General Lutz, who frequently shielded the impulsive younger officer against the

* See my book *Die Geschichte der deutschen Panzerwaffe, 1916–45.*

attacks which he so often brought upon himself when discussing professional matters.

With his appointment in 1938 as Commander in Chief Motorized Forces, Guderian seemed to reach his goal, yet it was not until the war that Guderian's genius in the creation of a panzer force became fully apparent and made him famous throughout the world, a fame which has lasted to this day.

However exaggerated it may sound, it was Guderian's revolutionary organizational skills and tactical thinking which transformed the whole military situation in 1940. He had his own ideas on the art of surprise, believing always in being ready before his opponent and then presenting him with a fait accompli. Guderian had a wide knowledge of technical matters and was deeply impressed by the range of possibilities opened up by developments in modern technology. His sound basic knowledge of radio-telegraphy, acquired during his service with a signals unit in 1912 and 1913, was also to stand him in good stead in the campaign of 1940. Added to this gift for organization, as well as for leadership, was his ability as an inspired teacher who enjoyed great popularity among those under his command, as well as a model family life. In military operations Guderian always believed in being at the front so that he could take personal control whenever necessary. His chief of staff would deputize for him with his tactical support staff in temporary headquarters which could be moved as required.

There can be no doubt that Guderian played a decisive part in the victory over France in 1940. It was his task to capture the Ardennes, and the areas bordering on the river Meuse, in a single thrust and then quickly make room for the deployment of the two mobile columns following close behind. Although he achieved this quickly, he was forced by an overcautious High Command into making unnecessary stops, first at the narrow bridgehead at Sedan on 15 May, again at the river Oise on 17 May, and finally just outside Dunkirk on 24 May.

The panzer successes were particularly notable as they were gained against an army which basked in the prestige of the victory and glory of 1918. In 1940 the French Army was still considered the most powerful in the world. Allied forces were stronger in terms of armor and superior in numbers to the Germans (3,376 Allied tanks against 2,680 German tanks). What the Allies lacked were new ideas. Despite what they had seen happen in the Polish campaign, the Allies still relied on the Maginot Line for protection and thought only in terms of defense and a slow, drawn-out campaign. In the event, Allied tank formations were split wide open as they were forced to spread themselves along the full extent of the front and were made to follow the pace of the infantry, instead of consolidating to fight a concentrated campaign.

With the forces on both sides fully engaged in heavy fighting, Guderian's corps, with air support from the Luftwaffe, succeeded in crossing the Meuse and establishing a bridgehead far enough forward to enable an immediate advance westward. On 15 May, however, orders were received from the panzer group commander, General von Kleist, to stay in position. Any further advance had to wait until reserves could be brought up in sufficient strength from the rear.

Guderian immediately protested vehemently to General von Kleist that they should take advantage of the areas abandoned by the enemy to carry the thrust still deeper. At this time, too, 2.Pz.Div found a set of French orders which contained the words "We must finally put a stop to this flood of German tanks." These orders showed how critical the situation had become for the French and added weight to Guderian's argument for continuing the advance deep into enemy territory.

Kleist finally gave way. Guderian could advance next day, 16 May, with 1.Pz.Div and 2.Pz.Div, but 10.Pz.Div was to remain in position for use in the fighting around Stonne. On 16 May Guderian and his staff arrived in Montcornet and met up with the 6.Pz.Div of General Kempff's corps approaching from the right. Close contact was maintained between Guderian and his 1.Pz.Div and 2.Pz.Div at all times.

Guderian had formed a firm conviction, based on previous strategic discussions, that they should push forward rapidly toward the Somme estuary on the Channel coast. The successful advances on 16 May now strengthened him in his belief.

But on the morning of 17 May General von Kleist announced that he would be flying in for a conference and that no further moves forward were to be made in the meantime.

The general arrived punctually. A heated but one-sided "discussion" took place during which Guderian asked to be relieved of his command immediately! Kleist's reproaches to Guderian reached their climax when he alleged that Guderian had deliberately chosen to ignore the plans of the High Command. Rundstedt, the Commander of Army Group A, eventually found a way out of the impasse between the two men by claiming that the order had originally come from Hitler and therefore *had* to be obeyed, though "reconnaissance in strength" was quite permissible as long as the headquarters remained in position. Nevertheless, a whole day, 17 May, had been lost and a great deal of personal unrest stirred up.

Despite this delay, Guderian's divisions reached the Channel coast on 20 May. The German Army had thus achieved its first goal—what Churchill later described as the "sickle-cut clean through the Allied forces." As a result the Luftwaffe was free to carry out raids which rendered the Allied-held sea ports of Boulogne and Calais useless for transport in or out. Dunkirk thus became the crucial port for the Allied forces.

On the evening of 22 May, Kleist decided to use Guderian's corps, with its 1.Pz.Div and 2.Pz.Div, for the attack on these three ports, but held back 10.Pz.Div in reserve, instead of letting it carry straight on at what was clearly a critical juncture.

Despite fierce Allied resistance, Guderian's 1.Pz.Div succeeded in establishing bridgeheads on the northern bank of the Aa Canal on the morning of 24 May. As other German forces were now approaching from the west, it was clearly possible to close off the Allies' last possible exit in time to stop the evacuation en masse of French and English troops from Belgium.

Then once again Hitler himself rashly took a hand in the matter. Having decided to save the panzer forces for the second phase of the campaign, he sent a personal order to Army Group A on 24 May, without consulting the Commander in Chief of the Army, stating that "no mobile units should proceed beyond a line drawn between Lens and Gravelines."

It was Hitler's notorious "order to halt" which allowed the Allies to evacuate their troops to England and, from them, to build the invasion army of 1944. With this order Hitler, the amateur, imagined that he could establish his role as Supreme Army Commander. In fact he simply destroyed the carefully considered plans of the German military command and gained merely an "ordinary victory," with none of the decisive results which might have been achieved had the British Expeditionary Force been captured.

As Len Deighton's book clearly demonstrates, this was the crucial and fundamental turning point in the war between Britain and Germany of 1939–1945. From the moment of crossing the Meuse and achieving that major breakthrough, it was essential for German forces to forge rapidly ahead, so denying the Allies any chance to organize their defenses. With the British Army trapped and the French on the run, it might have been possible to sue for a quick end to the war in the West.

Düsseldorf, March 1979

Hitler and His Army

"[Hitler] said it probably wouldn't harm the young fellows any if they had to enlist again, for that hadn't harmed anybody, for nobody knows anymore that the young ought to keep their mouths shut in the presence of elders, for everywhere the young lack discipline . . . Then he went through all the points in the programme, at which he received a lot of applause. The hall was very full. A man who called Herr Hitler an idiot was calmly kicked out."

—REPORT OF NAZI MEETING, Hofbräuhaus, Munich,
28 August 1920—from *Hitler*, by J. C. Fest

In modern times, war has usually brought accelerated social change. The Americans who survived the Civil War were different men from the "colonials" who had started fighting it. The Franco-Prussian War of 1870 changed Europeans from farmers into factory workers. But between 1914 and 1918 war changed the world at a pace that made precious history seem leisurely. The growth of literacy, governmental supervision of industry, conscription of men and women, and successful revolution, were each part of the legacy of the First World War. The weapons of that war were also a measure of changing technology, and the effects of this change were as far-reaching as the social changes.

In 1914 Europe went to war with armies designed for colonial "policing." The cavalry was armed with lances; uniforms were bright and buttons shiny. The infantry was more suited to eighteenth-century battles than to those of the twentieth. So were the generals.

Yet by 1918 a frightening array of modern weapons was in use: flamethrowers, four-engined bombers, machine pistols, gas shells, and tanks. New methods of waging war were tried. The European nations had become dependent upon overseas trade. German submarines sank Allied merchant ships on sight, and almost brought Britain to surrender. The British navy stopped ships bound for German ports and Germany came to the brink of mass starvation. After the war the Associated Medical Services of Germany estimated that 763,000 Germans had died of starvation as a direct result of the Royal Navy's blockade. Most Germans regarded it as a barbaric way of waging war on women and children, and resentment lingered in the German mind, and indeed still remains.

Germany in Defeat

There were many reasons for the final collapse of Germany in 1918. With loved ones starving at home and no foreseeable victory, German fighting men became demoralized. Even the German advances of that spring played a part in this, for when the Germans overran Allied rear areas they found abundant food and drink, fine leather boots, sheepskin jerkins, and a great deal of military equipment. It was a cruel contradiction of the stories told about a Britain on the point of starvation and surrender.

For General Erich Ludendorff, First Quartermaster General of the German Army and the most powerful man in Germany, the spring advances brought a more personal blow. He found the body of his stepson, shot down on the first day of the offensive.

By the summer of 1918 there were a million American soldiers in France and more were arriving at the rate of a quarter million each month. The Germans were now fighting the whole world.

To compound Ludendorff's problems, an epidemic of Spanish influenza caused his armies to report that they were too weak to repulse Allied attacks. The epidemic was affecting the Allied troops too, but the malnutrition of the Germans and the way in which the Allied armies were being constantly reinforced by soldiers from the United States meant that the Germans suffered most. Soon the Spanish influenza epidemic was to kill more people than did the war itself.

In 1918 Allied armies were using the newly invented tank in ever more skillful ways. On 8 August their resources were enough to put about 600 British and French tanks into the battle of Amiens. Light tanks and armored cars penetrated the German rear and attacked artillery positions, a divisional headquarters, and even a corps staff far behind the lines.

The German front did not collapse completely because the Allies had nothing with which to exploit the breakthrough. The Germans put their front line together again and even managed some vigorous counterattacks, but no one could doubt that it was the beginning of the end. Ludendorff himself wrote that as German reinforcements arrived they were jeered at as "black-legs" and asked why they had come to prolong the war.

"August 8th was the black day of the German Army in this war," wrote Ludendorff, and on 11 August Kaiser Wilhelm II, the German Emperor, said that the war must be ended and told his Secretary of State to begin peace talks.

The British official history says, "It pleased the Germans to attribute their defeat in the field to the tank. The excuse will not bear examination." Major General J. F. C. Fuller, tank pioneer and military historian, disagrees strongly with the official history, stressing that the morale effect of the tank gave it its importance. He selects— to support this argument—these telling words spoken by a German prisoner: "The officers and men in many cases come to consider the approach of tanks a sufficient explanation for not fighting. Their sense of duty is sufficient to make them fight against infantry, but if tanks appear, many feel they are justified in surrendering." As we shall see, these words echoed through France in May 1940.

Kaiser Wilhelm thought better of his decision to open peace talks, and his two senior officers, Ludendorff and Field Marshal Paul von Hindenburg, comforted each other with false hopes of a last-minute miracle. But it did not materialize. Instead, Ludendorff endured the agonies of failure and watched his army in its death throes. This, the death of his stepson—and his wife's inconsolable reaction to it—and the strain of overwork turned Ludendorff's mind. By the time of the surrender he was mentally deranged.

These three—the Kaiser, Field Marshal von Hindenburg, and General Ludendorff—were, respectively, the most senior in rank, the most exalted, and the most powerful men in Germany. They had inflicted a military dictatorship on the country but displayed no skill in statesmanship. Their final error of judgment was to wait too long before opening up peace talks. By now the army was at the end of its strength and the Germans had little choice but to accept any terms that their powerful enemies offered. Rather than suffer the humiliation at first hand, the army sent a civilian to ask for a cease-fire.

The American President, Woodrow Wilson, had already told the Germans that, unless they got rid of "the military authorities and monarchical autocrats," the Allies would demand complete surrender. In October 1918 Prince Maximilian, heir to the small provincial Grand Duchy of Baden, was chosen to assume the duties of Chancellor and Prime Minister of Prussia, as part of the transfer of power back to civil government.

At this final hour, Ludendorff suddenly had second thoughts about asking for peace and supported his plans to fight to the death with nonsensical statistics. It was enough to make the Kaiser regain his optimism. But Prince Max rejected their demands, saying, "The desire to perish with honour may well occur to the individual but the responsible statesman must accept that the broad mass of the people has the right soberly to demand to live rather than to die in glory." Prince

Max repeatedly advised the Kaiser to abdicate, and, when he did not do so, simply announced the abdication anyway, adding that the Crown Prince, Wilhelm's heir, had also renounced the throne.

Then, in one of the most casual transfers of power in modern history, Prince Max walked up to Friedrich Ebert, leader of the Social Democratic Party, and said, "Herr Ebert, I commit the German Empire to your keeping."

The Kaiser, who had so proudly led his country into this terrible war, now packed his many bags and ordered the imperial train to the Dutch frontier. In Holland he went to the chateau of Count Godard Bentinck and asked for a cup of tea—"strong English tea"—and shelter. It was a tradition of the Knights of the Order of St. John that one gave sanctuary to a brother. But finding space for Kaiser Wilhelm's retinue was more difficult; most of them returned to Germany.

The Spartacus Revolt

On 9 November 1918, the day on which Prince Max handed over the German Empire to Ebert, Karl Liebknecht, a forty-seven-year-old lawyer, onetime member of the Reichstag, and now Communist revolutionary, stood on the steps of the imperial palace and proclaimed a soviet of workers and soldiers. A red flag was hoisted overhead. With Rosa Luxemburg—an intellectual theorist, as compared with Liebknecht the agitator—he formed the *Spartakusbund*. This name, with its historical reference to the revolt of slaves in the ancient world, provides a clue to the nature of this Communist group. Idealistic, intellectual, and inflexible, its admiration of the Soviet Union matched only its hatred of the German generals and the rich. But it had no real policy that was not the subject of endless bickering. On 10 November, while the Spartakusbund was meeting in Berlin to adopt formally the new name *Spartakus Gruppe*, Ebert—already denounced by Liebknecht as an enemy of the revolution—was worrying about the more practical problems of food distribution, keeping the railways going, and upholding law and order.

While Ebert's Socialists were declaring an amnesty for political prisoners and granting complete freedom of the press, speech, and assembly, the Spartakus Gruppe were distributing leaflets declaiming "All power to the workers and soldiers" and "Down with the Ebert government." Liebknecht's news sheet, *The Red Flag*, was eagerly read everywhere and the demonstrations were well attended. Uncompromising as always, the Spartakus Gruppe was determined to see the sort of revolution that had transformed Tsarist Russia.

Friedrich Ebert, the new Chancellor (later to become President of the so-called Weimar Republic) was a moderate who had lost two sons in the war. He had no desire for violent revolution and no immediate desire to establish a republic, though he was determined to be rid of Kaiser Wilhelm and the Crown Prince. Ebert would probably have accepted Prince Max as Regent, and such a move would no doubt have been welcomed by a large part of the German electorate. Yet Kaiser Wilhelm's refusal to abdicate gave strength to the republican movements and was the main cause of the end of the monarchy. A monarchy would have provided an unending obstacle to the tyrant and a stability that Germany badly needed.

Ebert was attacked by men of the Right, who believed that only a return to military rule could provide the discipline and planning needed to make Germany prosper. More bitter were the attacks from the Leftists, who called him a traitor to Socialist ideals. Liebknecht was a vociferous enemy, whose middle-class background and privileged education persuaded him that extremist measures would bring simple solutions. Ebert, on the other hand, had a working-class background. He was a cautious pragmatist who knew that German workers were more concerned with hunger and unemployment than with polemics.

Germans knew well the feeling of hunger. Fearful lest they change their minds about the peace treaty, the Allies continued to apply the blockade of German ports long after the fighting ended. More than one million noncombatants had died in Germany and Austria in the last two years of the war. When the Armistice came, things got worse. There was no more food coming from the territories the Germans had occupied and now the Baltic ports were also closed. On 13 December, a month after the cease-fire, the Germans asked for essential goods to be allowed through the blockade. These included wheat, fats, condensed milk, and medical supplies. Permission was refused. In Bohemia in February 1919, 20 per cent of the babies were born dead and another 40 per cent died within one month. In March 1919, the general commanding the British Army of the Rhine reported to London that his soldiers found the sight of starving children unendurable.

On Ebert's doorstep that Christmas was an even more pressing problem. About 3,000 mutinous sailors from Kiel, the base of the High Seas Fleet, were demanding 125,000 marks from the government. Trouble had started in the German Navy's High Seas Fleet on 27 October 1918, when its commanders ordered it to sea for one last glorious battle. All the battleships and small cruisers were suddenly afflicted with mechanical trouble that prevented them from leaving. Marines moved in and 1,000 sailors were arrested. Some ships were deployed to fire upon the mutineers, but it made no difference. On the battleships *Thüringen* and *Helgoland* red flags were hoisted.

The next Sunday, 3 November, in Kiel, there was a public demonstration on behalf of the arrested sailors. A military patrol fired on the marchers, and by the following day systematic disobedience had become a revolution, complete with sailors' councils and red flags. This was not a result of exhortation by Liebknecht and Luxemburg; they were as surprised as the admirals. By 6 November the mutineers were in control of the whole coastal region, including the cities Lübuck, Hamburg, Bremen, and Wilhelmshaven, as well as some garrison towns inland. And yet the war was still going on, the ceasefire several days away. Troops arriving in Kiel to suppress the mutineers joined them instead. In Berlin the Spartakus Gruppe was gathering strength and preparing a congress to take place immediately after Christmas.

The law-and-order issue was crucial to Ebert's political survival. So far, his power had been unchallenged. Even Rosa Luxemburg admitted that the far Left had failed to win the masses away from Ebert. But a failure of law and order would certainly provoke a swift reaction from the middle classes.

Ebert's Berlin police were now under the command of Emil Eichhorn, who had simply gone to the police headquarters in Alexanderplatz and, without opposition, declared himself police president, releasing 650 prisoners who had been arrested during recent demonstrations. Eichhorn gave no help to Ebert in the matter of the mutinous sailors, and said that his policemen were neutral in that conflict.

The sailors had by now thoroughly plundered and vandalized the royal palace. They had received 125,000 marks in return for a promise to reduce their numbers and move into the *Marstall*, or royal stables, but they had failed to do so. Now they were demanding another 80,000 marks as a Christmas bonus. Ebert said he would pay, but this time they had to evacuate the palace before they got the money. On hearing this, the sailors broke into Ebert's Chancellery and would let no one in or out. They manned the telephone switchboard and took three officials hostage.

It was then that the besieged Ebert took the decision that was to sever him from the Left forever. He used the secret telephone link that connected his office to the army HQ in Kassel and asked the army for help.

Even after the soldiers had set up their artillery and machine guns, the sailors refused to move out, having heard that more sailors were on their way to help them. The battle was a short one and soon white flags came out. Thirty sailors were dead and about a hundred injured.

During the shooting, Karl Liebknecht's Spartakus Gruppe—which had given birth to the German Communist Party—was spreading the word that the army had started a counterrevolution. It was enough to bring crowds of men, women, and children to the royal palace and soon the soldiers withdrew in confusion.

Ebert dismissed the police president. Liebknecht had a response for this too. Having told the population not to cooperate with Ebert, Liebknecht then staged a demonstration to protest the dismissal, describing it as an act of provocation directed at the workers.

The demonstration was enormous—some said three quarters of a million people gathered—but as in all such demonstrations, it is difficult to guess how many were merely sightseers. However, it triggered the extreme Left into making a bid for power. Liebknecht and his followers proclaimed a general strike and distributed guns. It was the beginning of "Spartacus Week."

Irresolute and uncoordinated, Liebknecht's followers were successful in seizing some government buildings, most important newspapers, and the railway. A group attempting to occupy the Ministry of War were politely told that they must get some sort of written authority from their revolutionary leaders. They never came back. The soldiers and sailors in Berlin for the most part ignored the whole business. Soon the Socialist Minister for the Army gathered together enough loyal soldiers and some of the newly formed militia to turn the revolutionaries out of the buildings they had taken. There had been no real support for the Communists and they submitted meekly. Liebknecht and Rosa Luxemburg were arrested, quietly murdered by soldiers, and thrown into a canal.

Both sides withdrew and began to count the cost. Perhaps, at the time, no one concerned realized that the most important outcome was a permanent split between the Communists and Socialists. This division continued even when the Nazis became powerful, and it prevented any unified opposition to them.

The Spartacus Revolt had had little hope of success. The Communists were hated by the middle classes and distrusted by the larger part of the workers. On stage, Bertolt Brecht's portrayal of these events in his first play, *Drums in the Night*, includes a song "In November I was Red, yes Red. But it's January now." It was an epitaph for the revolt.

The Spartacists had no organized plan of takeover or disciplined force to hold on to what they got. They thought revolution would be easy, but they were wrong. The military mutinies in the north, which later spread throughout the country, persuaded the Left that the soldiers and sailors were on their side. It showed the total failure of the civilians at home to understand the mood of the fighting men. What the politicians thought was an army ready to die for Red revolution was just a collection of men without specific political aims other than getting out of uniform and going home. For the most part, the mutineers were good-natured and nonviolent. As a revolutionary force, they were nonrunners.

The Left made heroes of antimilitarist agitators and conscientious objectors who had stayed at home while millions of German sons and husbands were fighting at the front. The Right devoted its propaganda to restoring the pride of the latter. Inevitably this paid off in votes.

And yet the Right, too, had mistaken the mood of the soldiers. The misunderstanding dated from the time that the army withdrew from occupied territories as ordered by the Armistice. There was a deadline to meet, and such large-scale troop movements presented problems far beyond the capabilities of the newly elected soldiers' councils. By common consent the officers with staff training took over and their orders were not questioned. The weather was perfect, and the marching columns and transport services kept to the strict timetables. No one could fail to be impressed by the way in which Germany's armies returned to the Fatherland in good discipline and obedient to the commands of officers and NCOs.

But many hasty conclusions had to be revised. Content to be a disciplined army if that was what got them home quickly, the soldiers did not want to become a peace-keeping force for the new government. The fighting men who had marched through Berlin's Brandenburger Tor in December 1918 and been greeted and congratulated by the Republic's first Chancellor simply kept walking and went home. By Christmas the German Army in the Berlin area could muster only 150 soldiers.

Soon afterward, before the Spartacus Revolt, Ebert was invited to Zossen to see a new sort of military force that was being recruited —the *Freikorps*. It was to influence both the Nazi Party and the new German Army.

The Freikorps

There were plenty of German soldiers who had no great desire to return to civilian life, especially to the unemployment, hunger, and hardship they saw everywhere. As the war ended, a Major Kurt von Schleicher, later to become Defense Minister and Chancellor, proposed the formation of a new volunteer force to consist only of chosen veteran soldiers. They would be equipped with motor transport and organized into mobile "storm battalions." The plan was approved. The men were recruited secretly and signed short-term contracts, renewable every month. Influenced by the soldiers' councils that the rebellious soldiers had created, the Freikorps would allow its soldiers to vote for representatives, who would voice complaints about pay, leave, and even complaints about the officers.

It was 4,000 such well-disciplined soldiers that Ebert was taken to see on 4 January 1919. He was told that this Freikorps was at his disposal as a peace-keeping force. By 9 January, the Freikorps was fighting against the Spartacists in the streets of Berlin. The forces of the Left were defeated, and when the elections were held on 19 January, Ebert's Social Democrats won a large plurality—38 per cent of the total vote. In the first days of March, the Communists again tried to seize power. Sailors besieged police headquarters, and workers attacked police stations. The Ebert government declared martial law, and Freikorps units were sent into action. The uprising was put down in a series of bloody clashes.

The first Freikorps unit had been financed by special funds available to the German General Staff, but now the Ebert government financed them and recruiting posters appeared everywhere. The theme of the recruitment message—"Don't let Germany become a laughing-stock"—provides a revealing insight into what most troubled the German public at this time.

Schleicher's ideas about the Freikorps came at about the same time that Germany's eastern armies were asking for permission to recruit more men. A full-scale war continued along these eastern frontiers as Germany's neighbors tried to occupy more territory. The Germans fought back with the full approval of the Allies, who had ordered that the German armies in the Ukraine and Poland and the Eighth Army in the Baltic must remain in place as a barrier against the expansion of Russia's new army. But as news of the Armistice came, these German troops also wanted to go home and German resistance weakened.

The Freikorps, on the other hand, was to be a well-paid force dedicated to the defense of the homeland and unsympathetic to Communist ideas. Ebert's acceptance of this force produced another wave of bitter criticism from his left-wing allies, some of whom wanted nothing to do with the Freikorps even if the Republic perished as a result. But Ebert remained the pragmatist. He resisted cries for the suppression of the Freikorps just as earlier he had resisted a series of measures that would have changed the army beyond recognition.*

Vociferous objections to the Freikorps meant that the German Army's High Command had to be discreet in the administration and control of these dispersed units. To a large extent the Freikorps came under the individual control of each unit commander. Usually the commander was a tough, idiosyncratic war hero who controlled his men by strength of personality. Such men often gave their name to formations—and units were as varied as their leaders. There were well over a hundred Freikorps units, in all about a quarter of a million volunteers of a largely middle-class bias. At least one company was composed entirely of ex-officers, and in others there were many students. Not everyone was a volunteer. To boost initial recruitment, the final call-up of conscripts was assigned to the Freikorps.

The self-sufficiency of Freikorps units gave them the sort of independence and adaptability that was to become a characteristic of Hitler's army. They had inherited the ideas of the *Stosstrupp* (shock troop) formations which Germany had developed in the final months of the war. Those shock, or storm, troops had been mixed units of infantry and engineers using light machine guns, flamethrowers, light mortars, and also small artillery pieces that infantrymen could manhandle into position for use at close quarters.

Now the Freikorps modified the techniques of 1918. Called upon to fight guerrillas in open country, they used cavalry and armored cars. To dispose of the revolutionaries they quickly learned the business of street fighting. It was this fighting by the Freikorps that marked the change from the old style of trench warfare to the fluid breakthrough tactics of what came to be called *Blitzkrieg* (lightning war). So it was not surprising to find here, on Germany's eastern frontier, two men who were to fashion the new German Army. The Chief of Staff of Frontier Protection Service, North, where the most bitter

---

* The Supreme Command was to come under the authority of the soldiers' councils, all insignia of rank were to be abolished, troops were to elect their officers and demote them by vote. All these ideas, and many more, were adopted by a large majority at the 6 December 1918 congress of associated political parties. Ebert ignored these specific directives because he believed that such changes would make the army ineffective and mean the death of the Republic.

fighting took place, was Generalmajor Hans von Seeckt. The IA, the first staff officer, of the Freikorps's ruthless and formidable "Iron Division" was a young captain named Heinz Guderian.

Adolf Hitler

With that clarity of vision that only hindsight confers, we see all the ingredients of the great tragedy coming together. This highly disciplined nation—by 1900 the greatest industrial power in Europe—was now disintegrating.

The Ebert government, forced to obey the orders of the conquerors, was described throughout the land as a bunch of treacherous collaborators. The bitter revolutionary violence of the Left clashed with the organized violence of the paramilitary Freikorps. Instability and the threat of communism frightened investors, kept factories idle and men unemployed. Violence in the streets made the middle classes search for new political solutions. And the men of the General Staff bided their time and looked for new allies.

Into this unstable mixture one more ingredient had still to be stirred. A blinded Austrian corporal who spent the Armistice in a military hospital at Pasewalk, Pomerania, heard the news of final defeat and wept for the first time since he had stood at his mother's grave. Later Adolf Hitler was to say that this was the moment when he decided to enter politics.

Descended from a family of Austrian peasants, Adolf's father had distinguished himself by becoming a uniformed customs official. Adolf was the third child of his fifty-year-old father's third marriage. He was born on 20 April 1889 in a *Gasthof*, or tavern, in Braunau am Inn, an Austrian border town, 31 miles north of Salzburg.

At Linz High School his academic record was poor. Up until his final days in the Chancellery bunker, Hitler continued to complain of his early teachers and the way they tried to crush his individuality and mold his thinking. One teacher remembered him as a gifted and intelligent pupil who lacked industry. Perhaps it was the hope of escaping school discipline that helped form his ambition to be an artist or architect. Those ambitions were dashed when the Vienna Academy of Fine Arts rejected his entrance application.

Hitler's homeland was not the Austria of today but Austria-Hungary, a nation larger than Germany, in which Czechs, Slovaks, Serbs, Croats, Poles, and Ukrainians clamored and agitated for more power. It was Hitler's dislike of these "foreigners"—and perhaps his rejection by the Vienna Academy—that prompted him to cross the border to Munich, in Germany, rather than be drafted into the Austrian Army.

To prevent the Austrians finding him, Hitler registered with the German police in Munich as a "stateless person." But eventually the Austrian authorities tracked him down. On 18 January 1914 a Munich police official arrested him and took him to the Austrian Consulate. From there he was sent to Salzburg, in Austria, to enter the army, but military doctors rejected him as too weak and unfit even for service with an auxiliary unit.* Hitler went back to Munich.

In these months, immediately prior to the outbreak of the First World War, Hitler lived in Munich's bohemian world. He sold his sketches and paintings, mixed with intellectuals and crackpots, and sometimes spent a night in a doss house, but he was by no means penniless, as his tax records reveal. His income has been described as equal to that of a provincial lawyer.

War for Germany began on 1 August and Hitler was swept along in the hysteria that all Europe shared. Bavaria was still a kingdom within the German Empire. By 3 August, Hitler had written to the King of Bavaria requesting permission for himself, an Austrian, to join the Bavarian Army. He was assigned to the List Regiment. It took its name from its first commander and was composed mostly of volunteers, many of them students and intellectuals.

After only ten weeks' training the regiment was put into the ferocious first battle of Ypres and suffered terrible casualties. By December 1914 Hitler had been awarded the Iron Cross, 2nd Class. Later he got a regimental award for courage in the face of the enemy, and in August 1918 he was awarded the Iron Cross, 1st Class, a medal seldom given to men below officer rank.

Corporal—or more precisely, Private First Class—Hitler was employed as a runner, taking messages from regimental HQ to front-line positions. It was a dangerous job. Other soldiers believed Hitler enjoyed a charmed life. It was a belief many shared after the Führer had survived the attempts on his life that were to come.

Hitler kept apart from his fellows but was not unpopular. He read books whenever the circumstances permitted and claimed to have carried a volume of Schopenhauer during his front-line service.

Temporarily blinded, by a British gas attack south of Ypres in October 1918, Hitler ended the war in the Pasewalk military hospital.

---

* In 1938, when his army occupied Austria, Hitler ordered a search for the documents that would reveal his attempts to avoid military service. But the papers were not found until 1950.

By the time he got back to Munich the Kingdom of Bavaria was no more. This dynasty that had survived 1,000 years was toppled by the theater critic of the *Müncher Post*, who proclaimed in its place a people's state. This new ruler was assassinated and soon a "soviet republic" emerged, dominated by a handful of hard-boiled revolutionaries who kept control by means of brutal repression. This short-lived period of extreme Left power became more and more unpopular, so that when the Freikorps, together with local army units, gained power by force of arms, most Bavarians welcomed the change. There remained a legacy of anti-Communist feeling that would provide Hitler and the Nazis with sympathizers in the time to come.

But at this time Hitler, thirty years old, was uncommonly apolitical. In Munich he had willingly served the short-lived Communist military command and even wore a red band on his arm. When the army and the Freikorps overthrew the Communists in May 1919, Hitler was equally cooperative. He willingly gave evidence against them before the board of inquiry that the victorious army held. So well did he do this that the army employed him as a low-grade political agent. He was recruited as part of a scheme to prevent political agitators infiltrating the *Reichsheer* (the 100,000-man army that Germany was permitted under the terms of the Versailles Treaty signed in June 1919).*

Hitler and his fellow agents were given a short indoctrination course at Munich University. Lectures in political theory, banking, economics, and other subjects gave Hitler a chance to formulate his own ideas. Until now his opinions had been an incoherent mixture of hatred of Jews, Communists, and foreigners; pride and respect for the German Army; and lofty ideas about the role of the artist in society. Now he was able to dress up his bigotry in the jargon of the college lecturer, and a natural orator emerged. So obvious was his skill at speechmaking that the army assigned him to talk to returning soldiers—mostly ex-prisoners of war—about the dangers of communism, as well as to report on local political groups.

One such group was the German Workers' Party. It had been formed by men of the local railway workshops. It was typical of many such organizations in that it was more a drinking club than a political movement. Like all secret societies it had a generous measure of mysticism and folklore and there was much talk about the purity of the German blood. Its members grumbled to each other about the

---

* The *Reichswehr* was the combined German Army and the German Navy. The army alone was called the *Reichsheer* and the navy the *Reichsmarine*. The navy was permitted 15,000 men, including 1,500 officers. The Minister to whom the service chiefs reported was the Reichswehr Minister.

Jews, about big business, about Communist atrocities, the cost of living, and the moral decline of the country. The members wanted to be a part of a classless society (which perhaps meant only that they aspired to be accepted in middle-class circles) and believed in a vague sort of socialism but could not accept the sort of Russian-led internationalism that the Left wanted. It was a common enough point of view, and it was the reconciliation of nationalism with Socialism that was later to make the Nazi (National Socialist German Workers') Party so appealing to German voters.

After some hesitation, Hitler became member No. 555 and had no difficulty in becoming committee member No. 7 immediately. He was put in charge of propaganda and recruiting. Using the typewriter provided at his barracks, he gave his new task all of his immense energies and dedication. He wrote hundreds of letters, reactivated old memberships, and made personal approaches to likely recruits. None of his fellow members had either time or inclination for such feverish activity. But his role of political spy gave Hitler almost unlimited time to work for the German Workers' Party. It was this, as much as his ideas and energy, that enabled him to become the most dynamic member of one of the very organizations he was being paid to spy on.

Not only was Hitler the organizer of the weekly meetings, which soon were drawing crowds of some 3,000, but more often than not the principal speaker too.

It was through the German Workers' Party that Hitler came to meet Dietrich Eckart, a wealthy man who was to have an immense effect upon his life. Much older than Hitler, he was a mediocre poet, dramatist, and journalist. Obsessed with an all-pervading hatred of Jews, Eckart saw in Hitler a man who could spread his perverted philosophy. Hitler was exactly right for the task. A fighting man and medal winner, he did not have the speech or the appearance of an officer. On the contrary, Hitler's accent was that of the working-class ex-soldier, not frightened to voice the crowd's bigotry, fears, and hatreds. Eckart provided coaching and encouragement, influencing Hitler's reading and improving his diction. Then he used the wide circle of people he had met as a journalist to publicize Hitler and through him the Party and its need for funds. It was Eckart (together with Ernst Röhm) who in December 1920 raised the money to buy a news-paper—the *Völkische Beobachter*—for the Party. And it was Eckart who suggested "Germany Awake!" as the Party slogan.

Eckart also introduced Hitler to the Obersalzberg in the Bavarian Alps, where Hitler went for physical and spiritual refreshment and eventually built his magnificent villa at Berchtesgaden.

In order to appeal both to the Germans who voted Nationalist and those who voted Socialist (by far the majority), the German Workers' Party was, in that same year, renamed *Nationalsozialistische Deutsche Arbeiterpartei* (NSDAP, Nationalist Socialist German Workers' Party). Conveniently, this could be shortened to Nazi (from NAtional and soZIalist).

Ernst Röhm and the Brownshirts

Hitler's curious double life, as spy against the Party and its most active member, had not made trouble for him with his army employers. On the contrary, the army and the Freikorps units which now, in uneasy alliance, controlled Bavaria, saw Hitler as a valuable ally. The man who had created the intelligence department into which Hitler had been recruited joined the German Workers' Party as member No. 623. This man, Ernst Röhm—a thickset ex-General Staff officer with a scarred face and coarse manners—was a captain in the Reichsheer who acted as political adviser to the local Freikorps commander. Captain Röhm described himself as immature and wicked and made no secret of his homosexual activities. But Röhm had proved a fearless soldier in the war and afterwards had been entrusted with the task of organizing secret arms dumps all over Bavaria. Röhm was impressed by Hitler's activities and speeches and became close friends with him, one of the few who used the familiar "du" form of address. Röhm was able to supply Hitler with both finance and guns. No less important were the recruits he sent—tough ex-army men who were not afraid of physical violence.

This supply of ex-soldiers increased when the Berlin government decided to reduce the power of the paramilitary forces. In June 1921 the citizens' militia was disbanded, followed by the Oberland Freikorps in July. Röhm selected a squad of men from No. 19 Trench Mortar Company to provide physical protection for Hitler and then began to organize other such recruits into a proper formation. More men came from No. 2 Naval Brigade—the Ehrhardt Brigade—after the unsuccessful coup led by Dr. Wolfgang Kapp. Until now the ex-soldiers attached to the Nazi Party had been referred to as the "Sports Division," or SA, but soon, without changing its initials, the SA was renamed the *Sturmabteilung* (Storm Battalion).

The Communists had always outmatched the parties of the right and center. The middle-class liking for exclusivity made the latter accept into their party only people they liked. The Communists recruited from all classes of society and energetically sought new members; they organized a flag-waving uniformed body of men who chanted slogans, marched in step, and didn't shun street violence. Hitler learned both lessons. Responsible for recruitment, he opened the Nazi Party to all comers, and now he had a uniformed body of fighting men as formidable as the Communists.

But Hitler was disturbed to find that his SA men were not entirely his own. They were often unavailable to him because of maneuvers or drill parades. When Hitler went along to such events, he was received politely but not permitted to control the men. He was, in fact, being used by these men. Now that the Freikorps was being disbanded on orders from the Berlin government, whole formations were joining the SA intact. Röhm made sure that the military structure was preserved; there were motorized units, cavalry units, and even an artillery section. The SA was little more than the banned Freikorps under a new name. Its uniforms, its swastika badges, its rank system, and the raised-hand salutes could all have been found in the various Freikorps formations.

Senior officers of the Reichswehr watched this transformation with mixed feelings. Many saw it as a chance to build a secret reserve for the tiny 100,000-man force that the peace treaty permitted. Even its strongest opponents admitted that the SA—under whatever name its men marched—had by now become an essential part of the border defenses of Pomerania, Silesia, and East Prussia, where Polish forces were a constant threat. SA men themselves felt close to the army, in which many of them had served, and some had only joined the SA as a way of getting into the army. The tiny German Army was selective and turned away many applicants. Now it was being said that the SA would be incorporated into the German Army, as some of the Freikorps units had been.

In March 1923, aware of Hitler's misgivings about the SA, his friend Röhm provided him with a small bodyguard of SA men distinctively dressed in gray with black ski caps. They were called the *Stabswache* (HQ Guard). Hitler's relationship with the SA continued to be uncertain. It remained quite separate from the rest of the Party (the political organization) and refused to take orders from Party officials. Röhm's attitude was expressed in a memo he sent to Hitler: "Party politics will not be tolerated . . . in the SA." Only a couple of months after getting his Stabswache, Hitler quarreled with his SA and lost it again.

Now Hitler formed his own bodyguard of carefully selected men. *Stosstrupp Adolf Hitler*—as its name implies—was to be unequivocally loyal to Hitler. It was the beginning of the SS (*Schutzstaffel*, or Guard Detachment). Far from being apolitical, its members were to be indoctrinated with the Nazi creed to the extent of eventually policing, by means of the Gestapo and SD (*Geheime Staatspolizei*, or Secret State Police, and *Sicherheits Dienst,* or security service) the whole Nazi empire.

Meanwhile Hitler had no choice but to make concessions to the ever more powerful, ever more boisterous, and ever more independent SA. A consignment of shirts, intended originally for German soldiers in East Africa in the First World War, became available to the SA in Austria in 1924 and provided its members with a Nazi uniform that earned them the name "brownshirts," but it did not make them any more compliant to Hitler's wishes. And yet Hitler passionately believed that the power of Marxism came from its combination of ideology with violence, and his brownshirts gave him a way to counter Communist power in the streets.

Röhm and Eckart provided Hitler with the keys to power. Hitler himself added energy, intuition, a contempt for the public, and a fluent willingness to tell lies. As he himself was to say, "The receptive capability of the masses is limited, their understanding small. On the other hand they have a great power of forgetting." Or simply, "When you lie tell big lies . . . in the primitive simplicity of their minds they fall victims to the big lie more readily than to the small lie."

Austrians are not, and probably never were, the *gemütlich,* tolerant folk portrayed in song and story. The crude, embittered creed of Nazi prejudice found acceptance among the Austrians and their Bavarian neighbors in a way that it never did in northern Germany.

In Austria and Bavaria there were many who still treasured dreams of a Catholic monarchy. Hitler, a Catholic according to his application to the Vienna Academy of Fine Arts, hated the Habsburg monarchy. He certainly never wanted them back in power, but he readily used the prejudice and fears of both Catholics and monarchists. He discovered the political advantages of being anti-Protestant, anti-Jewish, anti-Communist, and above all anti-Berlin, for Berlin was historically regarded as the seat of Protestant-dominated Prussian central government. Hitler obliged his sympathizers by tailoring a creed to "prove" that all the voters' past troubles were caused by Berlin's incompetent Prussian generals and Jews paid by Moscow gold.

And even the word "Jew" was used by the Nazis as a catchall word to describe foreign immigrants, especially Russians and Poles, who fled to Germany after the First World War. The Nazi tirades against

Jews were designed to foment the fears of the xenophobes; the promises to build a strong Germany and defy the Versailles Treaty powers were intended to allay those fears.

Nazi slogans such as "Germany Awake" and other trappings were all primarily nationalistic. To the "Aryan" swastika of the Freikorps were added the imperial colors of old Germany (red, white, and black). Another imperial relic adopted by Hitler was General Erich Ludendorff, probably the greatest general of the First World War. Senile by 1923, when he announced his alliance with the Nazis, Ludendorff was devoting much of his time to "proving" that the First World War was part of a conspiracy that international Freemasonry, Jews, and the Pope had arranged. However, the old man's illustrious reputation was useful to the Nazis, and, when in November 1923, with Germany in a nightmare of inflation, Hitler made a crazy attempt to gain power at pistol point, the old general gladly led the march through Munich.*

Hitler thought that Ludendorff's presence would ensure for him the support of the army. It was a grave misjudgment; the German Army was controlled by General von Seeckt, who had modeled it to his own ideas. "Where does the army stand?" he had been asked by Ebert. "The army, Mr. President, stands behind me," Seeckt had answered arrogantly. Far from helping the Nazis, Seeckt offered the Munich authorities his help in crushing the revolt.

A cordon of police opened fire when the marchers tried to break through. Fourteen demonstrators died and so did three policemen. Most of the 9,000 marchers fled. Hitler escaped from the scene and was not arrested until two days later, when he was found some 35 miles away. Only Ludendorff faced the police rifles without flinching. He was arrested and stood trial with nine Nazi leaders. Hermann Göring, however, escaped to Austria.

It was Ludendorff's participation that gained worldwide publicity for the trial. Hitler used this chance to make political speeches, which were widely published in newspapers that had never before mentioned Hitler's name. One witness said that Hitler was "tactless, limited, boring, sometimes brutal, sometimes sentimental, and unquestionably inferior." But the prosecutor said that Hitler was "highly gifted," with an impeccable private life, that he was hardworking and dedicated.

---

* On the evening of 8 November 1923, Hitler took over a political meeting in the Bürgerbräukeller, a large Munich beer hall, and "arrested" the Bavarian state commissioner and the commander of the Bavarian armed forces. The next morning the Nazis marched to the Marienplatz in the center of Munich, but the demonstrators found their way barred by 100 armed policemen.

He was "a soldier who did his duty to the utmost and could not be accused of using his position for self-interest." With a prosecutor like that, a defense lawyer was hardly needed. Hitler's prison stay was short and his conditions in prison most comfortable. He was regularly visited by friends and supporters and used some of his time to dictate a book—*Mein Kampf*—to his faithful friend and helper Rudolf Hess.

Mein Kampf (My Struggle) showed that Hitler's ideas had already moved from national politics to world conquest. It is a curious and prejudiced ragbag of ideas. It devotes ten pages to syphilis and goes rambling on through art, history, and film without organizing the material to any conclusion. The book is dominated by vague anti-Jewish generalizations about Aryan man, mixed blood, and German heritage. Economic realities are avoided.

Hitler's prison experience brought about a change in his ambitions. No longer were they centered on Bavaria; his eyes were now on Berlin. He changed his tactics too. He abandoned ideas of violent revolution; the police and the army were too strong to oppose. From now on, Hitler's policy was largely decided by the attitude of the army. He was pleased, he said, that the police and not the army had fired at his marchers. It left open the prospect of an alliance with the army.

However, his chances of power, in any context, seemed slim when he came out of prison. The inflationary spiral, which had finally required armfuls of paper money to pay for a tram ticket, had ended with a drastic currency reform. The new paper money was just as worthless as the old, but the change provided an opportunity for people to believe in paper money once more. From that time on there was a new, optimistic mood in Germany. Britain and France were more conciliatory and the burden of war reparations renegotiated. There was investment from the USA. Economic stability began to provide more jobs for the unemployed, and by the end of 1924 radical and nationalist political movements were in decline.

Since Hitler's trial the Nazi Party had been put under severe restrictions of assembly and publishing. The SA was banned. But Röhm collected together his old brownshirts under the name of the *Frontbann* and began recruiting outside Bavaria for the first time. While Hitler was in prison, Röhm's force grew from the previous 2,000 to 30,000 men. By the time Hitler was paroled, Röhm was demanding more independence than ever before. The sudden growth of the brownshirts under Röhm gave him a new importance and threatened to overshadow Hitler and his political organization. On 30 April 1925 Hitler said goodbye to Röhm and his brownshirts. A press statement announced that the Nazis had no intention of setting up another such organization and would simply have a few men to keep order at meetings, as they had done before 1923. The "few men" were more or less the same ones as had made up Hitler's Stosstrupp, but now they wore the brown shirts, with black tie, and were to be called the Schutzstaffel (Security Squadron or SS). There were to be similar SS squadrons of ten men in other important towns. Only when Hitler had this tiny elite force organized throughout Germany did he resume connections with the brownshirts.

For the Nazis and the SA formations, the latter part of the 1920s marked a change in planning and method. No longer were they a provincial movement centered in Munich. More and more attention was given to northern Germany, particularly to Berlin, where the government and army high commanders were.

Thirteen Million Votes

Having prepared for a long uphill struggle, Hitler was suddenly provided with another period of chaos, like that which had benefited him at the time of the "Beer Hall Putsch," as his previous attempt to seize power was now mockingly known.* The new upheaval arose from the same economic depression that hit the United States in 1929 and went bouncing on through Europe. Austria's largest bank collapsed, closely followed by one of the big German banks. Factories closed and the number of unemployed rose to 6 million. The government sought emergency powers for drastic financial reforms, but the Reichstag refused and, in September 1930, an election was held.

As might be expected in such conditions, the Communists increased their vote. But the shopkeepers, managers, and ex-officers saw no solution in communism. The middle class, having officered the army and been unfairly blamed for its defeat, having husbanded their savings and been impoverished by inflation, were condemned as "class enemies" by the Communists. Apprehensive of the huge left-wing demonstrations and appalled by unending violence in the streets, they began to believe the Nazi claims that no one else could in fact restore order.

The German government, in what had become known as the Weimar Republic, was not strong enough to ride out the storm.† Its

---

* *Putsch* is a Swiss dialect word meaning "push" or "shove." It was adapted to mean a push for power or armed uprising.
† The strongest figure in the Weimar government between the great inflation of 1923 and the Reichstag of 1930 was Gustav Stresemann. He had negotiated the reduction

constitution had been drawn up in July 1919 in the small provincial town of Weimar. It provided for a bicameral government, proportional representation, and an elected President. The first holder of this post, Friedrich Ebert, a moderate Socialist, was succeeded in March 1925, in what was to portend the changing mood of the electorate, by Field Marshal von Hindenburg, warrior, nationalist, and monarchist.

Long since returned to Berlin, the Weimar government had few friends. The Monarchists, Nazis, and Communists all declared their contempt for this democratic federal system. The government was blamed for all the consequences of the peace treaty and the crushing reparations demanded by the Allies. The Weimar leaders were identified with the "November criminals" who had sought a cease-fire in 1918, for by now it was claimed that the German Army had never been defeated on the battlefield. Doubters were reminded of the way in which returning soldiers had marched through the Brandenburger Tor in December 1918, to be greeted by Ebert with the words: "I salute you, who return unvanquished from the field of battle."

Hitler promised a foreign policy that would restore Germany's rightful place in Europe, and he promised the middle-class moderates a place in that political future.

It was the middle-class recruits who transformed the Nazi Party and gave it roots in local government, in schools, universities, and professions, as well as in industry, commerce, and agriculture. The middle class provided the Nazis with a power base that the Communists could not hope to match. When the September 1930 votes were counted, the 12 Nazi Party seats had become a staggering 107 (while the Communists went from 54 to 77). The bourgeois parties— with the exception of the Catholic Center Party—had all lost votes to the Nazis. So had other right-wing movements. This Nazi landslide had no equal in German political history. After the Social Democrats, the Nazis were now the most powerful party in Germany. It was not only a vote for the Right, it was also a vote against the democratic system which the Nazis promised to destroy. For many it was the writing on the wall, and during the last ten weeks of 1930 about 100,000 people joined the Nazi Party.

Hitler had seen the way in which the German Army had consistently supported the Weimar Republic and decided that the only

in reparations and the Treaty of Locarno, as well as getting Germany a seat in the League of Nations. In 1926 he was awarded the Nobel Peace Prize. The death in 1929 of this Foreign Minister (who believed that Germany would dominate Europe but meanwhile should be conciliatory with the British, French, and Americans) left the government considerably weakened.

way to a totalitarian regime of the sort he advocated was with the support of the military. He concentrated his attentions upon the Reichswehr, artfully describing the politically subservient role it would have under a Communist regime (although that was exactly the role he also planned). In promising to rearm Germany in defiance of the peace treaty, he was promising the armed forces a new future. Money spent on modern equipment, including tanks, warplanes, and large battleships forbidden by the treaty, would give them the prestigious role they had enjoyed in the time of the monarchy.

The generals looked uneasily upon the ex-corporal. They would welcome the increase in expenditure and the new equipment, but under no circumstances would they welcome another war. Apprehensive lest required to subordinate their soldiers to the bizarre assortment of roughnecks and opportunists that made up the SA units, they watched Captain Röhm's growing ambition to be included on the General Staff. By 1930 there were more brownshirts than regular soldiers. Hitler strenuously assured the army that the SA was not intended to *replace* them, although, to Hitler's discomfort, that was exactly what Röhm was proclaiming.

Typically, a *Gruppenführer* of the NSKK (a major general in the *Nationalsozialistisches Kraftfahrer Korps*, brownshirt motor transport corps) would tell a regular army officer, in a friendly way, that although the Reichswehr would remain, the soldiers must expect brownshirts to be given choice jobs and high ranks. "That is the recognition of the success of our work."

Röhm was fond of saying that there was a new style of warfare and condemning the generals for being out of date. Although his instincts were the right ones, Röhm had no idea of how a new style of war might be fought. His theories were limited to the idea that the brownshirt was a new political soldier, freed of the autocratic discipline that characterized the Kaiser's army. Röhm's most radical idea about the new sort of army was that Röhm should command it. "I am the new army's Scharnhorst," he would brag, using the name of the man who had reorganized the Prussian Army after the collapse of 1806. But Röhm was no Scharnhorst; he was a noisy, self-indulgent homosexual who not only boasted of his amorous adventures but gave perverts senior jobs in his SA. The head of the SA's Intelligence Unit was paid a fee to supply Röhm with new boyfriends from the Gisela High School, Munich. Unfaithful partners were the target for assaults by SA patrols.

Hitler knew about Röhm's scandalous activities but turned a blind eye to them. For the time being, Heinrich Himmler, a prim young

1. Chancellor Adolf Hitler with President Paul von Hindenburg, 1933.

2. ABOVE, LEFT: Friedrich Ebert, Chancellor, and later President, of the first German Republic.

3. ABOVE: General von Seeckt (right) with Kurt von Schleicher, founder of the Freikorps, 1924.

4. LEFT: Dietrich Eckart, Hitler's mentor.

5. German soldiers and Freikorps men using an old British tank against rioters in Berlin in 1920.

6. Hitler with a group of supporters during the early days of the Nazi Party.

7. Ernst Röhm, SA chief of staff (left), with Franz von Papen.

8. OPPOSITE: Hermann Göring (left) and Heinrich Himmler, leader of the SS, who together plotted against the generals.

9. General von Blomberg in an official visit to England, inspecting an RAF bomber.

10. General von Blomberg, disgraced in marriage.

11. General Ludendorff being greeted by enthusiastic crowds at an army celebration.

12. General von Fritsch, victim of an SS frame-up.

13. Neville Chamberlain, the British Prime Minister, inspecting an SS guard when visiting Hitler in Munich during the Czechoslovak crisis in 1938.

14. German Foreign Minister von Ribbentrop signing the Nazi-Communist pact on 23 August 1939. Stalin, the Soviet dictator (right), and Molotov, his Foreign Minister, were to congratulate Hitler on his conquests in 1940.

SA man who had not been old enough to see fighting in the war, also overlooked Röhm's activities. Himmler idolized the swashbuckling, bemedaled Röhm, but he worshiped Hitler even more. In 1929, at the age of twenty-nine, Himmler had taken command of Hitler's body-guard units—now called the SS—and in keeping with his boyhood ideas of medieval chivalry, he enforced upon them a puritanical regime that distanced his private army from the brownshirt battalions.

Private armies, even part-time ones, cost a great deal of money. Most of the money—the Party was spending between 70 and 90 million marks a year—came from its large membership, but up to the end of January 1933 about 6 million marks had been donated by industry. Obviously this was only a tiny percentage of the Party income, but Hitler now had to find time to cultivate the industrialists, seeking both money and influence. From now on, the stakes would be large ones.

Nazi rallies became more and more theatrical: massed flags, military bands, fanfares, cannon fire, crowds chanting slogans such as "Germany Awake!" and complex rituals, including the "consecrating" of blood-stained flags, gained enormous audiences for the hard-sell political speeches.

In Germany aviation had progressed rapidly since 1918 and Hitler and his propaganda experts saw the drama of descending from the sky. It was for this as much as for the practical reasons that Hitler used aircraft so much. "Hitler over Germany" was the deliberately equivocal slogan. In 1932 the Nazi leaders flew 23,000 miles on Lufthansa aircraft. By means of its heavily subsidized airline, the Weimar Republic was in fact contributing to the election campaign of its most bitter enemies. Not content with this, the Nazis enrolled Lufthansa chief Erhard Milch as a secret member of the Party and so avoided payments of any airfares.

Air travel increased the importance of Himmler's SS, for it became necessary to provide Hitler with an escort in each of the towns he visited. Although technically still a part of the SA organization, the SS elite was becoming a powerful force in its own right.

The rallies, speeches, and personal appearances paid off in attract-ing the workers to the movement. Using proven Communist tech-niques, the Nazis went into the factories and—even more important during the Depression—down the long lines of unemployed. At the same time there was a deliberate accent on youth. Not content with paying lip service to the importance of young Nazis, the Party gave them senior jobs. Himmler had taken over the SS at the age of twenty-nine. Josef Goebbels was made a *Gauleiter* (district leader) at the age of twenty-eight. Of the Nazis sitting in the Reichstag, 60 per cent were under forty years old. After the July 1932 Reichstag election the Nazis held 230 seats of the total 608 (Communists got 89 seats). Although still without a majority, the Nazis were now the largest party there. In four years, the Nazis had amassed 13 million votes.

Alarmed by the growing power of the brownshirts, the army leaders, together with the police and other officials, played out a series of war games to examine the task of keeping law and order in the cities against the Communists and Nazis. They concluded that the shortage of motor vehicles would prevent them concentrating at trouble spots (they assumed that the railway would not be working normally). The Polish Army was building up in the Polish Corridor and along the East Prussian border at this time. Serious disturbances in the German cities might well tempt the Poles into a full-scale attack, which the German Army would also have to deal with.

The Reichswehr's *Planspiel* of November 1932 provided important lessons for anyone who cared to note them. The established German Army no longer had the physical power to overcome the uniformed private armies of Left and Right. This weakness was not due to a lack of rifles, machine guns, or artillery, or even to a lack of men, but to a shortage of trucks. The vital role of the truck had already been recognized by some military experts. In England Captain B. H. Liddell Hart greeted the six-wheel truck as a landmark in military evolution.

Germany had become the greatest industrial power in Europe and its army the strongest at a time when manpower, horsepower, and the coal-fired steam engine comprised the foundation of prosperity and might. Germany's coalfields were immense, its population large and hardworking, but there were no sources of oil at hand. Although only the spearhead of the army would get tanks and armored cars, the whole economy was fast becoming dependent upon motor transport. In spite of captured and controlled oil fields and synthetic fuel production, the fuel supply was to remain a constant problem for Germany.

Chancellor Hitler

Germany had more than its share of extremists and they would find no common accord. The Weimar Republic and its system of proportional representation tottered from one uneasy coalition government to the next. Politicians tried to reconcile workers, shopkeepers, Communist internationalists, powerful landowners, Prussian militarists, and industrial plutocrats. It often seemed as if the only thing that bound these disparate elements together was a dislike of the Weimar government.

Successive administrations were comprised mostly of men of good faith. Had they been given support from outside Germany, the Republic might have flourished. As it was, they did no better than survive from one muddled compromise to the next. The desire to impose upon the disorder of nature some orderly pattern or arrangement makes men into poets, painters, and gardeners; it also makes them prey to the illusion that a highly organized state will be civilized and preferable to a disorganized and muddled one. Men admired the neatly uniformed, disciplined Nazis, radiantly confident as they marched to military bands or chanted their slogans, and wanted to be a part of this parade before it passed them by.

By the time of the elections in January 1933, enough voters were attracted by Hitler's bold new experiment in politics to give him a chance to demonstrate his ideas. Without a clear majority, it was necessary for Hitler to form a coalition government together with the conservative Nationalist Party. Franz von Papen, who had been Chancellor until the previous November, agreed to becoming Vice Chancellor to Hitler and giving the Nazis Frick and Göring places in the Cabinet.*

While it is true to say that proportional representation gave the Nazis a chance to gain power, this can also be said of the whole democratic system. More important to Hitler's subsequent success were Vice Chancellor von Papen's personality and social skills.

Franz von Papen was a charming man about town. Ex-staff officer and Catholic aristocrat, he had married into a wealthy family of Rhineland industrialists. He therefore had links with the three most powerful elements of German political life: army, church, and industry.

Often ridiculed for his flamboyance, Papen was not unintelligent but his political skills were minimal. Some of his supporters believed that a man not so deeply committed to party politics might be able to

---

* Wilhelm Frick, lawyer and police official, had met Hitler when the Nazis applied for police permission to hold political meetings in Munich. He subsequently became Hitler's contact with the police and marched with the Nazis in the 1923 Beer Hall Putsch, after which he was arrested and sentenced to imprisonment. But the sentence was quashed, and in the same year—1924—Frick was elected to the Reichstag as a Nazi Party delegate. Frick was most responsible for establishing the Nazis' tight control of Germany and did this by introducing laws abolishing political parties, suppressing trade unions, and victimizing the Jews. In 1946 he was found guilty of war crimes at the Nuremberg trials and hanged.

unite the nation in a way that more dedicated dogmatists had failed to do. In any case, it was reasoned, Papen's influence with Hindenburg—already it had been stipulated that the President would only receive Hitler when the Vice Chancellor was also present—and his political controls of the Cabinet would be enough to contain the power of the Nazis.

Hindenburg hesitated before ratifying the agreement between the Nazi and Nationalist parties. One of the men he consulted about the decision was General Werner von Blomberg. For the proposed Cabinet, Blomberg had already been chosen as Defense Minister. One-time *chef des Truppenamts* (Chief of General Staff), he had recently been commander of Wehrkreis I (East Prussia), Germany's most sensitive and turbulent military region.* It was a job given only to the army's best men, and the SA units there, with many ex-Freikorps men, were integral to the military defenses. But a serious riding accident had caused Blomberg concussion of the brain and affected him to an extent that he requested to be released from active duty. His temporary assignment to a Geneva Disarmament Conference had given Blomberg direct access to the President in a way that few generals ever had. Blomberg told his President that there was little choice but to agree to the Hitler and Papen coalition. The German Army, he said, would be smashed to pieces if it came into armed conflict with the SA and SS.

Blomberg's view was not entirely objective. This excitable man, who looked like an aging film star and was so vain that he continued to wear his general's uniform throughout his life in spite of a law that prohibited ministers from holding army rank, supported the Nazis. A brief period in Soviet Russia had convinced him that the life-style and prestige of a general in a totalitarian society was something worth striving for. Now Blomberg had hitched his star to the Nazis for better or for worse.

President von Hindenburg gave his approval to the agreement that Papen and Hitler had made. It was assumed that some sort of deal would also be made with the Catholic Center Party, so that its seventy seats would be added to the coalition. Meanwhile the Nazis celebrated with torchlight parades and huge demonstrations.

In January 1933 Hitler held his first Cabinet meeting. It seemed that the Nazis were gradually adapting their totalitarian promises to the reality of democratic government. But Hitler was far too much of

---

* By tradition a *Wehrkreis* (Military District) commander was not only responsible for the training and administration of the army units in his district but also commanded those troops in battle.

an extremist and far too devious to be content with leadership through a parliamentary system. He deliberately sabotaged his negotiations with the Center Party so that there would be a clamor for new elections.

Now Hitler's plan became clear, for the Nazis already held key governmental posts and would continue to occupy them during the elections. Göring's position as Prime Minister of the state of Prussia, for instance, gave the Nazis control of the police of two thirds of Germany's total area, a huge region stretching from Poland to the Netherlands. Hurriedly Göring removed anti-Nazi police officials, promoted Nazis to positions of power, and authorized 40,000 Nazi Party members to be auxiliary policemen. Göring ordered that a small office in Berlin Police HQ, hitherto concerned only with the Constitution, should be reorganized as a secret police department. This was the beginning of the Gestapo.

Goebbels, the Nazi propaganda expert, wrote in his diary, "Now it will be easy . . . we can call on all the resources of the State. Radio and press are at our disposal. We shall stage a masterpiece of propaganda." Goebbels added, "And this time, naturally, there is no lack of money."

Already in January, before coming to power, Hitler had told the industrialists that this was the moment to give as much money as they could possibly afford. He promised that he would suppress the trade unions and that his plans for Germany would greatly benefit big business. Accepting, with varying degrees of enthusiasm, what they saw as inevitable, the banks, insurance companies, the Hamburg-Amerika Line, I. G. Farben, rubber companies, potash, coal, and steel interests, including Krupp, all helped the Nazis. Cynically, Göring told industrialists that this might be the last election for a decade, or even for a century.

About a week before election day, which was set for 5 March, the Reichstag building was deliberately set on fire. A mentally retarded Dutch anarchist was arrested for the crime. At one time it was widely believed that the fire was started on secret orders from Hitler, but now we can be virtually certain that the Dutchman alone was responsible.*

Hitler was in Goebbels's apartment when a phone call came to report the Reichstag fire. Goebbels was so certain that it was untrue

---

* The story about the Nazis' setting fire to the Reichstag is repeated by William Shirer in *The Rise and Fall of the Third Reich*. Even more surprisingly, *Germany 1866–1945*, by Gordon A. Craig, in the *Oxford History of Modern Europe*, continues to promote this ancient myth. Neither author gives any evidence to support it.

that he did not even bother to tell Hitler until more calls came with the same news. "Now I have them," said Hitler excitedly. Göring was already at the fire when they got there, his face flushed with heat and excitement. He screamed, "The Communist deputies must be hanged this very night. Everyone in alliance with the Communists is to be arrested. We are not going to spare the Social Democrats and members of the Reichsbanner either!"

Göring's wrath was soon turned into action. He sent his policemen to arrest some 4,000 people before morning. As well as members of the Communist Party, a wide variety of other opponents of the Nazi Party disappeared.

On 28 February, the day following the fire, Hitler went with his Vice Chancellor to see the eighty-six-year-old President von Hindenburg. It is perhaps a measure of the wild hysteria fanned by Goebbels and his propaganda machine that Papen helped Hitler get Hindenburg's signature on the emergency decree. This document delivered Germany into Hitler's hands. It restricted the press and rights of assembly. It enabled the authorities to intercept postal, telegraph, and phone services and made a "serious disturbance of the peace by armed persons" punishable by death. This decree and a supplementary one issued the same day meant that the Constitution was suspended and Germany was in a state of emergency. These "emergency laws" were the basis for the repressive, merciless regime of the Nazi state. Using their new powers, the Nazis arrested thousands of Communists and many Social Democrats and Liberals.

Detachments of brownshirts, some of them wearing the armband that identified them as auxiliary policemen and backed by senior police officers (who were mostly Nazi Party members), began arresting political opponents. Such prisoners included members of the Reichstag, although under the law they were immune from arrest. Amid this purge, all the trappings of Nazidom were organized: rallies, torchlight marches, speeches over the state radio, flags, posters, and intimidation. During the election period, fifty-one anti-Nazi politicians were murdered. Hundreds more were injured.

In spite of the Reichstag fire and the "masterpiece of propaganda," the Nazis got only 44 per cent of the vote on 5 March. (The Nationalists slumped to 7 per cent.) To govern the country would require compromises and cooperation with the parties of the center. But this was not what Hitler had in mind. With nearly 100 left-wing deputies arrested or in hiding, Hitler "guarded" the Kroll Opera House, where the Reichstag convened, with SS units and chanting armies of SA men, while he asked the assembly for dictatorial powers for four years by means of an "Enabling Act." Even without the arrests among the opposition, he would have got the 66 per cent vote such a bill needed. The Center Party (of Christian Democrats) voted for him and only Social Democrats against. He got 441 votes to 84. He persuaded President von Hindenburg to ratify the measure by promising that he would consult the President before making serious changes.

There remained only a few steps. He took away the powers of the sovereign German states, revealing how limited were his previous political ambitions in Bavaria. His biggest potential opponents were the trade unions and the army. He removed the power of the trade unions by forming them into the "labor front," a tool of the government. Thus there remained but one great threat to total Nazi control, the army.

Hitler's Generals

One of Blomberg's first acts as Minister of Defense was to bring his old chief of staff from East Prussia to Berlin. Colonel Walter von Reichenau became head of the *Ministeramt* (the Ministry Office of the Reichswehr). Reichenau had the same favorable attitude to the Nazis as his Minister, Blomberg. But he lacked the capacity for personal adulation which Blomberg showed for his Führer. No one could have nicknamed the opinionated Reichenau "the rubber lion" as they did Blomberg. Reichenau was a cold, calculating man, who combined considerable technological skills with the ability to lead his soldiers on punishing cross-country runs. Not only more intelligent than Blomberg, he had a wider experience of life than was commonly found among his peers. Reichenau was well traveled and well read and had translated some of Captain Liddell Hart's books into German. Like Blomberg he was a proponent of mobile warfare. A ruthless empire builder, Reichenau was later to develop a technique of gate-crashing Hitler's dinner gatherings in a way that only senior Party officials and Hitler's old friends dared to do. He was not very popular with his fellow officers, and doubtless they showed commendable judgment.

His rapid promotion from colonel to major general did not make more friends for him, but his job was a vital one and he was well equipped to do it. Hitler had given his generals plenty to do. Not only was the Reichswehr's full mobilization army of twenty-one divisions now to be the peacetime establishment strength, but it was also to prepare to receive heavy artillery and tanks. With this latter task in mind, Reichenau had Krupp in 1933 begin a proper program of tank production (under the guise of agricultural tractors). The first five tanks arrived in August. Studies were made in war production, raw materials, and pricing. Most important of all, Reichenau changed the name of his office to prepare for the work it would do in coordinating the Defense Minister's orders to the air force, as well as to the army and navy. It would henceforth be called the Armed Forces Office (*Wehrmachtsamt*, later *Wehrmachtamt*).

It was Hitler's plan to introduce national conscription, but meanwhile the army had to depend upon volunteers. Reluctantly the generals agreed that the SA and its allied Nazi organizations, such as the NSKK, SS, etc., must be its main source of recruits. To some extent this was an advantage. The SA men were able to march and most NSKK men could drive, but this arrangement meant that all the army recruits would be thoroughly indoctrinated with Nazi philosophy.

The army also resented the growing importance of the SA. By the end of 1933 the brownshirts had been given recognition as an official government organization. Even more disconcerting was the way that Ernst Röhm, its leader, had been given a place on the Reich's Defense Council, as well as a place in the Cabinet.

Yet the army did not want to see the brownshirts totally disbanded. The SA was still a vital part of the defense of the eastern borders and had in effect helped Germany to get round the limitations of the 100,000-man army specified by the peace treaty. But now that Hitler was in power, there was little for the brownshirts to do. "They were like an army of occupation," remembered more than one German. The army suggested that the best deployment for SA units was a militia under Reichswehr command.

Röhm's countersuggestion of 1 February 1934 was dramatic: he wanted the SA to take over all defense duties and relegate the army to the task of training his men. Now even Blomberg—whose adulation of and obedience to Hitler was legendary—realized that the army was in danger of total subjugation to the wishes of Röhm and his followers.

The events of that year moved swiftly. On 28 February Hitler called a conference of senior men of the army and the SA in the Great Hall of the Army General Staff building on Bendlerstrasse. He told them, in no uncertain manner, that the army would be the sole bearer of arms, although for the time being the SA would continue its frontier protection duties and premilitary training. The SA, said Hitler, could never be organized to carry out the rigorous program of training with modern arms that the army had to complete to be ready for a defensive war in five years and a war of aggression in eight years.

For those of the SA in his audience who had learned to take his words with a measure of reserve, Hitler had a surprise that was nothing less than shattering. He called Röhm and Blomberg to the rostrum and produced a pact. It laid down specifically that the role of the SA was confined to training and even that was to come under the direction of the army. He told both men to sign it there and then; they obeyed.

Röhm was beside himself with rage. To his senior staff he called Hitler "an ignorant corporal" and threatened to turn against him, all of which was reported to Hitler by Obergruppenführer Viktor Lutze (who eventually got Röhm's job). "We must allow the affair to ripen," said Hitler calmly. His decision to back the armed forces was a natural one, for the Führer—no matter that it was unprecedented—was going to become Germany's number one soldier.

While Röhm raged, the army celebrated. Hitler, with customary attention to detail, had chosen the day on which the Association of General Staff Officers held its annual dinner—i.e., the birthday of Count Alfred von Schlieffen, the military theorist. This was the one-hundred-and-first anniversary.

Defense Minister von Blomberg decided that the army must demonstrate loyalty to Adolf Hitler equal to that of his brownshirts. He ordered that non-Aryans (except men who had lost fathers or sons at the front in the 1914–1918 war or had served there themselves) were to be dismissed from the army immediately. Even more compromising was Blomberg's decision that the army would wear the Nazi eagle and swastika on its uniforms and that the swastika would be incorporated into army insignia. President von Hindenburg himself signed the order.

The far-reaching importance of Blomberg's action is clear. The army's role had been nonpolitical; now it was dedicated to keeping the Nazis in power and wore their badge lest any opponent of the Nazis forget it. (The Red Army wore the hammer and sickle, a device which had already served the Russian Communists well.)

John W. Wheeler-Bennett suggests that Blomberg's later willingness to support Hitler as a candidate for the presidency—and thus as Supreme Commander of the army—was settled aboard the pocket battleship *Deutschland* when Hitler, together with senior officers of the army and navy, sailed from Kiel on 11 April 1934 as part of the spring maneuvers. By that time, a secret bulletin had told Blomberg and Hitler that President von Hindenburg was close to death. On 1 May —a holiday celebrated enthusiastically by the Nazi Party—the army assumed the Party insignia, says Wheeler-Bennett.

Although this fits together neatly, the order about soldiers wearing

Nazi badges was in fact published in *Militär-Wochenblatt*, No. 32, dated 25 February 1934. Hindenburg had signed the order on 21 February. The orders about dismissing Jews from the army (for in this case, and most others, "non-Aryan" was another word for Jew) was promulgated on 28 February 1934, the one-hundred-and-first anniversary of Schlieffen's birthday, the very day when the highest ranks of the SA and the army listened to Hitler's decision in the Great Hall of the Bendlerstrasse. It becomes clear that this "concession" to the army, which was a shattering surprise for Röhm, was really the outcome of a secret agreement between Hitler and Blomberg.

There were men in the German Army who objected to these orders. Colonel Erich von Manstein (who figures largely in the story of the 1940 victories) wrote to the High Command, boldly declaring that the army had shown cowardice in surrendering to the Nazi Party on such an issue. He objected to discrimination against men who had proved, by voluntary enlistment, that they were prepared to give their lives for Germany. Blomberg saw the letter and told General Werner von Fritsch (who had just become Commander in Chief of the Army) to take disciplinary action against Manstein. Fritsch said it was not the Defense Minister's business and did not do so.

As this incident serves to indicate, Werner Freiherr von Fritsch was a soldier's soldier. Every profession produces men who are both gifted and totally consumed with their work, and the success of such men rarely evokes envy from their associates. Fritsch was such a soldier. Although one hesitates to use the word "popularity" of such an introspective personality, there was probably no one in the German Army who inspired in his men the same degree of confidence.

Selected for training at the Kriegsakademie in 1910, Oberleutnant von Fritsch, still only thirty years old, was the top of his class, with outstanding marks. His brilliance won him subsequent posting to the Great General Staff in Berlin.* During the First World War Fritsch, although at least once close enough to the fighting to be wounded by a hand grenade, was kept on staff duties. In 1926 he worked under Blomberg, as head of the Operations Section of the *Truppenamt* (Troop Office, a name used to disguise the forbidden General Staff). Fritsch was a conservative in every way. He believed that tanks and aircraft had a place in war but should be subordinated to the other arms.

Army life suited Fritsch. He was a solitary type who preferred his own company. For relaxation he liked to ride alone; horses were a

---

* The Great General Staff was named to distinguish it from the general staffs of smaller formations, e.g., divisional general staffs.

passion with him comparable only to his work. He was incapable of small talk and found it difficult to make friends. This probably accounted for the fact that he never got married. To one friend he expressed his regrets about this and said how much he would have liked to have had children.

For such a taciturn, truthful man, the noise, lies, and verbosity of the politician were extremely distasteful, and he was sometimes indiscreet enough to display his contempt for the Nazis, although he developed a grudging regard for Hitler. Just as Fritsch persuaded himself that, whatever his faults, Hitler was Germany's future, so did Hitler come to believe that this general (in whose presence Hitler became silent and withdrawn) was the German Army's future. When the time came for the Nazis to destroy this vulnerable man, it was not a plan of Hitler's making.

Fritsch's appointment in 1934 to the coveted job of Commander in Chief of the Army had been a compromise. Defense Minister von Blomberg put forward the name of his old friend Reichenau. A supporter of many Nazi ideas, Reichenau would have been welcomed by Hitler, but he was not popular with his fellow officers. (The two group commanders—General Wilhelm Ritter von Leeb and General Gerd von Rundstedt, who had to work under the Commander in Chief—said that they would not have Reichenau in that job.)

Fritsch was at that time stationed in Berlin, as commander of Wehrkreis III, and was content to stay there until his retirement. But President von Hindenburg and Vice Chancellor von Papen chose Fritsch for the job of Commander in Chief and he got it. It was to bring him a place in the history books and profound sorrow.

Hitler had made up his mind that the army must be his ally, whatever the cost to those round him. He was already thinking about the massive army that conscription would bring, once he decided to defy the terms of the peace treaty. The army would no longer need the SA as a source of recruits or as a supplementary force in the East—and neither would Hitler.

Obsessed with his own importance, Röhm failed to see this. He staged massive SA rallies and parades as a show of force and made excited speeches about the need for a "second revolution." Whatever Röhm intended, there were plenty of people who distrusted him enough to see this as a threat. His enemies were delighted to foment such fears.

Röhm knew too many of Hitler's secrets to be allowed to flee into exile or to stand up and answer charges in a law court. Hitler sent for him on 4 June 1934 and the two men talked for four hours. The result was that the 4.5 million men of the SA were to be sent on leave for the month of July and Röhm himself was to take sick leave for a few weeks.

It was a setback to Röhm's enemies. What chance was there of persuading anyone that a revolution was to take place while the revolutionary army was on leave and its leader in a rest home?

Hermann Göring—or "Captain Hermann Göring, retired," as he was contemptuously referred to by the generals—coveted the role of Commander in Chief of the Army. It was enough to make him an enemy of Röhm. But the man who had most to gain from Röhm's downfall was Heinrich Himmler, who commanded the SS, a force which had now expanded to about 80,000 but was still technically a part of Röhm's SA. But Himmler's sentimental feelings of loyalty to his old boss Röhm had him pass the conspiracy over to his subordinate Reinhard Heydrich, a man even more cynical, brutal, and devious than Himmler. Heydrich started to spread rumors about SA plans for a seizure of power. Forged documents, paid informants, threats, lies, and whispers all played a part in his scheme.

Hitler realized that the SA could become a rallying point for all anti-Nazi Germans. The presence of the ex-Kaiser's eldest son, Prince Wilhelm, in the SA was enough to conjure fears that the army's oath of allegiance—now sworn to President von Hindenburg—would, when the old man died, be given to the Crown Prince. And Röhm was a monarchist.

On Sunday, 17 June, Vice Chancellor von Papen made a speech at Marburg University, protesting about the Nazi control of the press and warning against further radicalism. Nazi Party leaders spent that Sunday with the Führer at a conference in Thuringia. To them Papen's speech sounded like a rallying call for counterrevolution. Publication of the speech was banned by Goebbels, who was a target for much of Papen's criticism.

Hitler flew to see President von Hindenburg, now near death. It was a hot day. On the steps, roasting in his full uniform, was Defense Minister von Blomberg. In a meeting that lasted only a few minutes, he told Hitler that unless he could bring about a relaxation of tension, the President had decided to declare martial law and hand over control of the country to the Reichswehr. If this happened, there was always the chance that the Reichswehr would restore the monarchy, something that would ruin Hitler's dreams of total dictatorship.

Most commentators suggest that this was the time when Hitler decided that Röhm's power must be reduced suddenly and violently. But I am unconvinced. We see nothing in Hitler's past or future behavior to suggest that he would abandon a gamble at this early stage. President von Hindenburg consistently wanted all fighting to end—would he have committed the nation to a civil war in the last days of his life? And what of the absurd Blomberg—would this obsequious puppet have led the army against his master, having already predicted that the army would be smashed in such a conflict? And would he have ordered his soldiers first to remove from their uniforms the Nazi Party badges like the one that shone on his tunic while he talked with his Führer?

Whatever decided Hitler upon the "Night of the Long Knives," it was not the threat of what Blomberg's Reichswehr might do to his millions of brownshirts. More likely it was because of what the brownshirts might do to the Reichswehr. Hitler would never conquer half the world with brownshirts. For that he would need professional soldiers and, like it or not, the generals.

The Night of the Long Knives

Röhm had more than fulfilled his promise to organize a uniformed paramilitary force for Hitler. By the beginning of 1931, the membership was marginally larger than the Reichswehr's 100,000 men. As unemployment grew, so did the SA, and by the end of that same year they numbered 300,000. By the summer of 1934 there were 4.5 million brownshirts. Such numbers presented more of a threat to the Nazi Party than to the rest of the nation. Its strength gave the SA leaders enormous power over their fellow Nazis, and Röhm was as powerful as Hitler.

It has been alleged that the SA—and more especially its leader, Röhm—was determined to continue the revolution to a truly socialist conclusion. But the brownshirts were not reformers. They simply felt that the part they had played in giving Hitler absolute power should now be rewarded by jobs in the civil service, positions in commerce, or ranks in a new sort of army. Throughout the SA there was a feeling of anticlimax. The great revolutionary battle for which they had marched and drilled and trained for years was not going to take place. Hitler had moved into power without it. Furthermore, Hitler had already decided that his plans for curing unemployment and encouraging the economy and rearming must on no account be disturbed. Hitler said, "We must therefore not dismiss a businessman if he is a good businessman, even if he is not yet a National Socialist; and especially not if the National Socialist who is to take his place knows nothing about business." That was not encouraging for old brownshirts who had broken bones and spilled blood for the Nazi revolution.

On Thursday, 28 June 1934, Hitler went to Westphalia to attend the wedding of an old friend. Hardly had he arrived than there was a phone call from Himmler in Berlin. He had alarming reports of an imminent SA uprising. Göring—at Hitler's side—fueled his anger. More reports followed, all equally alarming and equally false. Hitler returned to Berlin and alerted his SS-Leibstandarte Adolf Hitler (the elite unit used as his ceremonial guard). On Friday he phoned Röhm to tell him that he was coming to see him next day at 11 A.M. Röhm was to ensure that all senior SA officers were present.

Himmler continued to push his master to a decision. There was now evidence, said Himmler, that the SA units in Berlin were briefed to occupy government buildings on Saturday afternoon. In fact, the head of the Berlin SA had already left for a holiday in Tenerife. Another report from Himmler's SS told of brownshirts marching through Munich demonstrating against Hitler. Actually they were shouting, "The Reichswehr is against us." These two stories were enough to galvanize Hitler into action. By 2 A.M. he was in his private Junkers Ju 52 on his way to see Röhm. At 6:30 A.M. on Saturday, Hitler, gun in hand, forced open the bedroom doors of Hanselbauer Pension where Röhm and his SA men were staying. Hitler was visibly shaken to find male sleeping partners in some of the rooms. Hitler called Röhm a traitor and arrested him in person.

By 10 A.M. Saturday, 30 June, Hitler had returned to nearby Munich. To Göring went the codeword KOLIBRI (hummingbird). All over Germany senior SS officers opened their sealed orders and began the systematic murders.

At 5 P.M. Hitler sent for Josef (Sepp) Dietrich, Commander of Leibstandarte Adolf Hitler, and gave him a list of all the imprisoned SA leaders. "Go back to the barracks," Hitler ordered, "select an officer and six men, and have the SA leaders shot for high treason." Dietrich saw that six names had been ticked in green pencil.

Dietrich supervised the executions in person. As each of the men was led into the prison courtyard Dietrich impassively told him, "You have been condemned to death by the Führer. Heil Hitler!" before each was shot. One of the men greeted Dietrich warmly. "Sepp, my friend, what on earth's happening?" asked SA Obergruppenführer August Schneidhuber, who was also the police president of Munich. Dietrich gave him the same treatment as the others.

The killings continued over the weekend. Some were shot as they answered the door or in their offices. No less horrifying than the ruthless way in which men were sent to kill was the robotic way they obeyed. Sent to murder a director in the Ministry of Transport (Dr. Erich Klausener, also president of Catholic Action and one-time police chief), Heydrich's man killed him in his office and calmly phoned Heydrich on the director's phone to say that the deed was done.

And the victims were not all supporters of Röhm. A high-ranking SS officer was murdered on the orders of his rival. A lawyer was killed for having taken part in legal proceedings against Nazis. Gregor Strasser had received from Hitler the Gold Party Badge just a few days before. He was killed because, although no longer a rival to Hitler for control of the Nazi Party, he was still considered a rival to Göring and Himmler.

At 3 P.M. on 1 July Röhm was still alive in his prison cell, but eventually Göring and Himmler persuaded Hitler that the brownshirt leader must die too. An SS officer gave Röhm a loaded revolver and a copy of *Völkischer Beobachter* which gave details of the "purge in the SA." When Röhm declined to commit suicide, he was shot. "Aim slowly and calmly" were Röhm's last words, but it took three bullets to kill him.

Disconcerted by the proliferation of killings, Hitler gave the order to stop on the afternoon of 2 July. At least one SA leader was saved by a messenger arriving in the nick of time. "The Führer has given Hindenburg his word that the shooting is now finally over," the execution squads were told.

To what extent the army was surprised by the "Night of the Long Knives" is difficult to ascertain. Some units had made guns and transport available to local SS units to help keep order should there be an SA revolt. *Wachregiment-Berlin* (Berlin Guard Regiment) assigned a company of men to guard the Bendlerstrasse buildings (the Reichswehr Ministry and Army High Command were in the same block). Reichswehr Ministry officers were told to have weapons at their place of work. As late as 28 June Generalleutnant Ewald von Kleist, the army commander in Silesia, had had a meeting with the local SA commander and discovered that each was preparing for an attack by the other. Inquiries made that night revealed that this same situation was being repeated by SA and army units all over Germany. General von Kleist was sufficiently alarmed to fly to Berlin and tell Fritsch, adding that he believed that the alarm was being fomented by the SS. Fritsch told Reichenau, who said, "That may well be right, but it is too late now."

There is no evidence that Reichenau, or even Blomberg, had prior information about the planned murders, but it seems certain, from their subsequent actions, that neither of these men of the Ministry (as opposed to the generals in the High Command, next door on the Bendlerstrasse) was caught by surprise.

Fritsch, however, was certainly caught by surprise. General Walther K. Nehring remembers:

> On 29th June 1934 after work I found myself at my house near the Reichswehr Ministry in the Bendlerstrasse on the Tirpitz Ufer. Captain von Mellenthin (personal general staff officer to General Freiherr von Fritsch, the army C in C) asked me to come to Fritsch urgently. I went in my civilian clothes rather than take the time to change. Upon arrival there General von Fritsch seemed rather excited as news had just arrived about a putsch of the SA planned for tomorrow. Fritsch ordered security measures and urgently wanted from me all the armoured vehicles in the area of Berlin. At that time there were very few.
>
> It was quite clear that the General and his staff were completely surprised and could give no details. I suspected that he had been given very incomplete information by General von Reichenau of the Ministry.*

The killing that weekend of two of the army's own came as a shock to many officers who had been told that this business had nothing to do with the army. General Kurt von Schleicher, soldier turned politician, had been Chancellor when Hitler took over the post in January 1933. He was shot by an execution squad, and General Kurt von Bredow, his subordinate, was murdered soon afterward. Although neither of these generals was popular, it was generally expected that the army would condemn the murders and demand an investigation into the circumstances of the deaths. Such an investigation might have shown the Nazi leaders as the ruthless criminals that they were. Instead, without hesitation, General von Reichenau issued a communiqué saying that Schleicher had been proved a traitor to the state in both word and deed. His wife, added Reichenau, died because she placed herself in the line of fire. The truth was that even the Nazis, in trying to justify the murder, failed to find any evidence connecting Schleicher with Röhm or with any other treasonable activities.

Defense Minister von Blomberg praised Hitler. In his Order of the day for 1 July he spoke of the Führer's soldierly decision and the exemplary courage used to wipe out traitors and mutineers. The Defense Minister's congratulations on behalf of the army left Hindenburg, its Supreme Commander, little alternative but to add his own.

The next day Hindenburg significantly included the words "From

---

* In a letter to the author.

15. Erich von Manstein, probably the most brilliant general of the war.

16. Generaloberst Gerd von Rundstedt in 1939.

17. German tanks advancing into Poland in the early days of September 1939.

18. German infantry in Socharzow, a small town in Poland, in 1939.

19. German soldiers and a tank crewman (black uniform) chatting with the crew of a Red Army armored car (left) in Poland after the joint invasion.

20. A German infantry unit uses the town square of Policka, Sudetenland, as a vehicle park. Notice the strange collection of vehicles and the number of cycles.

21. Erwin Rommel, commanding Hitler's bodyguard, accompanies him at lunch (from a field kitchen) during the campaign in Poland, 1939.

22. Burning ships in the harbor at Narvik, Norway, 1940.

23. German infantry fighting in the snow near Narvik.

24. German infantry being taken into Oslo harbor by tender.

25. Rommel (circle) watching motorcyclists of his armored division practicing a river crossing on the Moselle, chosen for its similarity to the Meuse.

26. The German Army revived many old ideas and much outdated equipment. Carrier pigeons were widely used in 1940.

reports placed before me" in the message of thanks and appreciation he sent to Hitler for his gallant personal intervention.

"All catched" was the message in bad English that Reichenau sent to his counterespionage chief after the SA leaders were dead. Many other army officers could not conceal their satisfaction.

Hitler displayed his usual astonishing skill at squeezing every last advantage out of the situation. Having legalized the murders by means of a retrospective law consisting of a single sentence, Hitler took responsibility upon himself but did it in such a way that most Germans believed he was covering up for the misdeeds of subordinates.

Hitler had gambled that the army would not move against the murder squads and he had proved right. The generals had condoned murder, even the murder of two generals. They had been initiated into the dirty business of Nazi politics, but artfully Hitler had not involved them to the extent of owing them a favor.

While the army was celebrating the destruction of its rival, Hitler was arranging the emergence of a new one. Just one week after the murders, it was announced that Heydrich's *Sicherheitsdienst des RfSS* (the SS Security Service organization), which had done so much to prepare and foment the killings, would now extend its power to all Nazi Party organizations. In July, Hitler made the SS an independent organization. Contrary to Hitler's promise that the army and navy would be the only armed organizations, the SS was also now given permission to form armed units.

The SA continued under its new leader—Viktor Lutze—but it was no longer a force to be reckoned with. "Someday we'll . . ." its members could be heard saying late at night when the beer had flowed too freely, but their voices remained low. The days of the rowdy, violent bohemian brownshirts were over. In contrast, Himmler's SS men were silent, impassive puritans, their habitat not the street corner but the office. The day of the ultimate bureaucrat had dawned.

"I Swear by God"

The army selected 2 August 1934 as a day of parades and marches. Defeat in the First World War having deprived it of a victory date, it had chosen to celebrate the twentieth anniversary of the mobilization date for that disastrous war.

Paul Ludwig Hans von Beneckendorff und von Hindenburg, who had served in the Prussian Army during the Austro-Prussian War of 1866, served in the Franco-Prussian War of 1870–1871, retired in 1911, and then returned to service to become a Field Marshal and

Germany's most famous living son, died at 9 A.M. on the morning of 2 August 1934. Hurried orders changed army parades into memorial services.

The Enabling Act of March 1933 gave the National Socialist Cabinet—in effect Adolf Hitler—the right to make laws, even nonconstitutional laws, providing that the powers of the President remained undisturbed. Now President Hindenburg was dead and Hitler had no wish to disturb the powers of the President. He simply assumed them.

The power of the President had been made enormous by the otherwise rather liberal Weimar Constitution. Article 48 enabled the President to suspend the basic rights of any citizen. It was this that made it legal to set up concentration camps, three of which were opened in 1933. A law dated 28 February 1933 provided the Nazis with the right to put opponents into protective custody (*Schutzhaft*). Henceforth, anti-Nazis would simply disappear.

Even before Hindenburg's death, Hitler had arranged the way in which he would take power of President and Chancellor. "Der Führer und Reichskanzler," he called himself, modestly adding that the stature of Hindenburg precluded anyone replacing him. Technically, the post of President remained vacant during Hitler's time, enabling Hitler to avoid taking the oath to uphold the Constitution.

Meanwhile, the men in the Defense Ministry—Blomberg and Reichenau—had also been preparing for the day of Hindenburg's death. Reichenau had been laboring over the words of a new oath for the army and navy to swear to the new President. Instead of an oath that obliged the soldiers to uphold the Constitution, the nation, and its lawful establishments, Reichenau substituted one that pledged personal allegiance to Adolf Hitler.

Some believed that Reichenau and Blomberg were motivated by a desire to return to the old German Army tradition of swearing loyalty to a monarch. But Adolf Hitler was now more powerful than any constitutional monarch. He had virtually eliminated the power of the Reichstag, was empowered to ignore the Constitution, and commanded fierce loyalty from his huge Nazi Party and SA men. Now he took over the powers of the presidency, which included the rank of Supreme Commander of the Armed Forces.

To make quite certain that nothing went wrong in this vital step to total power, Hitler moved quickly and with great cunning. Knowing that in personal confrontation he was indomitable, he sent for Blomberg and the service chiefs. On the morning of 2 August, said Admiral Erich Raeder, testifying after the Second World War at

Nuremberg, Hitler had them in his study and read aloud the text of the oath before asking them to repeat it. If any of the men in that room had doubts about the legality or the morality of the oath, they did not show them. Raeder said it came as no surprise to him since he had sworn a personal oath to Kaiser Wilhelm.

To make the army swear unquestioning loyalty to a man who was not constrained by the Constitution, by monarchy, or by any legal restrictions made the army into a Nazi institution in a way that Röhm's SA had never been and still was not. The brownshirt oath promised only to obey orders that were not illegal acts.

The armed services swore to carry out any action—criminal or otherwise—that Hitler cared to try. There was not even provision for Hitler's sickness or insanity. To order the army to take such an oath was an act of folly. It was, moreover, an act for which Blomberg had no legal authority. But in Hitler's Germany anything could be legalized, as Blomberg's action was three weeks later.

On the evening of President von Hindenburg's death, every army unit held a religious service and every officer and man took the oath of allegiance on the flag of his regiment:

"I swear by God this sacred oath, that I will render unconditional obedience to Adolf Hitler, the Führer of the German Reich and people, Supreme Commander of the Armed Forces, and will be ready as a brave soldier to risk my life at any time for this oath."

That oath was to affect profoundly all attempts to remove Hitler as the war turned unmistakably against Germany. It would prevent withdrawals that might have preserved army units from destruction, delay capitulation in 1943 at Stalingrad until losses became catastrophic, and keep the army obedient long after its commanders were convinced that their Führer was unbalanced.

The Destruction of Blomberg and Fritsch

Largely due to the energies of Blomberg and Fritsch, the German Army had by 1937 grown to considerable size and strength, and to incredible quality. Hitler was, however, dissatisfied by the speed of the army's program of expansion. He sent for his military leaders to tell them so. The Hossbach Conference (called after Hitler's adjutant, Colonel Friedrich Hossbach, who, in the absence of a secretary, kept the notes of this secret meeting) was primarily intended to spur Fritsch into faster action.

The conference, on 5 November 1937, was attended by the Foreign Minister, Baron von Neurath, as well as by Blomberg, Göring,

Fritsch, and the naval Commander in Chief, Admiral Raeder. Hitler expounded his ideas about the way in which a policy of aggression should be timed. He believed that Germany's greatest strength would come between 1943 and 1945 and that war could not be delayed later than that. He wanted Italy to be encouraged into Mediterranean adventures, which would occupy the attention of France and Britain, while Germany moved against Austria and Czechoslovakia, using threats, bluff, and force.

Living space (*Lebensraum*) for Germans had been a constant theme of Hitler's ever since *Mein Kampf*, but his views about getting it by means of war were not shared by his advisers, with the exception of Hermann Göring. Blomberg believed that France and Britain would move against Germany at the first sign of expansion and bring defeat and misery as they had in 1918. Fritsch agreed—and had moral objections too. Furthermore, Fritsch disliked the way in which the army was becoming a political force.

Neurath was so appalled by Hitler's theme that he subsequently suffered a heart attack. Raeder sat silent, thinking only of the tiny navy he had managed to build and what was likely to happen to it in confrontation with the huge fleets of Britain and France. Only Göring spoke in favor of Hitler's ideas and, when Blomberg and Fritsch argued against them, there was a heated exchange.*

The Hossbach Conference was an historic moment in Hitler's determined move to war. There is little doubt that Hitler was surprised at the lack of enthusiasm for his plans shown by his generals. He had always assumed that all the army's generals wanted war, and now he could not find one who did. To what extent the conference persuaded Hitler to get rid of Blomberg and Fritsch can only be guessed. But Göring must have noticed how Blomberg—at one time Hitler's favorite—was no longer in such high regard. Blomberg's job, as War Minister, commanding all three services, was the one that Göring most wanted.

Heinrich Himmler, leader of the SS, also had a lot to gain from the removal of Blomberg and Fritsch, and he was by now as formidable an enemy of the two as Göring. Himmler's powers had increased enormously since Göring had helped him to get rid of Röhm. Himmler was now the head of the whole German police service and, during 1937, was in the process of merging it into the SS. As well as his

---

* By this time, Göring had been given the rank of general and was Commander in Chief of the Air Force as well as Air Minister. In addition, he had become the "plenipotentiary" for the four-year plan, which gave him complete control of the German economy and made him fabulously wealthy.

part-time SS units, he commanded all the *Totenkopfverbände* (Death's Head Units) guarding the concentration camps, which were also under his control.

But Himmler's contest with the army generals centered on his *SS-Verfügungstruppe* (Special Task Troops), which had been created on 16 March 1935, also the day on which conscription had been announced. These SS men were organized and trained as soldiers. By the end of 1937 there were three large infantry regiments— Deutschland, Germania, and Leibstandarte Adolf Hitler—plus a combat engineer company and communications unit. The SS-Verfügungstruppe (generally known as SS-VT and eventually called the *Waffen-SS*) had the same field gray uniforms as the army, the officers came from two excellent training academies, and to lead them there was retired Generalleutnant Paul Hausser, now SS Brigade-führer. All this had been achieved in the face of great opposition from the army, notably from Blomberg and Fritsch. What Himmler wanted now was heavy artillery and tanks for his soldiers and positions in the Army High Command for his senior officers. With the removal of Blomberg and Fritsch he might get his way.

It began by chance. In Berlin a small-time crook named Otto Schmidt specialized in spying on homosexuals and blackmailing them. During interrogation by the police he boasted that some famous people had his victims, including the Potsdam police president, the Minister of Economics, and "General Fritsch." The matter was referred to the Gestapo office that dealt with the suppression of homosexuality. There Schmidt was shown a photo of the Commander in Chief of the Army and asked if this was the same man (the name is not very uncommon in Germany). Schmidt identified Fritsch as the man he had seen committing a homosexual act with a youth picked up at Wannsee railway station in Berlin. Fritsch had paid blackmail money after taking Schmidt to a house in Ferdinandstrasse, Lichter-felde. After more statements, Himmler personally took the file to Hitler in the Reich Chancellery. Hitler glanced through the file and told Himmler to burn "this muck." There the matter might have ended except that Field Marshal von Blomberg got married.

On 12 January 1938 Blomberg, a handsome fifty-nine-year-old widower, married Fräulein Erna Gruhn, a typist from the Reich Egg Marketing Board. Göring and Hitler were the only witnesses at a civil ceremony. It was kept so secret that Fritsch—Blomberg's closest colleague—was virtually the only other person informed. There were no press reports, so few people knew the face or the name of the new *Frau Generalfeldmarschall*. But such ignorance did not extend to the head of the Reich Identification Office of the Criminal Police in Berlin. Across the naked bodies shown in some lewd photos a vaguely familiar name had been written. Reference to the files produced an identification photo of the girl and a change of address registration—the new address was that of Blomberg.

Scarcely able to believe his eyes, the police president deliberately by-passed Himmler and went to Blomberg's Ministry. Unable to find the Minister, he went to General Wilhelm Keitel, who was now in charge of the Armed Forces Office through which the Minister's orders went to the service chiefs.

Keitel said he could not name the woman in the police identification photographs. Although Keitel's daughter was about to marry Blomberg's son, Keitel had not been at the wedding ceremony and had seen Blomberg's wife only once, heavily veiled. Out of stupidity or malice, Keitel suggested that Göring—who had been present— would be the best person to look at the photograph.

The Field Marshal's new wife had posed only once for pornographic photos and only a few of them had been sold before the police took the vendor into custody. But a hasty reading of the police file could suggest that the girl was registered with the police as a prostitute. Although untrue, it was not a suggestion that Blomberg's enemies would be in any hurry to deny. Even today, many history books say incorrectly that she was a police-registered prostitute.

By the evening of 23 January, less than two weeks after the wedding, Göring was in a position to destroy the career of Blomberg, the man who was, in his opinion, not giving the Air Minister's new air force the priorities it deserved.* And if the War Minister was disgraced and dismissed, who would get the Ministry? There was little chance that an admiral would be considered. The most suitable contender would be Göring, Commander in Chief of the Air Force and controller of the Air Ministry and of Lufthansa, the German airline. But whatever Göring's claims, the man most *likely* to become War Minister was Fritsch, a man with whom Göring had had a bitter argument at the Hossbach Conference, when he had called Göring

---

* It is usually said that stories about Blomberg's wife were in wide circulation by the time that Göring saw the papers, but the actions of the police, in having to consult the files to aid their memory and then consulting Keitel and the time between these events, suggest otherwise. From all the many accounts of this bizarre episode, I have mostly used that in *The Order of the Death's Head*, by H. Höhne. R. J. O'Neill's *The German Army and the Nazi Party* says that the police president's visit to Keitel was an attempt to deal with the matter without Himmler's knowledge. This also suggests that rumors were not widely current, as does Göring's reluctance to let the scandal take its natural course.

a "dilettante." There was no reason to remove Blomberg unless Fritsch, his obvious successor, could be removed too.

Göring told Hitler about Blomberg's wife the following evening. Meanwhile, orders had gone to the Gestapo to reactivate the file on Fritsch. (Himmler's unscrupulous intelligence chief, Heydrich, had made photocopies of the file before obeying the Führer's order to burn the original.) After work that lasted all night, the Fritsch file was sent to Hitler, so that it arrived in the early hours of 25 January. Disobeying strict orders, Hitler's military adjutant, Colonel Hossbach, went to warn Fritsch that he was going to be charged on the basis of the evidence. "It's a stinking lie," said Fritsch, incoherent with indignation. Like everyone else who knew Fritsch well, Hossbach was convinced that the charges against Fritsch were false. He persuaded Hitler to see the Commander in Chief of the Army and judge for himself.

On the evening of 26 January, Hitler summoned Fritsch and, in the presence of Göring, confronted him with Otto Schmidt. Fritsch gave his word of honor that he had never seen Schmidt before, but Hitler was unconvinced by this. Delighted at the way Fritsch had failed to convince the Führer, Göring ran out of the room and threw himself onto a sofa, shrieking with delight.

The next day Blomberg resigned as War Minister and went to Italy. If he expected his army to show him some measure of support, or even compassion, he was to be disappointed. But Fritsch was not so easy to dispense with. He resigned as Commander in Chief of the Army, but he would not accept Hitler's offer to let the whole matter be forgotten. He insisted upon a hearing. Hitler suggested the secrecy of a "special court," but the Wehrmacht's Legal Section head insisted that Fritsch be treated in compliance with the Military Legal Code. For an officer of Fritsch's rank, this meant a court-martial with the Commanders in Chief of the three services in judgment. The Reich Minister of Justice—no close ally of Himmler—supported this demand. Hitler agreed but made Göring president of the court.

On 18 March the court found Fritsch innocent on all counts. His defense counsel had merely gone to the address in Ferdinandstrasse given in Schmidt's early statement. There they found a Captain von Frisch (retired), who calmly admitted to both the homosexual act and payment of the blackmail, which could be checked against his bank statements. The Gestapo, said the captain, knew all about it. They had found him as long ago as 15 January.

Colonel General Werner Freiherr von Fritsch had proved his

innocence, but he was not reinstated in his position of Commander in Chief of the Army. Those who still believed that the generals would provide any united front against the criminal activities of the Nazis had now to revise their opinions. Far from protesting at the way their Commander in Chief was dismissed, one of them (General Walter von Brauchitsch) accepted his job without even waiting for the outcome of the trial.

The resignation of Blomberg had marked another step in the Hitlerization of the German armed forces. Furiously angry at Göring, who so obviously arranged his downfall, and at his fellow generals, who had failed him in his hour of need, the wily Blomberg suggested that Hitler should take over the job of War Minister. Now Hitler had tight control of all three services, both as Supreme Commander (the President's title) and as War Minister.

So that there should be no mistake about his intentions, Hitler immediately changed the title of the War Ministry. It became the High Command of the Armed Forces (*Oberkommando der Wehrmacht*). General Wilhelm Keitel (whom Blomberg had described to Hitler as "just a man who runs my office") was given the grand title of *Chef des OKW*. He continued to be little more than an office manager, but now he worked under Hitler's direct control.

The resignations of Blomberg and Fritsch were accompanied by a drastic reshuffle of men who had shown little enthusiasm for Nazi ideas. Sixteen generals left the army and forty-four were transferred. General von Manstein, for instance, was moved from his vital job as Deputy Chief of the General Staff to command a division. Foreign Minister von Neurath also lost his job. To help Göring over his disappointment, he was made a Field Marshal.

For Fritsch the events of 1938 were a tragedy from which he did not recover. His brilliant but formal mind could not adapt to the evil that confronted him. Permitted eventually to return to the army, he went to Poland with his regiment in 1939 and contrived to get killed as soon as he possibly could.

"Ein Volk, Ein Reich, Ein Führer"

Unlike most political parties, the Nazis never offered the voter a well-defined program of politics and economics that would bring peace and prosperity. Rather, they warned of Jewish conspiracies that would destroy the world and Slavic invasions that would bring doom to pure-blooded Aryan man. Opponents were classified as Communists or Jews, or both. Vagueness was a deliberate basis of Hitler's fascism. Thus, as the Nazis assumed power, they had no coordinated machinery of government to impose. Hitler preferred that his lieutenants fought among themselves as they built empires. Nor were those empires always so specialized as Goebbels's control of press, radio, and propaganda. For instance, Göring's influence extended from the secret police to the Air Ministry. Vague policies and squabbling subordinates all served to center the power in one man.

Hitler's climb to preeminence is more sinister in the light of his continuing remarks about the gullibility of the electorate. By 1933 this abstemious forty-four-year-old Austrian had achieved almost unprecedented personal power. He had achieved it by systematically telling the German people the things they wanted to hear, while doing secret deals with anyone who could be of use to him, no matter how much difference there was between secret promises and public oratory.

Adolf Hitler's medical reports show him to be without any important physical or psychological handicaps. In 1939, at 5 feet 9 inches tall and weighing 155 pounds, he would have been considered a better than average risk by most insurance companies. His only serious surgery had been a minor operation to remove a polyp from his vocal cords in 1935, but this had fomented in him a terrible fear of cancer, from which his mother had died.

Stomach cramps, however, caused him considerable pain and loss of sleep. The trouble dated from June 1934, when he had had Röhm and his other old Party comrades murdered. Like his other ailments—ringing in the ears and eczema—these symptoms are commonly associated with tiredness, stress, and hysteria. A fashionable Berlin doctor treated Hitler with injections and pills—mild doses of glucose, vitamins, and caffeine in various proportions—and thereby made a fortune. Hitler was convinced that this medical care had saved his life and became dependent, to some extent, upon such shots before particularly important displays of energy.

Hitler abstained from alcohol and tobacco. Eventually he prohibited smoking in his presence. He was a vegetarian but ate eggs. His conversation was repetitive and monumentally boring—as reading the transcripts of his everyday conversation proves beyond doubt—but his listeners succumbed to his compelling personal qualities. The combination of boundless energy and immense charm is a quality often glimpsed in world-famous actors. Hitler was able to focus his entire attention on the people he met and, in doing so, persuade them that their problems were henceforth his too.*

Even in 1935 men came from meetings with Hitler convinced that the repressive totalitarian regime he had created was distasteful to him and that he was searching for ways to relax conditions. Whatever you wanted to hear, Hitler supplied it.

His reading provided a fund of "digest" information that gave him instant rapport with experts, prophets, and bigots alike. His military knowledge was limited and he had no real understanding of technical matters, but he could patch fragments together by means of his truly amazing memory. He liked to confuse his generals by arguing specifically about equipment newly issued to some remote regiment or talk about some other minute detail. But he would often fail to understand the larger-scale logistics or strategy about which he was deciding.

Most of his difficulties centered upon his social insecurities. The coarse voice, imperfect grammar, and strong country accent that had been essential for his early successes at the polls became short-comings as he moved into the highest circles of the land. Similarly, his war service as a Catholic Austrian corporal in a Bavarian infantry regiment put him at a disadvantage when talking to the Prussian Protestants of the Army General Staff, whose military antecedents peopled German history books. In the presence of Fritsch, for instance, Hitler was always subdued and ill at ease.

There is no evidence that he had any kind of sexual problems or was in any way abnormal. It is true that he loved his niece dearly and was shattered by her suicide in 1931. But armies of sensation mongers have tried, and failed, to find evidence of any sexual relationship between them. Hitler was not influenced by women in the way that so many of his contemporaries were. He had a mistress, but she did not seek to change history as did the mistresses of the French statesmen Paul Reynaud and Édouard Daladier. To think of Hitler as a deviant or a monster is to miss the point. He was the epitome of the common man. He went to the First World War in a mood of idealism. He returned home to a chaos of social inequality and became embittered. His knowledge lacked the pattern that formal education grants and was unsupported by languages or by foreign travel— Hitler saw the Slav races and the French that he hated so much only after his armies had conquered them.

Hitler's type of crazy rhetoric about Jewish blood, capitalist con-

---

* Published examples of such conversations are to be found in *Hitler's Secret Conversations, 1941–1944* and in *Hitler Directs His War*, by Felix Gilbert.

spiracies, and slave nations could be heard in every factory canteen throughout Europe, and perhaps still can be. It was the fact that the men took it seriously enough to commit murder, build concentration camps, and march against the world because of it that turned Hitler's mind. But it might have had just that effect upon you.

Hitler's instinct enabled him to sell his vague "National Socialism" to the German people, but once in power he concentrated on providing full employment and then on raising the standard of living. Deprived of effective trade unions, the unemployed were given jobs on public works projects and factories. The workers did not complain. A plebiscite to confirm Hitler's actions not only brought 95.7 per cent of the eligible voters to the polls, but got 89.93 per cent yeses.

Having no colonies, Germany's most pressing need was foreign exchange to buy raw materials. Short-circuiting all the normal methods of world trade, Germany exchanged goods with countries that could provide such things as raw cotton, raw wool, and iron ore. When necessary, the government subsidized the exports to make the deal more attractive. This gave the Nazis a tight control of the economy. They could subsidize whichever exports they chose; they could give the raw materials to whichever manufacturers they favored. Even more important, they could vary the value of the mark according to the climate of world trade and according to the bargaining power of the supplier. These ideas were those of Dr. Hjalmar Schacht, president of the Reichsbank and from 1934 until 1937 the Minister of Economics. However, Schacht's genius would have counted for little had it not been for the generous terms with which the creditor nations—particularly Great Britain—settled Germany's international debts.

In the three years from 1933 until 1936, Germany climbed from depression to a prosperity as high as that of any country in Europe. Its social services were incomparable, and, although from 1938 onward military expenditure increased rapidly, German living standards continued to rise and remain higher than those of Britain even into the early 1940s.

German economists found Hitler open to new ideas about money and barter, just as tank experts found him quick to understand their theories about tanks. The airmen soon realized that he was one of the few politicians who understood the importance of air power, and steel manufacturers realized that he was one of the few men who understood how much easier it was to make steel without the trade unions or Communist interference.

Helped by his propaganda experts, who were, needless to say, delighted that he understood propaganda, Hitler had managed to link the heroic appeal of self-sacrifice for the community with a system of elitism and privilege to which only such heroes could aspire. This was the essence of the National Socialist state. In a postwar world racked by cynicism, greed, and despair, it was the idealist nature of Germany's finest young men that beguiled them into joining the Nazi machine. Any attempt today to define the Second World War in terms of armies of "fascist barbarians" will fail, as surely as any attempt to see the U.S.S.R.'s victory as a triumph of communism.

If there was one factor above all others that was to lead to Hitler's downfall, it was his absurd obsessive hatred of Jews. In the field of science alone, the persecution of the Jews deprived Hitler of military technology he would desperately need. A Nazi regime without anti-Semitism would probably have had some form of atomic warhead and V-2 rockets to deliver them by the late 1930s. Thus I am of the opinion that but for his anti-Semitism Hitler might have conquered the world.

At first, Nazi anti-Semitism was regarded by many as an electioneering gimmick, one that would be dropped after an assumption of power. But when it continued, Europe was not shocked: Hitler's pogroms were simply a continuing and better organized outbreak of a disease that Europe had suffered and tolerated for centuries.

Gradually the lies, the ruthlessness, the brutality, and the depravities took effect. A subtle change of climate brought into anti-Nazi alignment many in other countries who would not have opposed them politically. It brought together disparate elements that would not otherwise have cooperated. Evidence of this is the conciliatory attitude shown to Italian Fascists during the same period. This hardening of anti-Nazi attitudes across a wide spectrum of European society was something that German diplomats and politicians failed to see.

Considering his background and his complete lack of training, Hitler's military skills were astonishing. The way in which he gained complete control of both the military and civil life of Germany while remaining, right up until his death, the most popular ruler that Germany had ever known* is perhaps unique.

But as the war continued, it was Hitler's political dogma that ensured the failure of his military aims. His worst military decisions— the refusal to let units withdraw to better positions, the obsession with towns that had strong psychological overtones (such as Leningrad

---

* According to the historian A. J. P. Taylor, writing in the *Observer* newspaper in October 1978.

and Stalingrad), and the political interference with the army—all these stemmed from his fears of *political* consequences. Politically motivated plans can be fatal to world conquest as to car factories. Worst of all, in promoting himself to command the army, he saddled himself with an incumbent he could not dismiss.

Men and women who spent time at Hitler's mountain retreat, the Berghof, remember the boredom, the monotony, and the oppressive silence. Hitler's day began when he unlocked his bedroom door and reached for the newspapers that were placed on a hassock outside it. The morning continued in silence as servants dusted the furniture and polished the marble and aides tiptoed about and spoke in whispers. After a frugal lunch, at which the world of theater and fashion were staple topics, Hitler, dressed in tweeds and soft hat, went for a stroll with his guests as far as the tea pavilion built to exploit views of the mountains. Rich cream pastries provided a temptation which Hitler found too hard to resist.

In the evening a spartan supper would be followed by a film show. Light comedies and sentimental stories were preferred, although *Mutiny on the Bounty* and *The Hound of the Baskervilles* were top favorites repeated again and again. Obedient servants catered to the Führer's every whim. His adoring mistress, Eva Braun, was kept out of sight until her presence was required, and the guests were chiefly old cronies who sat up with him until the small hours of morning, exchanging gossip and stories of the good old days. So might have been the life of any working man who had won a magnificent lottery.

Few men felt entirely at ease in Hitler's company, which was evident from the change in mood when the Führer got up from his place by the big log fire and went to bed. One man who did enjoy Hitler's company was Erwin Rommel, whose meteoric career in the military was a direct result of the Führer's favor.

Erwin Rommel

Born in 1891 in Heidenheim, the son of a schoolmaster, Rommel was above all a typical Swabian: thrifty, loyal, punctual, and industrious. In the First World War he had been so determined to win the *Pour le Mérite*, Germany's highest award for valor, that he had led his men into ferocious fighting time and time again until he was eventually recommended for the decoration that so obsessed him.

In the postwar army he won notice as an inspiring and lively instructor of tactics. Typically he used as the basis for his talks his own skills and successes in the Italian mountains where he had won his

medal. Eventually his lectures were published in book form—
Infanteri Greift An—and as a bestseller it brought him fame and
fortune and the attention of Adolf Hitler.

Loyalty and obedience were fundamental to Rommel's character,
and he accepted the Nazi creed lock, stock, and barrel. In 1936 he
was selected for Hitler's escort at the Nazi Party rally at Nuremberg
and subsequently was made the army's liaison officer with the Hitler
Youth service. Hitler continued to make use of Rommel on escort
duties, and by the time war began Rommel had been made *Generalmajor* with backdated seniority and command of the escort battalion
that the army provided to Hitler. This unit was made up of soldiers
of the elite Grossdeutschland Regiment assigned to Hitler's headquarters on rotation. Contrary to what has been written about him,
Rommel was in no way associated with the SS bodyguard unit
SS-Leibstandarte Adolf Hitler, which was a bodyguard of men rotated
from that Waffen-SS formation. Hitler's personal protection, like that
of Winston Churchill, was the responsibility of plainclothes police
officers.

Rommel found no difficulty in adapting to the stultifying life at
the Führer's headquarters. He had no interest in art or music and
admitted that a visit to the ballet had bored him. Rommel lived only
for his army career, but he never suffered from that dulling of the
brain that so often affects young officers in peacetime. As a young
company commander he had interested himself in such things as the
repair of motorcycles, stamp collecting, boats, and organizing unit
dances. The qualities he had displayed in mountain warfare in Italy
were extended as he became a skillful skier and huntsman. His
emphasis on physical fitness meant that his soldiers were sometimes
subjected to two hours of training in the early hours of the morning.
No wonder, then, that while a far more reserved officer such as
Guderian could be nicknamed "Hurrying Heinz," Rommel earned no
nickname from the troops who served under him.

Rommel's uncritical attitude to the Nazi regime and his devotion
to Hitler paid great dividends in early 1940 when, on the personal
instructions of the Führer, he was appointed to the coveted command
of a panzer division. He surprised the officers of 7.Pz.Div with a "Heil
Hitler" greeting and distributed to them copies of his book.

PART TWO

Hitler at War

"I am insulted by the persistent assertion that I want war. Am I a fool? War! It would settle nothing."

— ADOLF HITLER, from an interview in *Le Matin*, 10 November 1933

The maps of Hitler's Europe changed continually. In 1935 the population of the coal-rich Saar Basin, which had been taken over by France as part of the war reparations, voted to return to German rule. In 1936 Hitler repudiated the Treaty of Locarno and marched into the Rhineland, a large section of western Germany which had been demilitarized since the end of the First World War. Two years later, deploying some of his newly built tanks, Hitler sent his army into Austria, his homeland, to join it to Germany in what the propaganda afterward called an *Anschluss*, or union. From this unopposed victory, which the soldiers called a *Blumenkrieg* (flower war), the Third Reich gained iron, timber, a frontier with Italy, and 6 million German citizens to work and fight for Hitler. A plebiscite confirmed that Hitler's move was popular with Austrians. The reunification was welcomed by 99.8 per cent of the votes cast.*

Germany now extended over the road, river, and rail communications which under the old Austro-Hungarian Empire radiated from Vienna. It was a stronger geographical position. Within two days of Hitler's annexation of Austria, Churchill made a speech on the subject: "Europe is confronted with a programme of aggression, nicely calculated and timed, unfolding stage by stage . . ." In fact, Europe was confronted with a ruthless opportunist rather than by a plan, but the end result was the same. Flying home from his Anschluss triumph, Hitler had shown General Keitel how his mind was working. He put his hand across a small newspaper map of Europe so that his finger

* Of 49,493,028 people entitled to vote, no fewer than 49,279,104 did so.

and thumb covered Germany and Austria. He nipped Czechoslovakia
and then winked at Keitel.

Czechoslovakia

If the Western Powers were to halt Hitler, then the best time to do it
would have been in 1938 when he threatened Czechoslovakia.
France was already committed to helping the Czechs and so was
Russia. The Czech Army was well trained and Czech fortifications
along the German border were first class. Czech tanks and guns were
world-famous and its armaments industry—including the Skoda
works—was the second largest in the world.

Germany and Its Eastern Neighbors,
1918

MAP I
After the Russian collapse and the signing of the Treaty of Brest-Litovsk,
2 March 1918.

The German Army would require all its resources if it was to make war on Czechoslovakia, with little left to face France. General Alfred Jodl later admitted that only five fighting divisions and seven reserve divisions defended Germany's western frontier and that the unfinished fortifications "were nothing but a large construction site . . ." Even a weak and disorganized French Army would have been enough to overwhelm the Germans, and the shape of Germany was such that any bold thrust would cut it in half.

The German economy at this time could not have supported the war machine. The program to manufacture synthetic rubber and aviation fuel needed more time and there were problems in the manufacture of explosives.

Most important of all was the way in which Hitler's proposed Czechoslovak adventure was opposed by the German generals. Some were appalled at the idea of this unprovoked attack and others simply warned that it would lead to a war which Germany could not win. Any determined move by the French Army would have fulfilled the warnings, given the generals power to move against Hitler, and perhaps even triggered a putsch. As it was, Hitler's belligerence and bluff gave Germany a bloodless victory and made his generals appear as spineless, incompetent Jeremiahs.

Hitler found little difficulty in manufacturing grievances against Czechoslovakia. The Germans living in the Sudetenland, near the German border, were being ill treated, said Hitler, so this region had to become part of Germany.

In fact, the question of the Sudetenland Germans was far more complex than Nazi propaganda would ever admit. Czechoslovakia had been created from a defeated Austria-Hungary at the end of the First World War. For some time the Germans, like other minority groups in the country, were treated badly but, as Germany prospered, the Sudeten Germans had been treated more fairly. By the time of the crisis, they were probably the most pampered minority in the world. But Germany's prosperity under Hitler and the nationalistic Nazi propaganda (much of it specially designed for Germans living overseas) had become particularly appealing to Germans living in Czechoslovakia. The country in 1938 was in a temporary economic decline, and this had hit hardest the industrial regions in which the Germans lived. The disputed regions were not just strips of border land but well over a quarter of Czechoslovakia's area. These regions provided all Czechoslovakia's available graphite and zinc, well over half of its coal, copper, and paper, as well as half its chemical industry. Furthermore, these regions included almost all the border defenses,

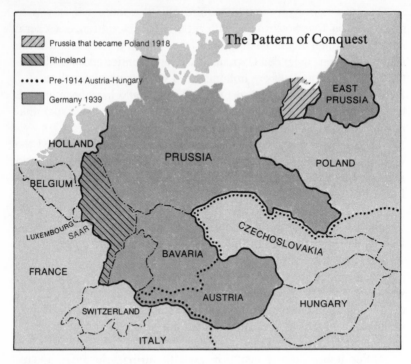

MAP 2

Germany plus Austria made jaws to bite Czechoslovakia, which in turn made new jaws to eat Poland.

the most modern forts in Europe. These were essential to Czech security. Faced with the choice between giving Germany such an area or going to war, the Czechs called upon France to honor the 1925 Treaty of Locarno, under which France guaranteed Czechoslovakia's territorial integrity.

Britain and France

At the time of the Czechoslovak crisis, Britain's Prime Minister was Neville Chamberlain, who had come to that top post from local government. His rise disproves the theory that all men are promoted only one step beyond their level of proven competence; it took him all the way from mayor of Birmingham to Prime Minister of Britain. A previous holder of that post—David Lloyd George—had described Chamberlain as "a pinhead." His most notable, and indeed popular, contribution to government had been getting the nation's defense estimates whittled down to the very lowest point for the interwar period.

Chamberlain was staid, honest, and efficient, but he had the mentality of the clerk and was completely out of his depth when faced with the techniques of dictatorship. Hitler broke his word, changed his mind, simulated rage, hammered the conference table, and used overt threats of invasion and bombing raids as a way to get concessions. Hitler used the telephone tapping operations of Göring's *Forschungsamt* (Research Office), which intercepted telephone conversations, Telex messages, and telegrams (with special attention to foreign embassies), and had extensive and efficient facilities for deciphering and evaluating information. Ever since 1933 when the Forschungsamt (FA) was created—hidden in Göring's Air Ministry organization—Hitler had used it to measure how far to push his victims.*

Chamberlain preferred to believe that Hitler was a reasonable and honest man, simply because he could think of no way of dealing with him if he was otherwise.

There was, at the time, little opposition to Hitler anywhere in Europe. The Conservative Party, in power in Britain, suspected that any direct confrontation with Germany might tempt Stalin to move westward. (When, in 1940, the U.S.S.R. invaded Lithuania, Latvia, and Estonia, these fears proved to have some foundation.) Britain's Labour Party, in opposition, although vociferously anti-Fascist, was bitterly opposed to the rearmament and conscription that were needed to resist them. Although in hindsight difficult to believe, many British Socialists voiced fears of a coup d'état if the army was given more money and influence.

The mood of the country did not encourage politicians to prepare to fight Hitler. Winston S. Churchill, Member of Parliament for Epping, was virtually a lone voice calling for sanctions, collective security, and rearmament. He was over sixty years old and generally considered well past his prime. His warnings and advice went unheeded. In spite of their large majority in Parliament, the Conservatives did not want to risk the possible unpopularity that such measures might bring. Churchill was shunned.

France, by common consent the greatest armed power in Europe,

---

* Although in *Breach of Security* David Irving says that Hitler would not read wiretaps, his more recent book *The War Path* shows a change of opinion. For instance, page 136 says that FA-tapped embassy conversations in Berlin told Hitler volumes about morale in London and Prague. Page 145 describes Hitler turning FA wiretaps over in his hands.

was even less willing to confront Hitler. Having been shattered morally and physically by the First World War, the French were in no mood to fight again. The extreme Left and Right fought in the streets, until a broad Left coalition, the "Popular Front," came to power. As Germany grew stronger and more bellicose, Stalin decided that a stable France would be to Soviet Russia's benefit. He instructed French Communists to ally themselves to the Popular Front.

The Popular Front courted popularity by reducing the working week to forty hours with no reduction of wages. It was claimed that this would reduce unemployment. It did not do so; it increased prices, decreased exports, and led to devaluation of the franc.

But, unlike Britain, France had a treaty that committed it to aid Czechoslovakia. Russia was also committed to help the Czechs, but only after France did so. Nearly all the high-ranking officers of the Red Army had already been murdered or imprisoned, on orders of Stalin. This weakened army and the way in which both Poland and Romania refused to let Red Army soldiers pass through their territory to Czechoslovakia made many Western experts doubt if Russia would or could give aid.

The French encouraged Britain to help settle Germany's claims peacefully and so get them off the hook. Chamberlain, seeing it as his chance to go down in history as a great statesman, flew to Munich in September 1938 to see Hitler.

The trip gave both the words "appeasement" and "Munich" new pejorative connotations. It was like asking a Sunday school teacher to put out a contract on Al Capone. Instead of confronting him, Chamberlain became Hitler's aide. He warned the Czechs of what would happen to them unless they gave up their territories to the Germans. Adding a warning not to mobilize, he demanded an answer within twenty-four hours.

For a moment it seemed as if there would be war. The Czech reply described the joint note as "a de facto ultimatum of the sort usually delivered to a vanquished nation and not a proposition to a sovereign state." But Chamberlain urged the Czechs not to publish their reply and told them that "the German forces will have orders to cross the Czechoslovak frontier almost immediately, unless by 2 P.M. tomorrow the Czechoslovak government have accepted German terms." From the tone of the note, the Czechs might have suspected that Chamberlain was Hitler's ally, rather than theirs. In the face of this, the Czechs gave way.

Not long afterward—in March 1939—Hitler's soldiers moved out of those large fortified frontier zones and occupied Prague, the Czech capital. Czechoslovakia as a nation had ceased to exist.

The Czech Army was disbanded and its officers pensioned off; the men were not conscripted into the Wehrmacht. Hitler now had a new selection of tanks, artillery, small arms, and aircraft to distribute to his Wehrmacht. The Skoda arms factory at Pilsen was almost as famous as that town's brewery. It supplied arms to Romania and Yugoslavia, who now had to negotiate with Hitler for replacements and spare parts. There was no lack of employment; the armaments factories began to supply the Nazi war machine.

Rapacious Nazi businessmen submitted their claims for Czechoslovak industry, as they had done for Austrian industry. I. G. Farben had taken over the largest chemical enterprise in Austria—Skodawerke Wetzler A.G.—having offered to replace all Jews in the management and bring this huge gunpowder plant into the German four-year plan. So went valuable factories in Czechoslovakia. The Dresdner Bank was entrusted, by Göring, with the task of controlling the most important Czech industries and thereby took over the big Czech banking chain Boehmische Escomptebank.

Poland Threatened

Every month the German Army grew in size and strength. In 1934 the 100,000-man army had had no tanks, no airplanes, and very little artillery, and Germany had been disarmed for fourteen years. But by 1939 Prime Minister Chamberlain was facing a Germany in the process of mobilizing 4 million men. Theoretically, in that four-year period, each of those 100,000 professional soldiers had trained forty men. In fact, not even the German Army could have done that, and only about one man in eight had even the briefest training before mobilization. The *Ersatz* and *Landwehr* divisions consisted mostly of middle-aged men who hardly remembered what a rifle looked like. The fact remained that Hitler now had the large army he wanted and was virtually in direct control of its operations.

Poland was a huge parcel of land which had emerged periodically from the mists of European history, but never in exactly the same place. Three times already Poland had been divided between Germany and Russia. Now it was to happen for the fourth time.

It was inevitable that the frontiers drawn up by Poland at the Treaty of Riga (which followed her victory over the Russian armies in 1920) would be disputed. The northeast region—apart from the

border areas taken from Lithuania—was occupied by a million
White Russians. The southeast quarter was populated by nearly
4 million Ukrainians. There were a million Germans living inside its
western border. The Poles—about 19 million of them—lived in the
western half of Poland. Two million Jews were dispersed throughout
the land but remained together in communities, principally because of
the murderous pogroms against them, which the Polish government
did little to discourage.

The Polish government was a combination of soldiers and right-
wing politicians. Their conquest of large areas of land from Russia

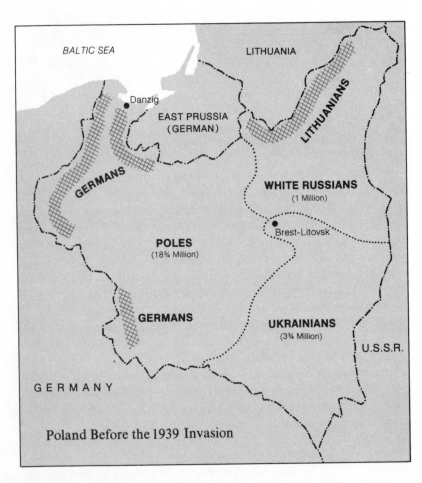

Poland Before the 1939 Invasion

MAP 3

had strained the Poles' relationship with their eastern neighbors, but they were friendly with France and friendly enough with the Nazis to help themselves to a piece of Czechoslovakia when, in 1938, that country succumbed to Hitler's aggression.

The British and French concessions to him at Munich convinced Hitler that he could screw a few more territorial demands from the men he scoffed at as "old coffee aunties" without much risk of war. He turned his attention next to Danzig.

Poland had been given a "corridor" to the sea, through Prussia, to Danzig, which was now a "free city," although its population was almost entirely German. Hitler wanted roads and railways across the Corridor and said that Danzig must become German again. By Hitler's standards, the demands were reasonable. Hitler reckoned that "the worms" who governed the western nations would never go to war for such trifling matters. Hitler told his generals to prepare for an attack on Poland.

But, as might have been expected, Hitler had a trick up his sleeve. This time it had that element of theater that Hitler so loved. Just three days before Hitler first planned to start the attack, the German-Soviet Non-Aggression Pact was signed. The Slav "monsters" upon whom all his years of abuse had been heaped were now prepared to divide Poland with him. Hitler reasoned that the news of the pact should be enough to deter the worms. Two days later the British issued a clear warning by signing an Anglo-Polish Mutual Assistance Pact. Hitler remained convinced that the Poles would not go to war and asked them to send a plenipotentiary to Berlin.

The British urged the Poles to negotiate and were confident that they would. The Germans, who were tapping the telephones at the French and British embassies and deciphering the secret telegram messages, shared that confidence. But the Poles would not even name a plenipotentiary. Hitler backed down; now he asked only for the return of Danzig to Germany and for a plebiscite to be held in the Corridor. The Poles still would not agree.

As long before as 3 April, the OKW had ordered the army to prepare plans for an attack on Poland. Commander in Chief of the Army General von Brauchitsch ordered General Franz Halder, Director of Operations for the Army General Staff, to work on them. Halder, a Bavarian artillery officer, ordered his planners to work.*

---

* A disproportionate number of senior German generals came from the artillery: Walter Warlimont, Ludwig Beck, Walter von Brauchitsch, Friedrich Dollmann, Alfred Jodl, Franz Halder, Walter von Reichenau, and Wilhelm Keitel. By the end of the war 40 per cent of the generals and six of the nineteen field marshals had come from

The Polish plain was a terrain ideally suited for mechanized warfare, even though the roads were very primitive. German intelligence
well knew that timing was vital; the rainy weeks of late September
and October produce thousands of square miles of mud that would
bog down any army. And then there were the broad Polish rivers.

Broad rivers are the most worrying of obstacles to military
planners. Even the mighty Vistula upstream from Warsaw was ford-
able at several places in that summer of 1939. But when the rains
started, such broad rivers could become an obstacle that would daunt
not only bridge builders but also the men who might have to cross
them under fire.

As the diplomatic wrangling went on, Hitler persuaded himself
that France and Britain were looking for a way out of their obliga-
tions. The Polish invasion was originally set for 26 August but, as
X-day approached, Hitler came to believe that he needed a few more
days to drive a wedge between the Poles and their Western Allies.
And yet with every day that passed, the wet weather that would
protect the Poles came closer. Hitler set the date for 1 September,
knowing that if the date was again changed, it would mean a delay of
some months. Many of the active army divisions had been brought
up to full strength by calling in reservists for their "annual training,"
while the regular army had been moved to the jumping-off points
under the guise of "summer exercises." But the summer could not
last forever.

By now Hitler did not want a *Blumenkrieg*. He wanted a real war
and military victory in Poland, but he did not want France and
Britain involved in the conflict. On the night of 28 August Hitler
dreamed up a series of demands that he knew would sound reasonable
to the Western Allies but be unacceptable to the Poles. These included
giving the Poles just one day to get a plenipotentiary to Berlin. Either
they would refuse to comply at such short notice or the negotiator
would arrive and find agreement impossible. This would enable Hitler
to start his attack on 1 September as planned.

With intercepts of the British ambassador's telephone conversations to London in his hands, Hitler felt sure that this final device
would be enough to sever the Poles from the West. At midday on
31 August he gave his army the provisional go-ahead. A few minutes

---

the artillery arm. Matthew Cooper, in his book *The German Army*, attributes this to
the brains required for gunnery and the much lower casualty rate that gunners suffer
in war. I cannot agree. Low casualty rates bring slower promotion, not faster. My
explanation is the way in which the sort of set-piece battle that characterized the
Western Front fighting of 1914–1918 made it essential that artillery commanders
were brought into the high-level planning.

later the Polish ambassador asked to see the German Foreign Minister. At 4 P.M. on that same day, 31 August 1939, with the Polish ambassador still waiting to speak to him, Hitler gave his army the final decision: the attack would begin next morning.

The Polish ambassador told Hitler that the Polish government was now favorably considering the idea of negotiations. But by this time Hitler was determined upon war and intoxicated with his own power. Dissenters were harshly reminded of how the Führer had been right about the Rhineland, Austria, the Sudetenland, and Czechoslovakia. In none of those cases had the worms acted. Hitler had a hatred for Poland that went far beyond any political ambitions. On 22 August he had told his senior commanders of his intention to send his SS units into Poland "to kill without pity or mercy all men, women and children of Polish race or language." He had told them that he would use his SS to stage a propaganda stunt to start the war.* And he told them that, after Poland, he would invade Soviet Russia.

Brauchitsch, who had replaced Fritsch as army Commander in Chief, did little or nothing to dissuade Hitler from aggression. When Hjalmar Schacht, former Minister of Economics and Reichsbank president, reminded Brauchitsch that his oath to the Constitution required that a declaration of war needed the approval of the Reichstag, Brauchitsch told him that if he tried to enter the Army High Command (now moved to Zossen, outside Berlin) he would have him arrested.

In the early hours of 1 September the German invasion began. For what seemed like an age, the British government hesitated as radio reports told of the Polish fighting. Hitler remained in Berlin, still clinging to the hope that Britain and France would find a way to avoid allying themselves to a country that was already doomed. But on 3 September Britain went to war and some hours later France did too. Hitler shrugged, got into his private train, *Amerika*, and traveled up to the front.

The planning for that attack had been going on all through the summer. The planning team was called *Arbeitsstab Rundstedt* after its leading figure, Generaloberst Gerd von Rundstedt. Sixty-four years old, Rundstedt had once been the army's senior general after Blomberg and Fritsch. But for his age, he would have been made Commander in Chief of the Army, according to what Hitler told Keitel. Rundstedt was an eccentric. He seldom wore a general's uniform (or later a field marshal's), preferring that of Infantry Regiment No. 18, of which

---

* The incident was to be an attack on a German radio station near the Polish frontier by SS men dressed in Polish uniforms. Concentration camp prisoners would be murdered to provide corpses for the newspapermen.

he was honorary commander. Because of his insignia he was often mistaken for a colonel and addressed as such, but he found that amusing. Recalled from retirement, he refused to purchase an overcoat on the grounds that he was too old to make the cost worthwhile. He was an avid reader of detective stories but self-conscious enough to read them in the open drawer of his desk so that they could be quickly hidden from sight.

Although in charge of the planning for the attack on Poland, Rundstedt remained in his house in Kassel through the summer and left the work to the two officers assigned to him. One of them was Erich von Manstein, who had spent almost his entire career in staff work, although at this time he was commanding the 18th Infantry Division at Liegnitz. Fifty-two years old, a stern-looking man with a large beaky nose and heavy eyebrows, Manstein had been chief of the operations branch of the General Staff and later its deputy chief. He had lost his job when, after Blomberg's resignation, senior officers with little liking for the Nazis had been moved to less sensitive positions. Guderian called Manstein "our finest operational brain," and more than one historian has called him the most skillful general of the war.

Manstein's participation in the planning has tended to obscure the contribution made by Colonel Günther von Blumentritt, who was at that time an officer on the General Staff as chief of the training section. The work these two men did is more remarkable considering that the army would not give them time off in which to do it. Both men, separated by many miles, continued with their day-to-day duties.

As the plan evolved, Rundstedt was ordered to take command of the southern group of armies for the attack and Manstein was made his chief of staff. Army Group North was formed from the existing Army Group Command I under General Fedor von Bock.

Manstein and Blumentritt were two of a small number of officers whose experience with the General Staff and as chiefs of staff to senior commanders made them preeminent in the skills of planning and gave them an importance beyond their military ranks. Other such officers included General Gustav von Wietersheim, who was to command the motorized units that followed Guderian in May 1940, and Halder, who was to oppose Manstein's ideas.

The Conquest of Poland

Germany needed a quick victory over Poland. In addition to the need for tactical haste to decide matters before the Poles could mobilize, and the strategic perils of a two-front war, Germany's fighting endurance was severely limited.* Already experts from German industry had decided which Polish factories would be most necessary to the war economy, and the military plan was designed to capture such plants intact.

The Poles were far too complacent about the danger threatening them, believing that German mobilization announcements would give them, and France, enough time to mobilize too. But the Poles were wrong. The German *Welle Plan* (wave system) enabled them to mobilize in secret. By the end of August, reservists had joined the active divisions and even the third and fourth "waves" of former Landwehr divisions had gone quietly to face France from the fortified West Wall.

The German plan depended upon overrunning the Polish railheads near the German border and the reserve deployment and assembly areas before called-up Polish reservists arrived there. By bringing the small regular Polish Army to battle near the German frontier, it would eliminate the chance that the Polish forces would retreat behind the Vistula and reorganize. And unless the German Army fought within easy distance of the German railheads in Silesia and Pomerania used in the previous war, the movement to battle would delay and exhaust the German infantry and stretch too far its horse-drawn supply lines.

At 4.45 A.M. on 1 September, five German armies in the north, west, and south attacked. At 6 A.M. Warsaw was bombed without warning. The air strikes against the Polish air force virtually destroyed it on the ground.† The Germans followed with attacks on railways and roads to hinder movement and mobilization.

Polish politicians thought it possible that the Germans would simply seize the free port of Danzig and a large piece of the Corridor and then stop fighting. Politically, such a success would have given the Poles the choice of letting the Germans keep what they had or carrying on the war and facing charges that they were the aggressors. It was for this reason that the Polish Commander in Chief was told to

---

* In June 1936 General von Fritsch ordered a study of materiel, financial, and manpower requirements. An appendix showed that oil fuel was the critical factor, in particular storage facilities of 1 million tons. At the estimated wartime rate of consumption (and taking into account synthetic oil production), Germany could fight for only seven months. Germany imported 90 per cent of its tin, 70 per cent of its copper, 80 per cent of its rubber, 75 per cent of its oil, and 99 per cent of its bauxite. It was only the resources from the Soviet Union that enabled the German machine to continue the war.

† Polish aviation was controlled by the army and navy. There was no separate air force.

put a large army in the Corridor. It has been estimated that about a third of the whole Polish Army was there when German spearheads came from both sides and cut it to shreds.

Manstein's plan was old-fashioned, but he had done his work well. The Poles fought like tigers, but the Germans knifed through Polish cavalry and infantry, who died fighting an even more old-fashioned kind of war. Polish cavalry charged the German tanks and died gloriously, although it was later suggested that the Poles thought that some of the tanks were no more than cars with wooden and canvas covers, the sort of thing the Germans had used on early exercises.

Everywhere the Luftwaffe subjected the Poles to machine-gun fire and bombs. Every account of the Polish fighting has to be read bearing in mind this German command of the air. It was a war of continuous movement; no front formed for more than a few hours.

In the south, the Fourteenth Army headed due east for the river Vistula. Should the Poles withdraw behind that river, they would be already outflanked.

In the original OKH plan, Reichenau's Tenth Army was also to head due east, but Rundstedt and Manstein calculated that the bulk of Polish forces was still west of Warsaw and redirected Reichenau's thrust to cut them off from the capital. From East Prussia the Third Army was sent to complete the pincer movement west of Warsaw. Only the massive Polish forces around Poznan came near to retreating fast enough to escape the jaws that were closing upon them.

The Poznan army had been virtually by-passed by the original attack. To withdraw an army is a considerable feat of staff work and organization; to fight at the same time comes close to the impossible. The fighting troops become entangled with transport columns and field artillery, while coming the other way along the country roads is everything from the wheelwright to the physical training inspector. In spite of all the problems, the Poznan army—with remnants of the survivors from the Corridor—turned southward and then attacked the German southern thrust with enough vigor to make its army commander call for help and force the whole German corps to swing its front northward and bring another regiment north by air.

The Eighth Army had been given the task of covering the flank of the Tenth Army's attack, and there was a certain amount of bad feeling about the failure to put out enough reconnaissance units to discover the danger from the north. There were very few motor vehicles available, and at this moment cavalry was not available either.

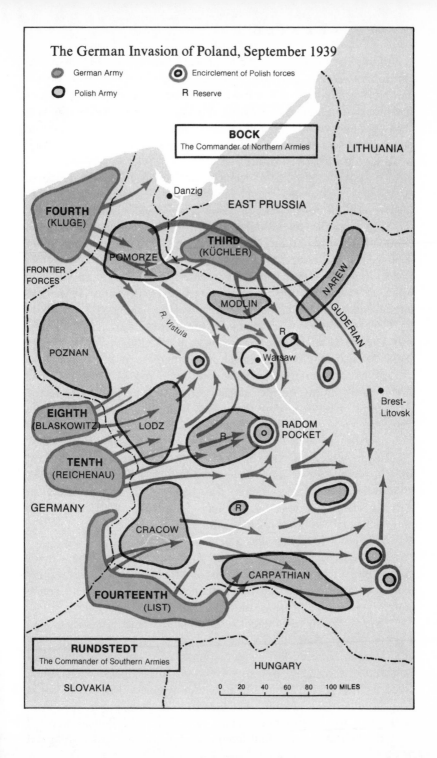

The German Invasion of Poland, September 1939

German Army
Polish Army
Encirclement of Polish forces
R Reserve

BOCK
The Commander of Northern Armies

LITHUANIA

Danzig
EAST PRUSSIA

FOURTH
(KLUGE)

THIRD
(KÜCHLER)

POMORZE

FRONTIER
FORCES

MODLIN

R. Vistula

NAREW

GUDERIAN

POZNAN

R
Warsaw

Brest-
Litovsk

EIGHTH
(BLASKOWITZ)

LODZ

R
RADOM
POCKET

TENTH
(REICHENAU)

GERMANY

R

CRACOW

CARPATHIAN

FOURTEENTH
(LIST)

RUNDSTEDT
The Commander of Southern Armies

HUNGARY

SLOVAKIA

0   20   40   60   80   100 MILES

Manstein was in no hurry to provide help to the Eighth Army. He did not want to send the Poles reeling, lest he knock them farther east. Instead, he told a Tenth Army panzer (armored) corps, which had got as far as the suburbs of Warsaw and was discovering that tanks became very vulnerable in street fighting, to wheel round and attack the Poles from the east. Manstein was now forcing the Poles to fight with a reversed front.

To assist in this encirclement—later to be called the battle of Bzura River—Manstein called into action the two reserve divisions that were following the Eighth Army. They were moved up to attack the Poles from the west. By now this battle had come under the direct control of Army Group South, so Manstein could ask the other Army Group to close the ring by sending a corps south against the Polish armies. Besieged were nine infantry divisions and three cavalry brigades, as well as the remnants of ten more divisions. It was the largest such military operation that had ever happened.

General von Bock, commander of Army Group North, argued with OKH and finally got permission to put XIX Panzerkorps under direct Army Group control. This was the highly mobile force of tanks and of infantry in trucks, under the command of General Heinz Guderian. In letting his mechanized forces race ahead, Bock created the world's first independent tank army. Hitler had intervened to make this northern pincer strong in armor; now he let them go in a longer sweep to the east than was ever envisaged in the original plan.

Risking attacks from the east, Guderian's tanks raced south toward Brest-Litovsk. In ten days they covered 200 miles. Polish reserve units were shot to pieces before they had even been assembled. At Zabinka, east of Brzesc, the Germans found one of the few Polish tank units. It was at a railway siding unloading its tanks and was destroyed before it could offer a defense.

On 17 September, just south of Brest-Litovsk, Guderian's tanks made contact with XXII Panzerkorps of Army Group South. Virtually the whole Polish Army—or what remained of it—was inside a gigantic double pincer. The fighting continued, but the war was over.

No legal Polish government survived to secure an armistice or sign a peace treaty. Years of frontier incidents since 1918 had produced bitter enmity between Poles and Germans. Much of newly conquered Poland was considered by many Germans to be liberated Germany. Guderian had routed his armored column in such a way that he could pass through his old family estates and the place where he was born. And when war began many German residents in Poland were ill treated; thousands were murdered. After German victory, vengeful local Germans added to the terror that the SS brought to Poland. As Telford Taylor points out in *The March of Conquest*, it was not a phony war in Poland at this time. Neither was it a phony war at sea.

Close behind the German armies came *SS-Einsatzgruppen* (Special Task Forces), which systematically murdered teachers, doctors, officers, churchmen, landowners, local government officials, Jews, and aristocrats. Following a message from Reinhard Heydrich of the SS, General Franz Halder confided to his diary the cryptic note, "Housecleaning: Jews, intelligentsia, clergy, nobility." By the end of the first week of war, Admiral Wilhelm Canaris of the *Abwehr* (Military Intelligence Service) reported that SS commanders were boasting of 200 shootings a day. By 27 September Heydrich said that only 3 per cent of the Polish upper classes had survived this massacre. It was all part of the plan to produce "a leaderless labor force" to serve Germany. Polish children were not to be taught to read or write. They would learn to count to a maximum of 500, write their names and "that it is God's command that he should be obedient to Germans, honorable, industrious and brave."

The Poles have been criticized for military incompetence, but it is hard to see what else they could have done. They had no modern weapons. Their frontier with Germany was very long indeed and made even longer with the Germans now in Slovakia. The Polish Army's railheads, the industrial centers, and the vital Silesian coalfields were west of the Vistula. All this would have been abandoned had they retreated behind the Vistula to avoid the German pincers. Abandoned, too, would have been the men to be mobilized in that vast area.

And what about the Russians? On the day that the German pincers closed, news reached the OKW that units of the Red Army had crossed into Poland over its eastern frontier. "Against whom?" Jodl, the OKW Chief of Operations, asked in alarm. Hitler's secret agreement, to split Poland down the middle with the Russians, had been so well kept that even his commanders were surprised by it.

The Poles also had a secret military pact. It had been made with the French only a few months before. It was agreed that in the event of a German attack on Poland, France would, on about the third day after mobilization, launch limited attacks, following this with a full-scale land offensive using the bulk of her available forces not before the fifteenth day after mobilization. (Similarly, Poland had agreed to attack Germany from the east in the event of a German invasion of France.) The Poles had every reason to suppose that the promised French attack would send the Germans reeling. For, as the German

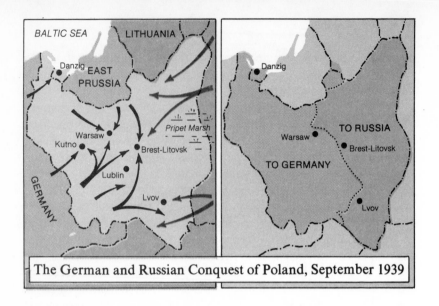

The German and Russian Conquest of Poland, September 1939

MAP 5

Chief of Staff later admitted, facing France in the West they had "no more than a light covering force, scarcely fit for collecting customs duties."*

But the French did not move; they were mobilizing. The French mobilization system was antiquated, slow, and inefficient, but French politicians and soldiers believed only in very big armies. They would do nothing until they were fully ready.

Even the greater proportion of France's artillery was in storage, and its generals would never go to war without their heavy artillery. So the French did no more than scatter leaflets over Germany and send some patrols into the virtually undisputed land between the French and German fortifications. After the war, General Maurice Gamelin, commander of the French Armed Forces, was asked about this secret

* It must also be said that others are of the opinion that France at this time was not strong enough to launch a major assault. At the Nuremberg trials, General Jodl said that he had been surprised the Allies did not use their 110 British and French divisions to attack the 25 divisions that the Germans had facing west.

The Swiss historian Eddy Bauer has pointed out, however, that Germany had 34 divisions facing west at the time of the attack on Poland, with the total brought to over 43 by 10 September. He also shows that Allied strength was far less than 110 divisions. No British troops were in position until October. France also had to cover the Italian and Spanish frontiers and had 14 divisions in North Africa. Bauer calculates that at the time of the declaration of war France had only 7 divisions available for the Western Front. Even on 20 September, with mobilization completed, there were only 57 divisions (and this includes the men manning the Maginot Line fortifications).

pact and France's failure to keep to it. He was unabashed. He claimed that France and Poland's failure to complete a parallel political treaty rendered the military treaty void.

Neither did the British attack Germany. The Royal Air Force was restricted to bombing German warships. When a British MP wanted to ask a question in Parliament about the inactivity of the RAF, Kingsley Wood, Britain's Secretary of State for Air, took him aside and told him not to do so, as it would be "dangerous." It was not revealed what form this danger might take nor whether it would be confined to the life expectancy of the Chamberlain government of which Wood was a typically inept minister.

In the West, the French and the British had declared war but did not fight it. This period of paralysis, which the French called "*drôle de guerre*," the British "twilight war," the Americans "phony war," and the Germans "*Sitzkrieg*," had been created by the development of the bombing plane.

The bomber had haunted Europe's politicians through the 1930s and into the first months of the war. Even after war began, it was hoped that the bombing of cities might be tacitly proscribed, as poison gas had been. This delicacy of feeling was not, of course, due to reluctance to inflict civilian casualties but rather to the prospect of retaliatory bombing. The scientists' predictions did nothing to allay these fears. The estimate of Britain's Committee of Imperial Defence was that the initial bombing attacks on London would continue for sixty days, kill 600,000, and maim well over 1 million people. In response to this, thousands of papier-mâché coffins were stockpiled and, with a nicely bureaucratic sense of priorities, 1 million burial forms had already been issued.

The Conquest of Norway: Air Power plus Sea Power

Probably the airplane changed the nature of warfare more than any weapon in use in the Second World War, until the atomic bomb with which it was ultimately armed. The importance of the airplane was due to its effect upon land and sea warfare, rather than to anything the strategic bomber could do.

Any navy could only survive as a fighting force if it controlled the air above its own ships. It could win battles by taking command of the air above enemy ships. These lessons had not been learned by the British High Command when in 1939 they went to war.

The RAF had been created as a separate service after German bombing attacks on London during the First World War. Perhaps it seemed sensible that all aircraft operated by the Royal Navy should come under the control of the Air Ministry. But, like so many things under the control of the Air Ministry in those times, this failed conspicuously.

It was 1921 before the Air Ministry would even agree to training naval officers as pilots. Even so, the Admiralty still had no control of the design of its aircraft and had to put up with land planes adapted to shipboard use and antique aircraft that were of little use for anything. By the end of 1938, a year after the Fleet Air Arm had returned to naval control, the Royal Navy had just three monoplanes—all Blackburn Skuas, originally requested in 1924.

The Air Ministry pursued a deliberate policy of keeping the Fleet Air Arm short of aircraft, on the grounds that in the event of war, land-based aircraft were always available to supplement naval air operations.

From time to time, exponents of naval aviation advanced the theory that the dive bomber and torpedo planes were best suited for use in naval actions. But the Air Ministry were unable to support this view, having staked the whole existence of the RAF upon the accuracy of the high-level bomber. The Fleet Air Arm ultimately went to war with a torpedo bomber and a two-seat fighter that doubled as a dive bomber, respectively described by one naval historian as "obsolete" and "obsolescent." No dive-bombing sight was fitted to the aircraft because, in spite of Admiralty requests since 1933, the Air Ministry had never produced one for them, fearing that any support for the dive-bombing theories would be taken as a retreat from official RAF strategy.

Little wonder, then, that antipathy toward all airplanes and the men who flew them affected the navy's decision-makers. The RAF's theory that bombers had made the battleship obsolete had been tested in those first hours of the war, when RAF bombers suffered heavy losses at the hands of the German defenders (20 per cent of the bombers failed to return), without doing more than superficial damage to German ships. Believing that the German air force might do rather better, the Admiralty hastily moved the Home Fleet from Scapa Flow in the Orkneys to the west side of Scotland. It remained there five months while anti-aircraft (AA) defenses were prepared at Scapa Flow. The RAF abandoned its attempt to destroy the German battleships.

Not only was the Royal Navy unprepared for the bombing airplane, it was similarly unready for the surface raider. The German Navy, like the German Army, had been forced by peace treaty limitations to produce a specialized and refined fighting force. Abandoning dreams of refighting the battle of Jutland, they had produced "pocket battleships" suitable to prey upon the merchant shipping of the Atlantic. The *Deutschland, Admiral Graf Spee,* and *Admiral Scheer*—limited to 10,000 tons by treaty but nearer to 12,000 tons—were among the best-designed ships of this century. These armored cruisers incorporated every new idea that could maximize firepower and speed and give them range enough to prowl the Atlantic. Their electro-welded hulls, armor belts, and immense internal strength gave them a chance to survive hits that would have destroyed contemporary ships of other nations. They were fast enough to outpace any ships with guns big enough to sink them. Luckily for the Royal Navy, the ships' designers had tried too hard to maximize the power—weight ratio and unreliable engines contributed to the destruction of the *Graf Spee* in Montevideo harbor in the South Atlantic in December 1939.

German warships' attacks upon British merchant shipping posed a problem for which the Royal Navy had no answer. Dispersed naval units were needed to find German raiders in the vast space of the Atlantic. Yet each unit had to be capable of sinking the raider, or it would simply fall victim to it.

Theorists had already pointed out that shipborne aircraft could enlarge the navy's search patterns by thousands upon thousands of square miles. Although large warships carried small floatplanes, such aircraft could not survive a landing in the open sea and so were unsuitable for search duties. If the sea lanes were to be kept open, it looked as if many cheap aircraft carriers might be the only answer to the fast commerce raider. The Royal Navy preferred to pretend that the airplane had never been invented.

Cooperation between the Royal Navy and the RAF's land-based Coastal Command was minimal (although the Royal Navy took the sensible precaution of assigning naval officers to assist with ship recognition). Coastal Command went to war without any training in antisubmarine warfare. Even German warships were able to get through the North Sea without detection.

The *Graf Spee* and *Deutschland,* as well as eighteen U-boats, had put to sea just before war broke out, followed in November by the battle cruisers *Scharnhorst* and *Gneisenau.* None of this activity was detected by the British Navy. Their first definite evidence that the German surface raiders were at sea had come a month after the outbreak of war, when the first merchant ship survivors came ashore in the Orkneys. The *Scharnhorst* and *Gneisenau* were fitted with the latest German radar (*Seetakt*), and at the end of November this enabled them to steam through the British patrol line in broad daylight. The British ships lacked this sort of equipment and the British Admiralty did not even suspect that any German warships had radar.*

It was the ineffectiveness of Allied naval resources and failure to control the North Sea that forced Allied strategists to look anew at neutral Norway. Had the Allies and the Germans both been quite certain that the other did not intend to occupy Norway, it is likely that it would have been permitted to remain neutral. Its advantages to the Germans, as a route for Swedish ore, had to be weighed against the cost of the large garrison that would have to be kept there. But both sides reckoned that Norway must on no account fall to the other side, and preparations to prevent this escalated.

Nothing could better illustrate the military and political illusions of the Allies than the 10,000-strong expeditionary force that was assembled to invade Norway. On the pretext of aiding the Finns, who were at that time fighting the Russians, the Anglo-French force was to cross Norway and seize the Swedish iron-ore mines that were vital to the German war effort. It was a foolish and provocative plan, and only the strong likelihood of military failure saved it from bringing Norway, Sweden, and the U.S.S.R. into the war, on the side of Germany.

Luckily for all concerned, the Finns made peace with the Soviet Union just as the invasion force was about to sail. However, these amphibious plans put the Allies in a good condition to fight off any German invasion of Norway. Or so it seemed to them at the time.

The most convenient route for Swedish ore to Germany was through the northerly—but ice-free—port of Narvik, Norway. The iron-ore ships sailed close to the Norwegian coast, thereby gaining calmer seas and the benefit of neutral waters. Ever since the beginning of 1940, German intelligence had been reporting that Winston Churchill, then the First Lord of the Admiralty, was seeking cabinet permission to mine those neutral waters. It was on the strength of this information that Hitler told his OKW Operations Staff to prepare *Studie Nord*, an invasion plan for Norway and possibly Denmark too.

Meanwhile, the Allies planned two separate operations. The first, code-named WILFRED, was to lay two minefields in Norwegian

---

* Royal Navy ships *Rodney* and *Sheffield* did have Type 79 radar at the beginning of the war. This was an air-warning set as compared with the German Seetakt, which was designed for surface work. The *Graf Spee* was almost certainly using hers in December 1939 to score hits on the *Exeter* when opening fire at 19,400 yards in the battle of the river Plate.

waters, with a third minefield marked as a deterrent but not actually laid. It was assumed that WILFRED would provoke the Germans into a move against Norway. Once they had landed "or showed they intended to do so," the Anglo-French force would occupy Narvik and seize the railway to the Swedish border. One historical study remarks, "The success of the plan depended heavily on the assumption that the Norwegians would not offer resistance, and strangely, the possibility of a strong German reaction was left almost entirely out of the account."

In Scandinavia tensions increased. The Swiss ambassador in Stockholm told his government, at the end of March 1940, that German and Allied landings in Norway were imminent. The German listening service, temporarily baffled by a British radio cipher change of 22 March, intercepted the message. Then came the most important coup in Forschungsamt history. The Finnish ambassador in Paris repeated a remark of the French Premier's about the British plan to sow mines in Norwegian territorial waters.

On the morning of 8 April, units of the Royal Navy laid mines in Norwegian waters. Hitler's intelligence had told him enough about British intentions for him to choose this same dark night of the new moon period for his invasion.

For their initial landings, German soldiers were packed into warships, followed by troopships and freighters.* Battle cruisers headed north to provide a distraction for the British Home Fleet while U-boats covered the landings against British naval interference.

Three hundred miles of sea separated Norway from the German attackers. Britain and France were confident that their large navies could deal the German invading forces a deadly blow. It was hoped that the subsequent loss of Swedish ore supplies through Narvik might prove fatal for the German war machine, but this too was wrong. German planners had calculated that the Swedes could stockpile ore through the icy winter and increase shipments in summer. By this means Germany could have imported almost as much ore per year direct from Sweden without using Narvik.

So confident were the British that when news came of the German invasion, Winston Churchill told the House of Commons, "[In] my view, which is shared by my skilled advisers, Herr Hitler has committed a grave strategic error."

---

* Some histories tell stories of German freighters in Norwegian ports, filled with infantry, waiting like "Trojan horses" for zero hour to disgorge their invaders. One history says that such freighters sailed but were sunk in transit. This is incorrect. Such ideas figured in early plans but were not in fact carried through.

The grim reality was that Hitler demonstrated once more a boldness of military ideas that surpassed those of his professional adversaries. And in doing so, he tightened his grip on the German war machine. The little ministerial office, through which Blomberg sent his orders to the service chiefs, had by now become the Oberkommando der Wehrmacht. Here Hitler had his own planning staff, under the direction of artillery General Jodl. No longer were all military ideas to originate with the Army General Staff.

Hitler had taken a close interest in his army's preparations for the invasion of Poland.* He had intervened a couple of times, giving Guderian more armor and sending him farther to the east. He had also shortened some of the times allotted for the initial objectives. These ideas for the most part had proved successful, but that did nothing to endear Hitler to the army, nor did it increase his faith in his generals. Now, for the first time, Hitler kept the planning all to himself. Instead of asking the army to prepare an invasion plan, he gave the task to the OKW, which, with General Wilhelm Keitel as his front man, he personally commanded. To do the day-to-day staff work for this campaign, the headquarters of XXI Corps was chosen. Since the Army High Command (*Oberkommando des Heeres*, or OKH) was by-passed, there was an unprecedented situation in which a corps staff was directly supervised by the Supreme Commander and the chief of the OKW. Only when told to supply the units needed did the OKH officially hear about the invasion plans. Göring, whose Luftwaffe units were given the same highhanded treatment, was even more angry than the OKH. The invasion of Norway established Hitler's authority over his army, navy, and air force. The success of it demonstrated his skill. "Hitler intervened to a very great extent," remembered Keitel in his memoirs.

Hitler's plan for the invasion of Norway required from the German Navy great daring and seamanship. Warships were to steam boldly into Norwegian ports and disembark assault troops. In the case of Narvik, this meant a long journey through waters where the Royal Navy was now extremely active. Once there, the dispersed German ships had to get away before the Royal Navy bottled them up and destroyed them.

The second stage of the invasion was support and reinforcement by Junkers Ju 52, three-motor transport aircraft. The entire Nor-

---

* Hitler's pet plan to seize the bridges that crossed the Vistula (from Danzig to Poland's Corridor) went wrong in spite of all his planning with air photos and scale models. But this failure was more due to the incalculable bravery of the Poles than to any fault with the ideas.

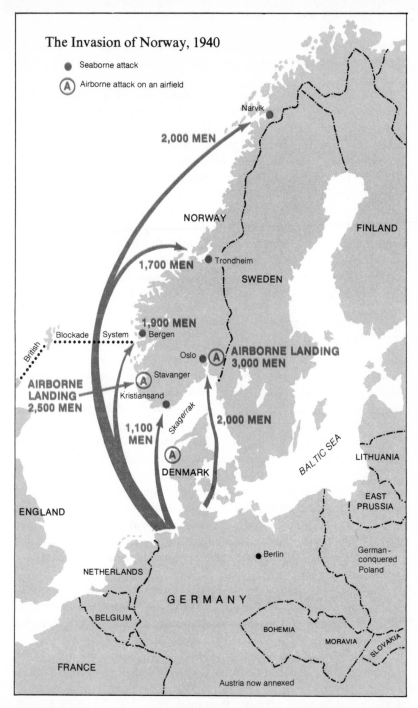

The Invasion of Norway, 1940

● Seaborne attack

Ⓐ Airborne attack on an airfield

2,000 MEN

NORWAY

FINLAND

1,700 MEN ● Trondheim

SWEDEN

1,900 MEN
● Bergen

Blockade System

British

AIRBORNE LANDING
3,000 MEN

Oslo ● Ⓐ

AIRBORNE
LANDING
2,500 MEN

Ⓐ Stavanger

Kristiansand ●

1,100
MEN

Skagerrak

2,000 MEN

Ⓐ

DENMARK

BALTIC SEA

LITHUANIA

ENGLAND

EAST
PRUSSIA

● Berlin

German-
conquered
Poland

NETHERLANDS

GERMANY

BELGIUM

BOHEMIA

MORAVIA

SLOVAKIA

FRANCE

Austria now annexed

MAP 6

wegian operation, including all subsequent land fighting, would be provided with air support and an umbrella of Luftwaffe fighter aircraft.

To say that the German plan worked without a hitch would be to exaggerate. At Narvik, for instance, the entire German naval force was sunk by the battleship H.M.S. *Warspite* and her destroyers, though not before the initial landings. The battle cruiser *Hipper*, en route to Trondheim, was discovered by a solitary Royal Navy destroyer— H.M.S. *Glowworm*—which rammed the German warship with enough velocity to tear a 120-foot-long gash in her side, through which poured 500 tons of seawater. In spite of a four-degree list, the *Hipper* continued to her destination with all vital equipment functioning. A troopship in the German force destined for Bergen, however, was sunk by a Polish submarine operating from Britain, and the German cruiser *Königsberg* was damaged by Norwegian coastal defenses. Later the *Königsberg* was sunk by Fleet Air Arm Skuas from the Orkneys, at the extreme edge of their range. It was the first major warship to be sunk by air attack.

At Oslo, the cruiser *Blücher*, carrying many of the German military staff, was sunk in the approaches. The seaborne force waited while a Luftwaffe attack was made upon the Norwegian capital. Because of muddled instructions, transport aircraft filled with German troops landed at the Oslo airfield while it was still in Norwegian hands. The infantry fought their way through and staged a parade in the Oslo town center. To the Norwegian onlookers the war seemed lost. The bluff worked and the occupation of the country went forward.

German losses were heavy. The *Blücher* was a particularly grave loss, for it was one of the few German ships with range enough to operate in the Atlantic. Other German seaborne attacks were more successful, and soon the large Norwegian towns were all in German hands. Thus they held the administrative centers, where defense mobilization would otherwise have been taking place, as well as the ports and airfields.

So, long before any Anglo-French forces were landed, the Luftwaffe had command of the air and was operating from Norwegian airfields, making Norwegian coastal waters extremely dangerous for Allied ships.

Lacking a Norwegian airfield, the Allies improvised. RAF Squadron 263, using antiquated Gloster Gladiator biplane fighters, sailed to Norway in the carrier H.M.S. *Glorious*. In a snowstorm, while still 180 miles offshore, they made their first-ever deck takeoff. By a miracle of air navigation, they found the frozen lake that had been chosen to serve them as an airfield and landed without accidents. But the absence of oxygen equipment prevented the Gladiator pilots getting to the German aircraft that were bombing them from 20,000 feet and, by the end of the second day, only one Gladiator remained serviceable, and for that there was no fuel. In due course, the airmen returned to Britain by cargo ship.

Another Allied fiasco was that of the French troops, landed off Namsos from the auxiliary cruiser *Ville d'Alger* without artillery, tanks, AA guns, mules, skis, or snowshoes, since the ship was too long to get into the harbor. The planners had not thought to check it, as any shipping-office clerk would have done.

For the first time, a battle was being fought and won by co-ordinated operations on land, sea, and in the air. The Germans were proving that the Luftwaffe could neutralize sea power when enemy ships were in "narrow seas" within range of land-based aircraft. The German successes in Poland and Scandinavia demanded that the Allies totally revise their theories of war.

From overconfidence, British naval policy swung to extreme caution. The Chiefs of Staff abandoned their plans for an amphibious assault upon the Norwegian coastline with a suddenness that angered Churchill. "I was indignant," he said. "It was soon plain to me that all professional opinion was now adverse to the operation which only a few days before it had spontaneously espoused."*

With no adequate air cover, the Anglo-French land fighting could not succeeed. The Allied evacuation of Norway started after only two weeks, with the Narvik units taken off after a month. It was obvious that, quite apart from air cover, Allied soldiers lacked the initiative that proper training and suitable weapons would have given them. They had been beaten by German soldiers who were, man for man and commander for commander, superior. Churchill saved some of his harshest words for the British general at Narvik, who declined to stage a direct assault upon the town. "He continued to use every argument, and there was no lack of them, to prevent drastic action," Churchill said bitterly.

No longer could excuses about the "tank country of Poland" account for the success in Norway of the Germans. Here they had fought in the snows and in the mountains, and still they had won.

The contribution that the small German Navy had made to the Norwegian campaign was a particularly bitter pill for the British and French navies to swallow. The Germans had begun the war with only

---

* Winston Churchill, *The Second World War*, vol. I.

13 large warships, even if light cruisers are included in the total. Britain and France had 107, plus 7 aircraft carriers, of which Germany had none. Germany started the war with only 27 long-range submarines, when the Allies had 135 such boats.

There were other bitter pills. Not only did their system of radio interception provide the Germans with better information about British naval movements than the British were able to obtain from ships, ship-based aircraft, and long-range air reconnaissance, but the Germans were prepared to move forward even when their information was incomplete. Allied commanders, on land and sea, stuck to the old naval maxim "Find, fix, and strike." Used as an excuse for inaction, the advice was just as wrong applied to tanks as it was to ships, just as disastrous in Norway as it was later to be in France.

It was such a mixture of caution and poor intelligence that almost proved fatal to the Allied withdrawal from Norway. On 5 June the Admiralty sent four Royal Navy cruisers—*Renown, Repulse, Newcastle,* and *Sussex*—to find a nonexistent enemy near Iceland, while nervously reserving units near Scapa Flow. This left the final evacuation of 25,000 troops and their equipment to sail across the North Sea with only the battleship H.M.S. *Warspite* to protect them. The carrier H.M.S. *Glorious,* making the same crossing, did not sail in the convoy, for which it could have provided air cover.

Informed by air reconnaissance and radio interceptions of the presence of the Royal Navy forces, two of Germany's most formidable ships, *Scharnhorst* and *Gneisenau,* accompanied by the newly repaired *Hipper,* were hunting for the Allied troopships. On 8 June they surprised the carrier H.M.S. *Glorious* accompanied by only two destroyers. Although it was a clear day, with almost unlimited visibility, the *Glorious* had no aircraft on patrol and so failed to get warnings of the approaching enemy ships.

The *Scharnhorst* used its Seetakt radar. It opened fire at a range of 14 miles and succeeded in hitting the flight deck, flipping sections of it up "like a box lid," as the German admiral described it. All three British ships were sunk, with only 46 survivors out of 1,561 sailors. Only the suicidal riposte of the escorting destroyer *Acasta,* which put a torpedo into the *Scharnhorst,* turned the German force back to port before it found the ill-protected convoy.

Probably it will never be known why there were no air patrols flying from H.M.S. *Glorious* on that beautifully clear June afternoon. H.M.S. *Acasta* had offered itself as a target, as well as dealing a crippling blow to a formidable enemy. The self-sacrifice of the two destroyers saved the whole Allied evacuation force. It was expected that there would be medals or a mention in dispatches. But there was nothing. The Admiralty's silence was interpreted as a sign that the tragic fiasco was to be forgotten as soon as possible.

Up to then, the British losses had been comparable to those of the Germans—two cruisers, seven destroyers, eight submarines, the German Navy three cruisers, ten destroyers, eight submarines, plus transports and supply ships.

It was the damaged ships that substantially reduced German sea power. The pocket battleship *Deutschland* (now renamed the *Lützow*, because Hitler feared the psychological effect of a sunken *Deutschland*) was badly damaged, as were four cruisers. This left the German Navy with only the battle cruiser *Hipper*, two light cruisers, and four destroyers.

British ships had escaped lightly considering what had really happened in the sea war. Many more Royal Navy ships had been brought into the cross sights of the U-boats but had escaped because of the malfunction of German torpedoes. They were running about 6 feet too deep, which meant that any ship with a draft of less than about 17 feet was safe from them. In addition, the German magnetic pistols which detonated the torpedoes were grossly inefficient. Without these two design faults, the Allied shipping casualties would have been even higher. For instance, the battleship *Nelson* had been hit by three dud torpedoes on 30 October 1939. Only when the German U-boat fleet reverted to contact pistols and rectified the depth-keeping mechanism of the torpedoes in late summer of 1940 did the submarine arm become fully effective.

In the vast expanses of the Atlantic, where an even more vital battle was being fought, the Admiralty had made comparably bad decisions about the protection of Allied merchant convoys. Asdic, a submarine-detection device, on which the Royal Navy's strategists had based all their thinking, was proving of limited use against submerged U-boats and of virtually none against surfaced ones. German submariners turned this to such advantage that the second half of 1940 was to be called "the happy time" by the U-boat crews, who perfected the technique of surface attacks on convoys by night.

The first of the Royal Navy's Flower-class corvettes came into service in May 1940. They were desperately needed—so desperately that everyone concerned had to overlook their grave faults, including a top speed of only 16 knots, which was less than that of a surfaced U-boat.

Even more far reaching was the Air Ministry's decision, in April 1940, to abandon experiments with a depth charge that could be dropped from the air. Only energetic pleading succeeded in getting the project going again.*

The Royal Navy had failed to prepare for war and now was failing to respond to the changing nature of the war. The Russo-German Pact was providing Germany with oil, cattle, grain, and coal overland from the East, but still the naval authorities would not be deterred from their ideas about a sea blockade, like that of the First World War. Pursuing this mood of logistic megalomania, the Royal Navy began to lay a gigantic minefield stretching from the Orkneys to Iceland. Only after the mine-laying had started did anyone calculate the prohibitive number of mines that would be required to complete it. The partly laid minefield was then abandoned.

Again ignoring the lessons of history, the Royal Navy was organizing its precious warships in "hunting groups" that roamed around the Atlantic in the hope of encountering submarines. This was clearly illogical; German submarines were of no account unless they attacked shipping. It would have been more sensible to use warships to protect the convoys and wait until the German submarines sought them out.

The German invasion of Denmark, which took place with virtually no resistance on 9 April 1940, did not make that country an ally of Britain; there never was a Danish government in exile. However, the invasion provided an excuse for an Allied occupation of Iceland, a Danish possession with a strategic location. From there, naval forces, and, more important, long-range aircraft, could be brought into action in the battle of the Atlantic. This was one of the few consolations to be wrung from the Scandinavian setback, which toppled the Chamberlain government. The French said the Allied failures were entirely the fault of the British. German morale soared as the Allies argued and nursed their wounds. But by the time the Norwegian naval campaign was over, the French and British armies had suffered an even more humiliating defeat.

The Western Front

In 1870 France had suffered a devastating defeat at the hands of German invaders. The residual humiliation helped to convince the French Army that when the chance came, the army must attack with all the strength, zeal, and blind fury that could be mustered. And this

---

* The pleading of Air Marshal Sir F. W. Bowhill, Air Officer Commander in Chief of the RAF Coastal Command. The airborne depth charge was vital because the anti-submarine bomb in use at this time had to score a direct hit on a target to sink it and so was very ineffective.

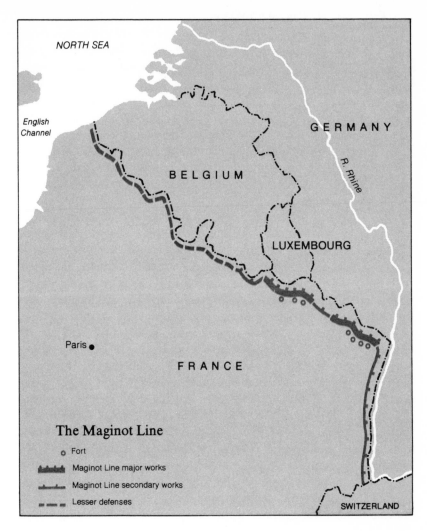

NORTH SEA

English
Channel

GERMANY

BELGIUM

R. Rhine

LUXEMBOURG

Paris ●

FRANCE

The Maginot Line

○ Fort

Maginot Line major works

Maginot Line secondary works

Lesser defenses

SWITZERLAND

MAP 7

is exactly the spirit in which France went to war in 1914. In their brightly colored uniforms, they charged forward into machine-gun fire and acres of barbed wire. The terrible casualties that France suffered that year, and continued to suffer because the Allied generals continued to cry "charge," finally convinced even the generals that the new weapons had made offensive warfare suicidal and that the art of fortified defense must be fully exploited.

After the First World War, the French Army remembered the elaborate underground shelters from which the Germans had emerged to decimate the Allied attacks. The Germans, for their part, remembered the tanks that had several times brought the Allies close to victory. And so the French and German armies gave their priorities to different weapons. But once again the French were one war behind the times.

The Germans—like any defeated army—searched their souls to find the reasons for failure. The Allies preferred to believe that their eventual victory in 1918 proved that their methods were satisfactory. So the changes in German theory were radical, but the French changes were only in emphasis.

No man is in a hurry to conclude that the skills and knowledge to which he has devoted a lifetime are obsolete. During four years of war on the Western Front, generals had become expert at the technique of attack and counterattack in localized conditions. Complex staff work was required to concentrate near the front line the men, food, and equipment necessary for an assault. The artillery preparation alone required immense dumps of shells, and bombardment before attacks often went on for days. After it, the infantrymen, each carrying 60 pounds of equipment, and keeping to rigidly prescribed intervals, marched through mud churned by artillery shells headlong into devastating machine-gun fire. If, by sheer weight of numbers, there was a breakthrough, both sides had the same formula for containment. Thinly spread reserves were used to "seal off" the breakthrough region. Patrols were sent forward to discover the exact dispositions of the enemy. Then the opposing general staff began building up supplies for a counterattack. This First World War formula provided the method by which the French command attempted to deal with the German blitzkrieg—lightning war—of 1940.

The Maginot Line

The First World War left France dispirited and depleted in manpower. By 1939 there were 300,000 fewer men to defend France than had been available in 1914. Missing were the unborn sons of the men who had died assaulting the German lines. So the French built an elaborate chain of subterranean forts. It was, by any standards, a considerable feat of engineering. Almost all the official visitors compared the installations with those of battleships.

The casemates were carefully sited to provide extensive fields of fire, and provision was made to shoot at the neighboring casemate should it fall into enemy hands. Still to be seen along the frontier, overgrown with weeds and stained by sooty rain, these massive buildings—none of them with less than 3.5 meters of concrete as a roof—are almost indestructible. Each casemate is a two-story block with metal observation cupolas (and in some cases retractable artillery cupolas) on top. The upper floor was given over to guns; below were sited the generator and ammunition supply, with troop accommodation and stores alongside. Usually such casemates are protected by tank traps and anti-infantry ditches. Sometimes there are underground tunnels to connect to a neighboring casemate.

At certain places along the line there were built big forts (*ouvrages*). Such enormous underground works were photographed in the 1930s for the newspapers and are what most people think of as the Maginot Line. Here were the underground railways, cinemas, and recreation areas. Here soldiers were photographed having sun-ray treatments, sitting down for lunch, or riding on the electric trains. The air was conditioned and slightly high in pressure to keep out enemy gas. The fuel supplies were held in massive underground reservoirs and the water tapped from deep wells. There were automatic fire doors and cross-connected power lines that could feed extra power to nearby forts. Some of the forts accommodated 1,000 men. Everything had been carefully thought out. The propaganda said that soldiers manning the forts could stay inside indefinitely.

In fact, the underground works were not the paradise that propaganda depicted. The living quarters were extremely cramped and men slept on narrow three-tier bunks. The glare from the light bulbs hurt their eyes, and men complained of deafness from the echoing sound of the generators and other machinery. Even worse was the drainage; septic tanks were not specially ventilated and the stench in some of the forts was overwhelming. Still worse, damp proved such a problem that the equipment had to be regularly damp-proofed and the men had to be moved out of the subterranean dwelling and put into tents and later huts. Eventually they only went into the fortifications when on duty.

Whether the Germans would have been unable to invade France by direct assault on the Maginot Line is still debated. However, in 1940 they did not have to do so, for the fortifications protected only the central part of France's northeastern frontier. The frontier from Basel, Switzerland, to Haguenau in the Vosges followed the river

Rhine. Defense depended upon this river obstacle, and the Line was less formidable there than along the next section, from Haguenau to the corner of Luxembourg at Longuyon.

Everyone who looks at the map of the Line asks why it did not continue west all the way to the sea, especially since this flat area of the northwest had always been the route of the invader. Here France had fought for her life since the Romans and the Franks. Spanish armies from the Low Countries, Marlborough, Prince Eugene, Wellington after Waterloo, and, in 1914, the Kaiser's armies had all come this way. And Paris was a temptingly short march from this frontier.

So why was it not heavily fortified? Certainly this lowland region would have required special engineering, and any deep fortifications would have had to be constantly pumped to keep them habitable. But the deciding objection was the closeness of French industry to the border. The Maginot Line could not be run north of the French industrial region without crossing the Belgian frontier; it could only go through the industrial region or pass south of it. In the case of war, and particularly in the case of the 1914–1918 style of war the French envisaged, the alternative seemed to be having the industries pounded to pieces in the fighting or abandoning them to the enemy before the fighting started.

The Allied Solution: Plan D

There was a third alternative: for the Allied Army to advance and meet the invading Germans in Belgium. This is the plan that was adopted. As well as ensuring that France's industrial and mining areas along the frontier were well behind the lines, it would deny the Luftwaffe advanced airfields for attacks upon Paris and London. But where in Belgium? The Belgians had already cashiered their Chief of the General Staff for closing the barricades on the Belgian frontier during an invasion scare on the night of 13 January 1940 and followed this with an apology to the German ambassador for this unneutral act. The French and British commanders had never even met their opposite numbers in the Belgian Army, let alone staged military exercises with them. No fronts had been allotted to the various commands. There were no prepared communications, no lines of supply or ammunition dumps of any kind available for the British and French armies. All of this would have to be worked out after the Germans struck. When the Allied armies reached their defensive positions, they would have to build their own fortifications.

With the Allies facing such a monumental task, it is tempting to say that they would have done better to build and man a defense along the Franco-Belgian frontier and wait there for the expected German attack. But this would have granted the Germans air and sea bases along the Channel. It would also have resulted in the Franco-British armies sitting behind a defense line watching Belgium's twenty-division army locked in battle with the Germans. Whichever way the Allies played it, it was going to be a mess, a mess stemming directly from the Belgian refusal to cooperate for their own defense. The ultimate expression of this attitude came when the Belgian ambassador in London, some hours after the Germans had invaded his country, made an official diplomatic protest that the British armies had crossed the Franco-Belgian frontier to fight the invaders without having received an official invitation to do so.

The Anglo-French plan to move armies to a defense line that followed the rivers Meuse and Dyle—Plan D—meant that the whole Allied force must pivot upon the 9th French Army of General André-Georges Corap. The army that was to perform this complex movement was not only spread more thinly along its front than any other army but was far below strength in antitank and antiaircraft guns. It was also short of the transport needed for the movement, so that when the time came, most of the men had to march to their new positions. Some units marched 75 miles, a grueling task for an army on the eve of battle, especially an army comprising mostly middle-aged reservists.

It was of a unit in this vitally important Ninth Army that a British inspecting officer wrote, "Seldom have I ever seen anything more slovenly and badly turned out. Men unshaven, horses ungroomed, clothes and saddlery that did not fit, and complete lack of pride in themselves or their units. What shook me most, however, was the look in the men's faces, disgruntled and insubordinate looks, and although ordered to give 'Eyes left' hardly a man bothered to do so."

Inactivity, propaganda, and drink have been cited as the three main causes of demoralization of the French Army in 1940. Drunkenness among the soldiers during the months of inactivity had caused the railway authorities to arrange for sobering-up rooms to be available at big railway stations. However, there were many first-rate French divisions with high morale and first-class equipment. The low standard of the reservists was more indicative of the *extent* of France's mobilization—one man in eight—than of the state of its regular army formations.

The French had called up so many men that they crippled their industrial production. Consequently, skilled men had to be released from the army, causing not only new disruption but a lowering of

MAP 8

The advance of Anglo-French armies from the French border to meet a possible
German attack along a line in central Belgium. Note the way in which General
Corap's 9th Army has to advance and bend its left wing and make a stand along
the western edge of the Ardennes Forest. This army of weak reservist divisions
was to be in the path of the panzer attack through Luxembourg. The Allied
armies were to move into position along the Meuse, from Sedan to Namur, and
northward along the river Dyle, which gave the plan its initial.

morale among men who were not released. Their discontent was
fomented by the lack of military equipment and of any training for
modern war. The British mobilized only one man in forty-eight, but
war production had not yet properly started there. On what was now
being called the "home front," vast numbers of engineers were still
looking for jobs, and there was a total of 1.5 million unemployed.

The British Expeditionary Force (B.E.F.) in France was tiny, but it was entirely motorized. General Bernard Montgomery, then commander of the B.E.F.'s 3rd Division, said of it, "The transport was inadequate and was completed on mobilisation by vehicles requisitioned from civilian firms . . . they were in bad repair and, when my division moved from the ports up to its concentration area near the French frontier, the countryside of France was strewn with broken-down vehicles."*

Montgomery says the entire British Army was unprepared for a realistic exercise, let alone a real war. The B.E.F. had Britain's choicest military equipment, but it had not been possible to put together an armored division to include in it. The British antitank 2-pounder guns were in short enough supply to prompt the hasty purchase of 1-pounder guns from the French. They were mounted on handcarts. There were no heavier antitank guns and very few light antiaircraft guns. But in Britain, the Secretary of State for War proudly told the nation that the B.E.F. was "as well if not better equipped than any other similar army."

The French Army depended for the most part on horse-drawn transport. No doubt it seemed logical that those French units given motor transport should be on the outer rim of the Plan D movement on the Dyle River, for they had farthest to travel. The British held the central part of this moving front, while Corap's aforementioned unfortunates were the pivot.

There was no strategic reserve. France's only three armored divisions were in the rear areas, rather than part of the front, simply because they were still undergoing their initial training.

The High Command

Because the British Expeditionary Force was so small, there was no Allied command as such. British soldiers came under the direct command of French commanders in the area in which they were stationed.

. The great catastrophe that was about to engulf France would call for quick thinking and flexible reactions from local commanders and all the way up to the top. But the structure of the French Army's command system was so rigid that no quick reactions could possibly be transmitted through it.

The French Army has always been obsessed with a rigid, inflexible,

---

* From his book *Memoirs*.

legalistic chain of command, which men did not dare to challenge or by-pass. The remarkably poor support given Brigadier General Charles de Gaulle when he tried to continue the fight against the Germans was largely accounted for by the fact that the French Army's chain of command led back to the men who had signed an armistice on 21 June. But in the French Army of early 1940, even the chain of command had gaps and blurred edges that left some commanders wallowing in uncertainty. When, during the attack, it became necessary to define the chain of command from the British troops in France through the French command and back to the British government, the legalities of the system could not be agreed upon.

At the pinnacle of the French Army's command system was the sixty-eight-year-old General Maurice Gamelin, who had been France's youngest divisional commander during the First World War. In 1939 he was still regarded as one of the world's most brilliant military commanders. He had been Commander in Chief of the French Army for nine years, and its equipment, training, and disposition—to say nothing of the retirement age of its senior commanders—was his to decide. He was a tiny doll-like man who had become an intellectual, devoted to culture, philosophy, and the history of art. It was widely believed that Gamelin's sophisticated tastes had led him to choose as his HQ the Château de Vincennes, conveniently close to the pleasures of Paris. It was a gloomy thirteenth-century bastion, where England's Henry V died of dysentery in 1422 and where, on Napoleon's orders, the Duc d'Enghien was executed in 1804.

Gamelin evolved the strategy, appointed the commanders of the units, and gave orders to the French armies in the Alps, Syria, and North Africa. But he had no General Staff. Operational control of the great armies in northeastern France was the responsibility of General A. L. Georges, who had the old, and ill-defined, Napoleonic title *Major-Général des Armées*. Even Georges's chief of staff admitted that Georges was not absolutely certain where Gamelin's responsibilities ended and his own powers began. This was not made simpler by the bad feeling that existed between Gamelin and Georges. Perhaps because of this, the latter had his own HQ 35 miles away from Gamelin's. To make matters worse, General Georges spent a great deal of his time at what was described as his "personal command post" near his residence, at a third location some 12 miles from his HQ.

In any case, the majority of General Georges's staff were not at any of these places. They, under General Aimé Doumenc, were located at the GHQ Land Forces in a mansion belonging to the

Rothschilds at Montry, about halfway between the HQ of Georges and the HQ of Gamelin. General Doumenc, like many of his subordinates, compromised by spending his mornings at Montry and his afternoons at Georges's HQ, whether the general was there or at his personal command post.

The military telephone service being no better than the French civilian telephone service, messages were usually conveyed by motorcycle dispatch riders. There was no teleprinter communication between the HQs and the army commanders. At Gamelin's HQ there was not even a radio. Gamelin's usual way of communicating with Georges was to go to him by car. Questioned about the lack of radio, Gamelin said it might have revealed the location of his HQ. Questioned about the speed with which he could get orders to the front, Gamelin said that it generally took forty-eight hours.

PART THREE

Blitzkrieg: Weapons and Methods

"A perfected modern battle plan is like nothing so much as a score for an orchestral composition, where the various arms and units are the instruments, and the tasks they perform are their respective musical phrases. Every individual unit must make its entry precisely at the proper moment, and play its part in the general harmony."

—LIEUTENANT GENERAL SIR JOHN MONASH,
Commander Australian Corps, France, 1918

Blitzkrieg (lightning war) came into common use as a word after the German armies had quickly encircled western Poland in September 1939. Yet the resemblance between that campaign and the attack on France in May 1940 is no more than superficial.

The Polish campaign had been planned, fought, and won in accord with the most conservative of German military thinking. The same German railway system had decided where the same railheads would be, and therefore where the attacks could be launched and supplied, as in the previous century. The heavier concentration of attacking forces was in the south because they could be supplied through the best of the railway systems. The dramatic movements of two armored corps drew attention away from the fact that most of the German armor was distributed piecemeal to the battle. The shock power of concentrated armor was not used; the old doctrine of *Kesselschlacht* (encirclement battle) had settled the outcome of the campaign.*

The Germans needed to engage the defenders close to the frontiers. The fighting had to be well within range of the old-fashioned foot soldiers and horse transport, which constituted 90 per cent of the German Army. Although German armor went deep into eastern Poland, no major battles were fought there. The German propaganda service made much of the tanks and the screaming *Stuka* dive bombers (Junkers Ju 87s) and of those rare occasions when the German columns were supplied by air, but in fact the German Army and its methods were very conventional.

When the time came for the Germans to examine the lessons of the

---

* *Kessel* means "cauldron," "kettle," or "container"; *Schlacht* is "battle."

Polish campaign, there was more concern about the way in which German Army horseshoes had proved unsuited to splay-footed farm animals requisitioned at the time of mobilization than to the way in which the Model 1934 machine gun had suffered frequent stoppages from dust and mud. Already the shortage of horses had driven the Germans to buying those offered for sale by the British Army as its motorization continued in the 1930s. At the time of the fall of France, one British prisoner of war noticed British Army markings on the hoof of a German officer's horse and was told that all the horses in that particular artillery battery originated from the British Army.

Back to Schlieffen

The German campaign in Poland was little more than a replay of Alfred von Schlieffen's ideas of the early 1900s, modified by General Helmuth von Moltke, namesake and nephew of the hero of the Franco-Prussian War, for use in 1914.

In those opening days of the First World War the Germans had almost conquered France as quickly as a generation later they took Poland by the same method. In 1914 the German First Army force-marched its infantry 300 miles from the Meuse to the Marne via Brussels, but the supply services could not keep up with them. Any army's rapid advance is a supply officer's nightmare. As the German soldiers moved farther and farther away from the railheads, supplies dwindled. The Germans could not get the damaged railways into working order fast enough, and commandeered motors were not enough to supplement the work of the horse-drawn supply columns.

Moltke's mistake gave the French a chance to mobilize. They quickly redeployed their armies, using railways and road transport (including even a few Paris taxicabs). The German infantry, exhausted by its long march and desperately in need of supplies, reeled back disorganized at the first signs of counterattack. The 1914 blitzkrieg had failed: Moltke, now a sick man, was relieved of his job.

The German miscalculation of 1914 was decisive. Failure to knock France out of the war at the outset condemned Germany to that long, two-front struggle its General Staff feared. The armies on the Western Front adopted the methods of siege warfare, the Allied sea blockade began, and Germany lost all hope of victory. But the Schlieffen Plan had not proved a total failure. The German advance in 1914 meant that the war devastated a huge region of northern France, not Germany, and the German occupation deprived France of the iron, coal, and agricultural produce of that region.

By 1939 the German General Staff had once again dusted off the old plan and found some of its basic reasoning applicable to a military invasion of Poland. They had not forgotten their logistic failure that had given the French Army a chance to mobilize.* This time there would be no mistake. The Germans now had the Welle Plan, which enabled them to mobilize in secret. The Poles believed that public German mobilization orders would give them good warning of a German attack, so the invasion achieved complete surprise, overrunning many of the Polish troop induction centers before they had begun their task.

That done, the Polish campaign became a battle of logistics. The German foot soldiers with their horse-drawn wagons marched as much as 30 miles in one day to engage the Poles and hold them close to the frontiers, while the mobile forces and the Luftwaffe prevented the Poles from getting their whole army into the field and deployed to fight. In 1914, the strategy had been an attempt to win in the West before turning the German Army eastward; in 1939 the German General Staff risked everything to get a decision in Poland before France was able to mobilize and attack from the West.

In the previous century, Chancellor Otto von Bismarck's diplomatic skills had enabled him to choose one enemy at a time, but Hitler was no Bismarck. Although he had knocked Poland out of the war before France was ready to attack, Germany now faced an alerted enemy. The next battle would not be able to exploit undeclared war on unprepared foes. If the element of surprise, vital to Prussian military ideas, was to be found in the next stage of the war, it would have to be a stroke of genius—or madness. It was. That is why the battle at the river Meuse in May 1940 will be listed among the decisive battles of the world long after the tactics of the Polish fighting are forgotten.

The Fallacies of 1939

There are no signs that anyone in the West learned much from the 1939 Polish campaign. In fact, there was little sign that anyone had yet digested the lessons of the 1914 Battle of the Marne. Detailed accounts of the Polish fighting were available, but many interpreted them to mean that Poland had been crushed in a gigantic battle of attrition, speeded up by the superior material might of the Germans.

---

* The word "logistics" is now applied to all matters relating to the movement and supply of troops, although the famous Swiss military theorist Baron Antoine-Henri de Jomini (b. 1779), who coined it from the word for "quartermaster" (*maréchal des logis*), used it to mean "the science of Staff."

In Britain and in France, where the earliest tanks had been pioneered, there was an ambivalent attitude to the German victories in Poland. It was a chance for the advocates of armor to reaffirm that the tank had brought victory in 1918. Now, they said, great armies of heavy tanks had ripped open the Polish front in just the same manner. Some experts went further and claimed that the German tank armies had won their victory by following meticulously the writings of Englishmen such as J. F. C. Fuller and B. H. Liddell Hart. Other commentators said that the decisive factor was the armies with which the Russians invaded Poland on the seventeenth day of the fighting.

To what extent the Red Army's brutal participation brought the final collapse of Polish resistance must remain a matter of conjecture, but most of the other interpretations of what had happened were wrong. The tank had been a failure in the First World War, and in 1939 the Germans used mostly thinly armored, lightweight models. There were no great tank battles, no sizable tank concentrations, and certainly no tank armies. The German encirclement, accomplished with mobile forces, was a direct development of traditional German military theories, as was the simultaneous Kesselschlacht of the frontier regions.

The word "blitzkrieg" has been attributed to Hitler, *Time* magazine, and Liddell Hart. Guderian's chief of staff, General Nehring, is sure that the word is not of German origin.* Whatever its etymology, the ideas behind the word are certainly German. Lightning-fast war had been an essential part of Prussian military thinking since long before Bismarck. It arose from the fear that if Prussia engaged one enemy in a lengthy war, other enemies would have joined in. A fast decision avoided this danger. In more modern times, supply lines threatened by the naval forces of France and Britain and Germany's lack of raw materials made long wars even more hazardous.

In addition to this strategic idea, "blitzkrieg" became a convenient way to refer to the tactical methods used. The American Heritage Dictionary defines "blitzkrieg" as "a swift, sudden military offensive, usually by combined air and land forces." The words has also become a catchall term with which to refer to the large body of material—much of it contradictory—produced between the wars by theorists and

---

* Kenneth Macksey, the biographer of Guderian and well-known expert on armored warfare, says that the word "blitzkrieg" was coined by Hitler in 1936 (see his *Guderian: Panzer General*, page 68). Larry Addington, in *The Blitzkrieg Era and the German General Staff, 1865–1941*, credits the first use of the word to *Time* magazine's issue dated 25 September 1939. Liddell Hart's *Memoirs* (vol. I) refers to "the new technique of what I called 'lightning war'—*Blitzkrieg* in German," but he gives no date. General Nehring's opinion was given in a letter to me.

prophets. It is the nature of such writing that it always claims strategic rather than tactical importance.

In this book I have used "blitzkrieg" according to the above dictionary definition, giving special attention to the military methods evolved by Heinz Guderian and used by his forces in May 1940.

The mistaken idea that the blitzkrieg concept was of British origin was given new credence by German generals when the war was over and their views were made available by Basil Liddell Hart. Liddell Hart, one of the finest military theorists of our time, remained always a historian, and whenever possible he expressed his ideas by means of historical example. His most famous book, *The Strategy of Indirect Approach*, originally had the title *The Decisive Wars of History*. Neglected, if not to say rejected, by his countrymen during the Second World War, Liddell Hart was, in its aftermath, provided with a chance to question the captured German generals and a great deal of his subsequent writings drew upon information gathered at this time. It was natural that Liddell Hart's interest should center upon the extent to which his theories had been proved correct by the panzer generals, and perhaps to emphasize these aspects of the war. The defeated German generals responded to the scrupulously fair way in which Liddell Hart wrote of them, and to some extent he became their spokesman.

When Guderian's memoirs appeared in English, Liddell Hart wrote the foreword. But, as the well-known British tank expert Kenneth Macksey has pointed out in his biography of Guderian, the passages in which Guderian praises Liddell Hart as his principal source of inspiration did not appear in the original German edition. Neither had Liddell Hart's name appeared in the bibliography of *Achtung! Panzer!*, which Guderian published in 1937.

Whatever sort of ideas the British theorists gave the Germans, there is no doubt that the blitzkrieg was a development of Prussian military thought. It can be seen in the regulations about flank attack that the great Prussian Marshal Helmuth von Moltke provided to his soldiers in 1869 and the encirclement theories of Schlieffen. The demand for a well-supplied, faster marching army came from the failure in 1914. In Poland the infantry had marched more than twice the daily distance their fathers had managed in France and were not too exhausted to fight afterward. The need for trucks to supplement the horse-drawn supply columns was emphasized by General Hans von Seeckt's theories of mobility. If Guderian was spurred by the writings of Liddell Hart, it is equally true that the infiltration tactics of the German infantry in 1918 provided the starting point of Liddell Hart's writings.

The Invention of the Tank

Napoleon's victories depended entirely upon offense. But while the world's generals in after years studied them and trained their armies accordingly, every military invention and development strengthened defense. In the second half of the nineteenth century, Henry Bessemer's process for manufacturing steel made it cheaper and better. With steel, guns became more efficient and barrels could be rifled to spin the missile so that its gyroscopic effect provided greater accuracy. Machine guns and barbed wire made frontal assault by infantry more and more hazardous, while iron, brick, and masonry gave way to concrete and reinforced concrete that made fortifications immensely strong.

It was defensive strength which brought a stalemate to the Western Front in the First World War. Massed armies faced each other in a siege warfare that depended upon naval blockades for each belligerent to starve the other into submission. But for many years all the components of a mobile armored weapon—which held out a promise of breaking the deadlock—had been available. The invention of the steam engine led to wheeled vehicles used on roads. By the time of the Crimean War (1853–1856), steam tractors, with flaps on the wheels, were being used to haul heavy guns into position more quickly and more efficiently than horses. Although the British Army was using "mechanical horses" as prime movers in the Boer War of 1899, the design for an armored version was filed away in 1912 and forgotten.

By that time the Holt Company in the United States had got a good linked track onto the steam tractors that were used in the soft delta land of Louisiana. After the First World War began, more than one soldier suggested armoring a Holt tractor for use as a weapon, including a French colonel, J.-E. Estienne, and Lieutenant Colonel E. D. Swinton, an Englishman, who was told that such a weapon would be too vulnerable to enemy artillery fire. Most things that the Allied High Command did, or refused to do, at this time were based upon the belief that everything was vulnerable to enemy artillery fire.

In 1914, when British naval aircraft were based in Belgium to fight the German airships, armored cars with Royal Navy crews were assigned to the role of airfield defense. This provided Winston Churchill, then First Lord of the Admiralty, with reason to take an interest himself in land warfare. He also took up the idea of fitting armor to artillery tractors and asked if they could be modified to cross trenches.

Churchill would not take no for an answer and insisted upon a

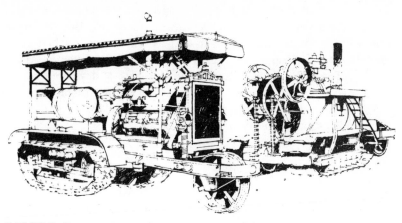

FIGURE I

The Holt "75" caterpillar tractor used for towing heavy artillery on the Western Front (left), developed from the first regular production model crawler of 1906 (right).

demonstration. In February 1915 his committee watched a Holt tractor, its performance impaired by bad weather. The committee decided that the machine was useless, but Churchill ignored their advice. He ordered work to proceed.

> I thus took personal responsibility for the expenditure of the public money involved, about seventy thousand pounds. I did not invite the Board of Admiralty to share this responsibility with me. I did not inform the War Office, for I knew they would raise objections to my interference in this sphere, and I knew by this time that the Department of the Master General of the Ordnance was not very receptive of such ideas. Neither did I inform the Treasury.*

So it came about that the tracks of the new vehicle were designed by Lieutenant W. Wilson of the Royal Naval Air Service. He worked with Mr. W. Tritton of Fosters of Lincoln, using American parts and boiler plate as armor. Dissatisfied with their first machine, the men assembled a much-improved version. Their second design was of the more familiar diamond shape. On Lord Salisbury's golf course the great monster demonstrated its ability to cross 9-foot-wide trenches. The army ordered 100 of them, describing them as water tanks for security reasons. The name stuck.

Colonel Swinton remained the most important protagonist of the

---

* Winston Churchill, *The World Crisis.*

tank. He saw its value as a surprise weapon and was convinced that it could deal a swift and mortal blow to the Germans. But the higher commander disagreed. Sir Douglas Haig, Commander in Chief of the British Army in France, told the Tank Supply Committee in August 1917, "[The] tank at any rate in its present state of development, can only be regarded as a minor factor . . . an adjunct to infantry and guns . . ." For Lord Kitchener, Secretary of State for War, the tank was no more than a "pretty mechanical toy."

The Failure of the Tank

The tank's "present state of development," of which Haig spoke as if it were the climate or some other act of God over which he had no influence, was largely due to the army's indifference. Half the tanks carried only machine guns; the rest carried 6-pounder guns. As one commentator wrote:

> They carried these particular guns because they were naval guns which the Admiralty found it possible to spare; the War Office did not find it possible to spare, or to make, any such armaments for tanks. In fact the War Office attitude to tanks was mainly confined to cancelling the orders given to construct them, whittling down the construction programmes when these were forced through by Cabinet Ministers, and staffing the Tank Corps with officers who had in some way gained a reputation for "difficulty." Luckily this type of officer was, under the social conditions then reigning in the British Army, often the best available for a new arm developing new tactics.*

The Royal Navy, the motor trade, and the army all contributed talented individuals to the tank units. Their commander, Lieutenant Colonel Hugh Elles, combined both intelligence and valor in measures that seldom go together. He soon got J. F. C. Fuller, a middle-aged major, who was later to become one of the world's foremost tank experts, as his chief staff officer.

Long before the tank reached a battlefield, its advocates were more or less agreed on certain essentials for its practical use. Months before the first tank action, Swinton advised that tanks should be deployed in a dawn attack "in great numbers and massed secretly . . ."; there must be no preliminary artillery bombardment, he said, because the ground captured must remain relatively undamaged so that ammunition and other supplies could be made available to the advancing forces.

Swinton was appalled when he heard of Haig's intention to use just

---

* Tom Wintringham, *Weapons and Tactics.*

forty tanks to prop up his unsuccessful battle on the Somme. It would reveal the secret weapon to the Germans with no chance of a break-through. Haig responded to this argument with characteristic zeal. He got rid of Swinton and then replaced the tank unit commander with a man of his own choice. The tanks were not concentrated; they were issued to infantry units, as support, over miles of front. There were a few individual successes, but the chance of a great victory had been squandered. From now on the tank could promise local successes but could never again be expected to end the war.

Haig had thrown the tanks into his failing offensive, in spite of pleas from the War Minister and the Minister of Munitions: "Pawned to pay for a local success which might draw an encore from the public —and, incidentally drown the growing volume of criticism," wrote Liddell Hart in his *History of the World War, 1914–1918.*

The first sight of tanks looming out of the mist was terrifying for German infantry and, although there was no breakthrough, there were many newsworthy stories of local success. This did little to endear the tank arm to the British brass hats. They resented the publicity that the tanks got and did everything to restrict the growth of the Tank Corps. The General Staff got the War Office to cancel an order for 1,000 new-model tanks and the War Minister was not informed. Artfully the War Office put opponents of tanks into the most crucial jobs concerning them.

Cambrai

What ended up as the "battle of Cambrai" was originally envisaged by Major Fuller as a tank raid upon the headquarters of Crown Prince Rupprecht of Bavaria some miles behind the German lines. The tanks were to strike at one of the most vital communication centers in the German rear and retire after twelve hours.

Now that Haig's premature use of the tank had alerted the whole German Army to its dangers, Fuller's "tank raid" idea could perhaps turn the loss of surprise into an advantage. One successful raid of this sort could keep every German unit constantly fearful of another one. And, of course, the tank men were not blind to the fact that a success-ful raid would ensure wonderful publicity for the tank units.

To what extent the actions of Haig and his fellow brass hats were influenced by a resentment of the attention that the Tank Corps had already attracted we cannot be certain. In any event, Haig squashed Fuller's plan and carried on with his third battle of Ypres. After ten days of artillery bombardment he sent his soldiers into reclaimed marsh. Nearly a quarter of a million men were lost in what went down in history as the British Army's most costly advance and gave many families—mine included—a new word to shudder at: Passchendaele.

When even Haig began to realize that Passchendaele would give him no glory, he reconsidered Fuller's idea of a tank raid at Cambrai, rolling downland where the Germans sat behind the formidable fortifications of the Hindenburg Line.

In the initial stages the tanks achieved complete surprise. Specially modified tanks bridged trenches, breached barbed wire, and brought supplies forward. Radio-equipped tanks reported as the attackers rolled forward no less than four miles in a war where progress was usually measured in yards.

But Fuller's ideas for a raid had been changed into a full-scale offensive, with unrealistic objectives and poor planning for the followup. There were no reserves ready to hold the captured ground, and the cavalry, who had spent years clamoring for a chance to exploit a breakthrough, were now not clever enough or quick enough to do so.

The Germans rushed to close the gap in their defenses and the British victory turned sour. Significantly, the British General HQ gave special prominence to any German successes against the British tank force. But "the incentive of a mention in despatches was not accorded to enemy feats performed at the expense of the infantry or cavalry," notes Liddell Hart dryly in his *History of the World War, 1914–1918*.

Soon the British had lost their newly captured ground, and more. Yet enough publicity had been given to the initial success for England's church bells to peal, for Haig to redeem his reputation, and for Cambrai to be written into history books as a British victory.

Anxious to escape censure for the staff shortcomings displayed at Cambrai, British senior officers tried to shift blame onto their own fighting men. The official court of enquiry supported this libel, using false accounts of the fighting to add credence to it.

The New German Infantry Tactics

Just as the tank attack at Cambrai revealed the method the British would use for the great offensives of 1918, so the Germans' counterattack was a test of the methods they would develop for their offensives in the spring of that year.

The Germans were being organized into assault (*Stoss*) divisions. The infantry used light machine guns and light mortars, together with flamethrowers, to seek out and attack weak spots in the British line. These specially chosen soldiers were trained to infiltrate the defenses and to avoid pushing the enemy line back. Strong points were by-passed and left for the follow-up units. The objective was always the artillery positions which, if overrun, would prevent the enemy's withdrawal to a new defense line.

The German infantry manhandled light artillery pieces forward to provide constant supporting fire. Aircraft gave close support to infantry. It was the first example of "battle groups," mixed teams working in very close cooperation. Tanks had no place in these tactics, which did not have the same dramatic impact that the tank displayed and so did not get the same attention. But this new tactical method revolutionized warfare and was not far short of what was later called "blitzkrieg."

Such infantry tactics, modified according to local conditions, were used by the Germans on all fronts. Especially noteworthy was the victory gained in November 1917 at Caporetto against the Italians. Rommel, then a young captain in the German Army, had received his *Pour le Mérite* after his battalion had captured 9,000 prisoners and 81 guns at Caporetto. In 1940 he was to win world fame in command of a panzer division.

More British tank-led battles were fought, notably at Hamel, Amiens, and Albert, while the French (who had by now developed tanks of their own) used armor in the St.-Mihiel and Meuse-Argonne offensives.

As long as the tank moved at a slow walking pace, there would always be enough time for the Germans to move up their reserves and re-form a defense line. Obviously something faster was needed to exploit the breakthrough, but the cavalry proved so vulnerable to small-arms fire that it was useless in this role. Armored cars, less vulnerable to machine guns, were not organized or equipped for such work. Crews were not trained to do it and there were not enough such cars. In any case, they depended too much upon undamaged roads. And German gunners were learning how to knock out tanks, and their engineers were learning how to build better traps and ditches to disable them.

The great tank-led battle at Amiens in August 1918 is often said to be the battle in which the tank won the war. But, after an initial advance of no less than 12 miles, aided considerably by a heavy mist over the battlefield, the Allies still could not break through the front. During the first four days of battle the Tank Corps was almost wiped out as a fighting force, having lost 72 per cent of its tanks (from various causes).

The Germans had rejected the idea of tanks because of the scarcity of the material needed to manufacture them. By the end of the war, only a few rather crude models had come from the German factories, and some captured Allied tanks were also used in battle. The Germans had no alternative but to fight the tanks with artillery; and this they did with notable success. As 1918 wore on, the Germans were knocking out tanks faster than British factories could manufacture them. In spite of frantic efforts made by base workshops, fewer and fewer Allied tanks were available to fight. In sixty-four days after the start of the Amiens battle, the number of tanks lost was equal to 41.4 per cent of Britain's entire production up to that time, including those assigned to training, and even those for which contracts had been signed but which were not so far made.

By October 1918 the Tank Corps was counting its machines on the fingers of one hand: four tanks were available at the Selle River on 20 October and three at Maubeuge on 2 November. By 5 November the Tank Corps, with only eight tanks left, admitted that it was at the end of its resources.

The French and the Americans were in no better position. On the Argonne-Champagne front, for instance, they had lost 367 French and 70 American tanks. (Of these 22 per cent were lost to artillery fire, 2 per cent to mines, 20 per cent were captured, and 56 per cent had mechanical failures.) Crew casualties were about 40 per cent. The final week of the war was fought without tanks.

Ludendorff's greatest concern during September 1918 was not the tank, nor even the Western Front; it was a series of events that had started with the loss of Jerusalem to General Sir Edmund Allenby in December 1917 and ended with the destruction of the last Turkish army at Megiddo in September 1918. Allied armies at Salonika were also on the move and, at the end of September, the Bulgarians signed a separate peace with the Allies. Without sufficient armies to protect Germany against this new threat, Ludendorff advised his government to ask for an armistice. The war was coming to an end.

Whatever had brought an end to the war, it was not the tank. The Royal Navy had probably made the most vital contribution to Allied victory. The U-boat had been countered and the sea lanes kept open to supply the Allies with food and munitions while blockading Germany to a point of starvation. When America's participation tilted the scales against the Germans, it was the Royal Navy which guaranteed that the American soldiers would arrive.

J. F. C. Fuller

"Boney" Fuller, chief staff officer of the British Tank Corps, admitted that "the war was brought to an end, not by fighting, but by famine and revolution." It was the Germans who insisted that they had been defeated by the tank; the generals considered it honorable to be defeated by a new weapon, just as the infantrymen could flee from the tank with no guilty feelings. This moral reversal that the tank inflicted on the enemy provided a tactical value out of all proportion to its firepower, but as long as it crawled so slowly it would never be capable of more than pushing the enemy back.* The tank in 1918 was not a war-winning weapon.

In the final months of the war there was much speculation about what might happen if tanks that could travel at 20 or 30 mph were delivered in large numbers to the army. Experts suggested that such a weapon would revolutionize tactics in a manner comparable with the introduction of armored foot soldiers at the battle of Plataea in 479 B.C. or the great victory won by heavy armored cavalry at Pavia in A.D. 774. It would alter the fundamentals of war, since thereafter no army could afford to leave its flanks exposed. Now, perhaps, the world was to embark on its third armored period.

J. F. C. Fuller's ideas had come to maturity in March 1918, at a time when German infiltration tactics were threatening British Fifth Army rear areas. Divisional, Brigade, and Army HQs were "panic stricken"; chaos spread through the whole command system as it lost contact with the fighting troops.

The Germans failed to exploit this success, just as the Allies failed on several occasions before and afterward, yet Fuller's ideas began with the German tactics. He realized that a fast tank was just the weapon with which to pursue such an assault. At this time, German Army HQs were, on average, 18 miles behind the line. Corps and divisional HQs were closer. Using tanks and close air support, the Allies should have no great problem in attacking the HQs of the enemy's commanding generals. Deprived of its "brain," the enemy front line would collapse within "a matter of hours," predicted Fuller.

Fuller's base workshops had already demonstrated that it was possible to build a tank that could go at 30 mph and keep going for 100 miles. Now he wrote out his ideas in full and sent them back to England with an engineering officer who had worked out a spring suspension for such high-speed tanks. (Until this time tanks had no suspension.) In its final form, Fuller's imaginative proposal was known as "Plan 1919." Before the plan could be put into use, the Germans had asked for an armistice and the war was over.

---

* The idea that there were fast tanks in use at this time persists because some lighter tanks were called "Whippets." But even the most optimistic specification claimed for them no more than a maximum speed of 8.3 mph.

B. H. Liddell Hart

During 1918 another British officer had started to think about how the deadlock of trench warfare could be broken. Captain B. H. Liddell Hart was not a tank officer and never became a tank expert in the way that Fuller was. But like Fuller, and the German Captain Heinz Guderian too, he was from a light infantry regiment, imbued with all the respect for mobility that such regiments have.

Liddell Hart firmly rejected the brainless human battering-ram tactics of General Haig and his fellows and reintroduced the notion that battles are won by ideas. There was always an indirect approach, he argued, always an unexpected place or unexpected way to hit the enemy. His book *The Strategy of Indirect Approach* exemplified such ideas in a history of warfare that started with the Greeks and Persians. It was to become his most widely read work.

After the war, Liddell Hart was chosen to revise the British infantry training manual, and, like Fuller, he used German tactics as his starting point. He added many ideas of his own, stressing the advantage of reinforcing success rather than sending aid to where the fighting was hardest. Turn opportunism into a system, he advised. He expounded these ideas at lectures. Although the War Office cut and changed the draft he had written for the official manual, his original version was published as a separate volume and Liddell Hart became an influential voice almost overnight. Generals came to hear him talk; the aide-de-camp of Marshal Ferdinand Foch, who became Supreme Allied Commander in April 1918, contacted him. In India one general had the lecture printed for the British troops at his own expense.

Boney Fuller was unconvinced by the indirect-approach theory, calling it "the strategy of evasion." But the two men saw eye to eye on many matters, and it had been Fuller's Plan 1919 (reprinted in *Weekly Tank Notes*) that first made Liddell Hart formulate his theories into more specific terms. Both men agreed that modern armies must achieve mobility by means of mechanization, and it was Liddell Hart who extended what were essentially tactical movements (hitting a headquarters 20 miles or so inside the enemy's territory) into the philosophy of "the expanding torrent," which spread disorder up through the army commanders to the enemy government.

There were many other theorists describing what the future held. The American Army's General (then Colonel) William Mitchell had used hundreds of airplanes to drop an unprecedented 80 tons of bombs onto German rear areas in one day to support an offensive. As the war ended, he was proposing more such bombing offensives and wanted 12,000 infantry soldiers dropped into the German rear and air-supplied. Mitchell advocated the dive bomber and demonstrated after the war that battleships were vulnerable to bombing aircraft.

In Italy Colonel Giulio Douhet went on to claim that wars could be decided by fleets of bombers. As with all such theories, these writings were more often used in support of vested interests than as a basis for rational discussion. And the theorists were too ready to go to extremes in their writings so that predictions became fantasies set in a science-fiction world.

A Changing World

The tank had been invented in order to break the deadlock of trench warfare. Used as a mobile armored pillbox, it could advance in the face of machine-gun fire and crush the vast fields of barbed wire that filled no man's land. Ability to cross trenches was considered far more important than firepower, and protection more important than speed. The war ended with very long, very heavy tanks, which were so slow that they became vulnerable to artillery fire. No matter how much the theorists insisted that a really fast tank (in the 20 to 30 mph category) would transform the very nature of war, the fact was that the war had ended with the tank no more than a rather ineffectual infantry support weapon. For the staffs of most armies, it remained so until the next war began.

The nineteenth-century world of peasants and gentry, in which horse and carriage marked the divide, was being undermined. Cheap motorcars poured from the factories. Henry Ford's Model T went on sale in 1908; by 1915 the number had risen to a million and by 1924 no less than 10 million Fords had been made. Mass production began a social transformation which is still continuing.

But the men of the postwar armies did not want to believe that their world might change too. When the First World War ended, the French and British professional armies resumed a peacetime life-style that centered on the cavalry regiment. It was a time when all professional soldiers had to make do with obsolete equipment and small budgets. It was inevitable that the newly formed tank arm should be squeezed hardest, and requests for new equipment or a chance to experiment were usually answered by reminders about the old tanks left over from the war. Having given the slow tanks to the infantry, any new faster tanks were given to the cavalry to be used as tin horses.

Perhaps governments would have given more support if tank experts had all agreed about the role of the tank in future warfare. Every permutation of tank, infantry, and artillery was advocated. Many were tested in peacetime exercises. During this time it was usually the infantry which emerged as the strongest detractor of the value of the tank in battle. The cavalry, which had had little or no fighting role throughout the First World War, was beginning to realize that unless it adapted to this new armored vehicle, its regiments would become extinct and finally be disbanded. But the infantry had done almost all the fighting, in appalling conditions, and many infantry generals were jealous of the publicity, funds, and promotions that the new tank arm had received during the war. Opinion polarized as the dispute continued. The extremists among the tank men wanted armies composed solely of tanks with no supporting arms whatsoever. On the other hand, the infantry demanded very heavy tanks that could move no faster than a fully equipped infantry soldier and would remain under the infantry officer's direct control.

The more perceptive of the tank theorists were stressing the importance of versatility. They believed that infantry, signals, engineers, and artillery should all be equipped with armored fighting vehicles on caterpillar tracks, thus giving the whole army "cross-country capability." It could be supplied either by air or by other tracked vehicles.

There were also fears for tanks that attempted to operate beyond the range of artillery. In May 1937 Marshal Mikail Tukhachevski—soon to be a victim of Stalin—wrote that "tanks, like infantry, cannot successfully act in combined troop combat without mighty artillery support." This idea, shared by the French High Command, was responsible for much of the French complacency before the German advance of 1940.

All the arguments contained a large measure of vested interest. Many senior officers, with allegiance and nostalgia for the chic regiments to which they had devoted their youth, did not relish the idea of divisional—or even corps—conferences at which a tank man in oily overalls gave the orders, for tank armies would have tank generals in command. The "old guard" preferred to have tanks dispersed throughout the army and used in the support role, thus making it as difficult for a tank man to command a division as it already was for the other specialists.

The dilemma facing the planners at that time must not be underestimated. How could these expensive motor vehicles and tanks be integrated into the army? There were several alternatives. First, the speed of the mobile forces could be kept down to that of marching men. But slow tanks had failed in 1918, and with the promised improvement in antitank weapons, they would probably prove an even more dismal failure.

Second, trucks and tanks could be given to the whole army. Here the cost—to say nothing of the availability—of raw materials made such a plan prohibitive even for a small professional army. And what became of men mobilized for war?

Third, part of the army could be separated off and given motor vehicles while the remainder marched. But which part of the army needed mobility most? And how would the mobile army get its supplies? Would such relegation demoralize that part of the army denied motors? In France such a course would almost certainly bring an end to the policy of peacetime conscription.

Cost was the ever-present limitation. Before Hitler came to power, there seemed very little prospect of the British Army being called upon to fight a European land battle. Theorists spoke of "the expanding torrent" in which armored forces, with close air support, made deep penetrations through fortified fronts. Such expensive ideas were far too Napoleonic for an army mainly concerned with putting down riots in the colonies.

For the British and French armies, the interwar years were a time of policing. For dealing with rebellious Indians or Arab tribesmen nothing was better than the fast, cheap, lightly armored little tanks with one machine gun. Smart cavalry regiments reluctantly reequipped with them. Such tanks could chase horsemen, climb steep outcrops of rock, and easily deflect the low-velocity bullets of the rebels' muzzle-loading rifles. On a European battlefield, however, nothing could have been less suitable, except perhaps a horse.

There were political considerations too. The major powers had to keep a broad industrial base if they were to continue to manufacture their own weapons. Still today, governments prefer to subsidize inefficient shipyards or profligate aircraft factories than face the political pressure that invariably comes from countries which sell armaments. It remains unwise to ban the sale of armaments to nations whose policies one wishes to change; they will need spare parts, repairs, and replacements and will have to bargain for them.

The cost of maintaining an industrial base can be relieved by foreign sales. So between the wars, British and French tanks were likely to be a compromise between what the armed forces wanted and what could be sold overseas.

In the British Army, despite some promising experiments, the exponents of tank warfare were totally vanquished by the combined efforts of advocates of the old school. By modifying infantry and cavalry units to take tanks, they had been able to frustrate all attempts to form permanent armored divisions. They winkled Fuller from his job as adviser to the Chief of the Imperial General Staff. They shamelessly rigged the autumn maneuvers of 1934 in order to discredit the improvised armored force that took part in it. The director of army maneuvers that year had more or less announced his intention beforehand, saying that he wanted to restore the morale of the older types of troops. To consolidate this campaign, the Royal Tank Corps experiments were discontinued and its best leaders sent to other jobs, with infantry or anti-aircraft units or to administrative posts in India.

The men who opposed the tank arm rationalized their opposition by believing every claim about the development of antitank guns. It was said that antitank guns were so powerful that they had made the tank virtually obsolete. Like so many other dire warnings of the same kind, these claims proved unfounded. The German 3.7 cm Pak (*Panzerabwehrkanone*, or antitank gun) was the best in general use anywhere in the world, but after 1940 the Germans gave urgent priority to getting improved ammunition and a bigger and better antitank weapon, the 5 cm Pak.

Hugh Elles, the first commander of the Royal Tank Corps, who had personally led his tanks into battle in the First World War, later lost faith in tanks. In 1934, when Master General of Ordnance, Elles decided that tanks would be of little use in future in any role other than the one they had had in those early battles. He ordered new tanks to be built to withstand all known antitank missiles. It was an absurd stricture, impossible to apply to any item of war, from battleship to bomb shelter.

This order resulted in the Infantry Tank Mark I, which went to war in France in 1940. It weighed 11 tons and had a top speed of 11 mph. Its commander aimed, loaded, and fired its sole armament, a machine gun, as well as commanding, navigating, and operating the radio. The only other member of the crew was the driver. As a war weapon, it was even less effective than the German PzKw I (*Panzerkampfwagen*) training tank.

In March 1938, believing war to be imminent, General Sir Edmund Ironside, soon to be Chief of the Imperial General Staff, noted in his diary that his army had no cruiser tanks, no infantry tanks, and only obsolete medium tanks. When war began and the Ministry of Supply had taken over from the Master General of Ordnance, Ironside asked the ministry about new tanks. He was given the astounding answer that there were two committees going their separate ways on tank design.

FIGURE 2   Matilda Mark II
infantry tank.

Neither had any contact with the General Staff, so they knew nothing of the army's needs.

The RAF cared even less about the army's needs. An RAF unit that obliged the army with a demonstration of "ground strafing" got a sharp letter of complaint from the Air Ministry. RAF cooperation with the army, the Air Ministry decided, must be solely confined to reconnaissance flights.

The RAF, long since a congenial haven for the worst sort of "Colonel Blimp," was terrified that any cooperation with the army or navy might reduce its status as an independent arm of the fighting forces. Not interested in the theories or practice of air support, which had been proved so vitally important in the First World War, it clung tight to the crackpot prophecies of men such as Douhet, who said that bombing fleets could win wars without the help of other services.

The same spirit of Colonel Blimp kept the RAF resolutely opposed to dive bombing. In late 1937, the chief test pilot of Vickers returned from Germany where he had flown the excellent Junkers Ju 87 Stuka. The Vickers chairman thought his enthusiastic report important enough to pass on to Britain's Air Minister but he was advised to "kindly tell your pilots to mind their own bloody business . . ."

So many decades after the event, it requires a considerable effort of mind to re-create that Europe of 1940, when France was a mighty power and her frontiers impregnable. Yet without that effort there is little chance of understanding the initial German victory.

The almost universal opinion that the war would continue in a stalemate provoked many into wondering if the belligerents would eventually be forced to come to terms. Liddell Hart had consistently advised against British participation in any European land battle, and he opposed sending the British Expeditionary Force to France. This was because he saw no chance of a breakthrough by either side and wanted Britain kept out of a long exhausting war of attrition like that of 1914–1918. Far from predicting the German armored thrust through the Ardennes, Liddell Hart specifically said in 1939 in his book *The Defence of Britain* that a large-scale movement through the Ardennes was not possible because of the terrain.

In Liddell Hart's view, the French Army did not need assistance from Britain; the French Army was more thoroughly trained than that of the Germans, which had expanded too much and too quickly. He interpreted the fighting in Spain and China as showing the increasing strength of the defensive, so that even poorly equipped and poorly organized armies could defeat an attacker. He did not move far from this view even after the German invasion of Poland.

Liddell Hart suggested that British economic pressure was her best weapon against Germany, with the added use of naval blockade and strategic bombing. In fact, as Germany extended her territories and traded with the East, the naval blockade affected her less and less. Strategic bombing proved a catastrophe, and Liddell Hart's suggestion that psychological warfare might be the indirect approach that would overthrow Hitler also proved a fiasco.

Such conclusions are not intended to belittle Liddell Hart, but to re-create a time when blitzkrieg seemed impossible, even for a man who had spent his life thinking about it.

Heinz Guderian, Creator of the Blitzkrieg

Perhaps it is unique in military history for one man to influence the design of a weapon, see to training the men who use it, help plan an offensive, and then lead his force in battle. Heinz Guderian did just that.

Guderian was born in 1888 at Kulm, a Prussian town on the river Vistula (now Chelmno, a Polish town on the river Wista). Born in a Germany that is now Poland, he went to live in a Germany that is now France—Colmar in Alsace. This region was annexed by Germany after the Franco-Prussian War of 1871 and returned to France at the end of the First World War.

Guderian attended military schools in Germany before being sent as a *Fähnrich*—an NCO aspiring to become an officer—to the battalion his father commanded at Bitche in Lorraine.

As a young officer, encouraged by his father, he elected to serve with a telegraph battalion. It was an unusual choice for an ambitious young infantry officer to make, but Guderian found the technical work interesting. When war began in 1914 he took charge of a heavy wireless station working in conjunction with cavalry.

With every week that went by, wireless was improved. Its application to warfare was changing the whole system of command. Since Napoleon's time, commanders had been moving farther back in order to control the battle, but wireless enabled a commander to be anywhere he wished, even in an airplane or a tank. From this time onward, radio communication was a top priority in all Guderian's theories.

In the latter part of the First World War Guderian had served as a staff officer, progressing from divisional staff appointments to the staff of a corps and attending a General Staff officer's course in Sedan. Again he found himself in that region of France where he had lived as a child and young man. During the 1914–1918 war, Luxembourg and the Ardennes were well behind the German front line. He knew the terrain well.

After 1918 Guderian remained in the postwar army. He served on the eastern frontier, working as a senior staff officer with the Iron Division, and also as a lowly company commander with his own regiment, before being selected for a staff job with the Inspectorate of Transport Troops. This office was responsible for studying the possible tactical uses of motorized infantry in combat, as well as the more mundane use of motor transport. The inspector intended to use Guderian in connection with motorized infantry studies, but the Chief of Staff changed this assignment and sent him to a technical job concerning construction work, workshops, and fuel supply. Guderian was "astonished" at being assigned to such humdrum tasks and even asked to return to his company command, but there was no escape.

Later, Guderian realized that this enforced experience was valuable to him, but at the time it was a great disappointment, assuaged to some extent by a self-imposed course of study. He read the works of the armored warfare theorists, in particular J. F. C. Fuller. This was the first time that Guderian had encountered the theory of mechanized forces striking deep to hit the enemy's "brain" and communications, rather than clashing with front-line enemy troops.

Guderian's experience of the infiltration tactics of the First World War fitted well with his new interest in tanks, in just the same way as these two factors had come together in the mind of J. F. C. Fuller in 1918. And to this was added a vital third element—Guderian's war experience with military radio. Here were the vital ingredients of blitzkrieg.

In 1927 the British Army was leading the world in tank-warfare techniques. The French and American armies had not permitted their tanks to form a separate corps as the British had done. Under the terms of the 1919 peace treaty, the Germans were not permitted to have tanks. The British Army had an "experimental mechanized force." It combined some little "tankettes," armored cars, Vickers medium tanks, a motorized infantry battalion (using half-tracks and six-wheel trucks), engineers, and an artillery regiment, with some self-propelled 18-pounder guns. It was a brilliant innovation. Even in 1940 this would have sounded formidable, but the army disbanded it after a couple of years and in Britain the promising experiments were forgotten.

They were not forgotten in Germany, however. By 1928 the Germans had found a way of having some tank experiments of their own and made a secret agreement with Soviet Russia to share the facilities of a testing ground at Kazan, on the Volga. The Germans brought expertise and the Russians provided some tanks, including the little British Vickers-Loyd type, some ideas from which were seen in the early German tanks.

Guderian remained in Germany and became well known in the army for his lectures on military history and his ideas about the future role of tanks, aircraft, and motorized infantry. By this time he was in the Troop Office (or *Truppenamt*, the name used to disguise the existence of the forbidden General Staff).

In the summer exercises of 1929 he used some small cars rigged up to represent tanks. Little was accomplished beyond establishing a desire for real tanks. When Guderian was given command of a motorized battalion, the need for make-believe continued; his men used motorcycles to supplement the antique armored cars and wooden sticks to represent antitank weapons. But there was no substitute for real radio, and in 1931 the British Army again led the world by installing newly developed crystal-controlled radios to exercise 180 tanks under one command.

It all worked perfectly—so perfectly that some observers suspected it was a hoax brought off by means of previously rehearsed drivers. Guderian knew better. He saw that radio command was now a primary requirement for the sort of warfare he envisaged.

"That's What I Need"

When, in 1933, Hitler became Chancellor, events in the German Army moved swiftly. By December of that year, Krupp submitted a tank-

FIGURE 3
The inexpensive PzKw IA tank.

chassis design, based upon the little British Carden Loyd Mk VI, which the Germans had tested in Russia. Its superstructure was designed by Daimler-Benz. Just a few weeks later, in February 1934, the drawings had become reality. The first prototype PzKw I was working and full-scale production began. Exactly one year later, Hitler was able to visit the army ordnance testing ground at Kummersdorf and see some of Guderian's tanks in action. It was here that he made his well-known aside, "That's what I need. That's what I want to have." Often cited to prove Hitler's early intention to wage war, it is more likely, as Kenneth Macksey suggests, that the crafty Hitler recognized something he could use to impress the world with his power and importance.*

While other politicians were discovering that rearmament was very unpopular with the voters who were asked to pay for it, Hitler was capitalizing on promises of international prestige and prosperity. He

* There is some confusion about the date of Hitler's remarks at the Kummersdorf army ordnance testing ground. Guderian, in his book *Panzer Leader*, suggests that the visit was in 1933, and Robert J. O'Neill in *The German Army and the Nazi Party* also gives this date. But no tanks existed at Kummersdorf then. Kenneth Macksey, in his excellent biography of Guderian, quotes early 1934. In fact, the very first prototype of the PzKw I ran on 3 February 1934. David Irving says in *The War Path* that Hitler visited Kummersdorf for the first time on 6 February 1935. It seems certain that 1935 is the correct date. Hitler would have watched production models of the PzKw IA (about 300 were manufactured) and perhaps the very first PzKw IB, in which the 6-cylinder Maybach engine replaced the low-power 4-cylinder Krupp power unit in the earlier tanks.

exaggerated the strength of his army, navy, and air force. He preferred small aircraft to big ones, so that he could have more of them. Half-tracks and small cheap vehicles could be paraded past the newsreel cameras and the foreign visitors. These light tanks were exactly right for this purpose.

There was intrigue and backbiting in the German Army of this time, as there was, and continues to be, in every other army. But it is as well to remember that opposition to Guderian was not always opposition to the tank arm, although it is understandable for Guderian in his memoirs sometimes to confuse the two. In fact, the support he got was incomparably better than that enjoyed by the tank experts of any other army. Even the lack of enthusiasm shown by the Army Chief of Staff—his most notable opponent—was due more to Germany's lack of fuel, limited steel production, and rubber shortage than to his opinion about tanks.

According to Liddell Hart, Blomberg, Germany's War Minister, had done more than anyone except Guderian to circulate Liddell Hart's writings and propagate his ideas. And Blomberg and Reichenau, head of the Armed Forces Office, had collaborated to produce translations of Liddell Hart's books for private circulation among German officers rather than wait for the ordinary translated edition.

Very little of Guderian's basic theory was ever challenged by his superiors. His emphasis on mobility was considered a legacy of the mighty Hans von Seeckt, while so much of the theory of blitzkrieg not only conformed with Prussian military thought since the elder Moltke, but was in direct line with the highly successful storm-troop tactics of 1918. The tank theorists of other armies were nonconformists in a hostile world. Guderian liked to think of himself in the same way and subsequent writings have encouraged this view. But this is not true of Guderian, who was bringing to fruition ideas that were widely acceptable to the men about him.

By October 1935 Guderian, forty-seven years old, was a colonel and chief of staff to the newly created Armored Force. Hitler, a year younger, had done even better. He was Chancellor, Führer, and Supreme Commander. Already Hitler was bringing his Party organization into closer association with the armed forces. The NSKK (Nazi motor transport corps) was training young men to drive. By 1939 it could provide about 187,000 trained drivers for trucks and tanks.

In 1935 the French had put together the world's first armored division. That the Germans scrambled to put together three such formations in that same year was a sign that Nazi megalomania was now affecting the army too.

Germany did not have the wealth or the industrial capacity to equip three armored divisions. The normal complement of 500 tanks of one such division was more than the entire German tank output to date. And all the tanks available were lightweight training tanks. (The PzKw IV was only just in prototype and the PzKw III was a year behind it.) As well as tanks, each division would require about 3,000 other vehicles plus the motorcycles, which were everywhere used to supplement armored cars and tanks.*

Even so, the rest of the army were discontented at seeing the Armored Force getting the lion's share of the motors. The artillery needed more towing vehicles, the infantry wanted trucks to ride in and to tow their small guns. The cavalry wanted some tanks. In fact, the whole army desperately needed more motor transport.

The artillery got the bulk of the half-tracks to tow and position the big guns that now began to arrive. The cavalry formed "light divisions" (a poor man's panzer division) using some of the tanks, and some infantry units were motorized. In the face of this competition, a panzer division's foot soldiers had to be content to go to battle in ordinary trucks; there could be no question of giving them the tracked, armored vehicles that Guderian wanted. They would simply have to keep to the roads.

By 1936 conscription had enlarged the German armed forces enough to give Guderian the bright red trouser stripe of the general, but it also brought into being an army far bigger than anything that German industry could equip with motor vehicles. From now on, those men who wanted a small professional army on wheels knew it was out of the question. Apart from a tiny elite, the German Army was to be a mass army of conscripted foot soldiers with horse transport and would remain so right through the war.

Hitler's decision to get rid of Generals von Fritsch and von Blomberg led to a massive shake-out of senior officers unsympathetic to the Nazis. One such victim was Guderian's chief, General der Panzertruppen Oswald Lutz, who had played a most important role in the creation of the motorized and mechanized forces.

There was no chance that Guderian's career would be similarly ended. In 1937 his hastily written and rather bland book *Achtung! Panzer!* contributed little to the theory of tank warfare but clearly established its author as a supporter of Hitler.

---

* In the face of conflicting personal accounts of the tank complement of the original armored divisions, my estimate is based upon the dates on which the factories changed over to building the PzKw IB model (1935). Only 300 of the previous PzKw IAs were manufactured, as noted before.

Then, in February 1938, a surprise message delivered late at night gave Guderian only a few hours in which to get his uniform changed so that he could wear the insignia of a *Generalleutnant* before attending a meeting at which Hitler was to preside. Guderian had been appointed to command of the world's first armored corps and had got the job over the heads of several officers senior to him.

Little more than a year later Guderian was asked to take command of the spearhead force for the Anschluss, or annexation of Austria. It gave him a chance to demonstrate the capacity of his armored units in a long cross-country movement, deployed in preparation for battle, since opposition to the Anschluss could not be entirely discounted.

Ever since the German reoccupation of the Saar in 1935, some men of SS-Leibstandarte Adolf Hitler had been included in such military operations so that the Nazi Party should be represented. So it was with the Anschluss, but by this time this SS ceremonial unit was wearing the same field-gray uniform that the soldiers wore. As the unit was motorized, it was best suited to accompany the panzer division. This formed the corps which Guderian commanded from a mobile headquarters.*

For Guderian's corps the Anschluss was a political success and a military failure. Guderian's own suggestion that the vehicles be decorated with flags and greenery contributed to the friendly way in which the invading Germans were greeted in Austria. But the journey of over 400 miles—from Würzburg to Vienna via Passau—completed in 48 hours, showed up the weaknesses of the armored formations.

Organization was poor. En route, Guderian had to threaten violence in order to use a fuel depot, and the complete absence of fuel-supply columns caused them to commandeer trucks from the mayor of Passau. On the other side of the frontier, the tanks only kept going because they were fueled from roadside service stations. (All the German tanks had petrol engines.) From this time onward, Guderian integrated the supply services into his divisions, so that between three and five days' supply of fuel, food, and ammunition could be carried by the fighting units. One close associate of Guderian has described the way in which he was already extending his tactical ideas into strategical ones. Now he began believing that fast, deep penetrations of enemy territory (of the sort that several days' supplies could make possible) would bring about a complete collapse of the enemy's entire military system.

---

* A corps usually consists of a corps HQ (with appropriate signals units plus attached engineers, artillery, and antiaircraft units) and two or more divisions.

The mechanical failures of the Anschluss were not so easily over-come. It was reported that 30 per cent of the tanks suffered break-downs. The true failure rate was certainly higher, and no amount of preparation would change this in any future operations. All that could be done was to train men from the divisional workshops to recover and repair tanks as fast as possible.

Rash as a Man

Although Guderian did not become one of Hitler's immediate circle, the Führer cultivated him to the extent of having him to dinner and sharing a box at the opera with him. Guderian was considered reliable by the Nazis, but, like many of those who occupy military positions of power, he was naïve. His concern was solely with the development of the panzer force and the petty arguments and rivalries that involved it. Writing to his wife after the occupation of the Sudetenland, he de-scribed Hitler as "a very great man . . . a courageous man." But in the same letter he reveals his understanding of the way in which Hitler had used him and his tanks to seize this territory: "It was of course only possible because of the new sharp sword in our hand and the will to use it, had peaceable means not been possible."

Guderian was an impatient man, seldom waiting to consider all sides of a dispute before giving orders to resolve it. During the open-ing stage of the Polish campaign, his corps contained only one armored division plus two motorized infantry divisions. The temptation to inter-fere with the detailed working of the panzer division proved too much for him. Friction arose between him and his divisional commander. There was an especially bitter exchange when the tanks were getting near to what had once been the Guderian family home. Using his fully equipped half-track command vehicle, he went ahead with the leading tanks. It was the first time such a senior officer had accompanied tanks in this way. He found the division halted at the river Brahe. The com-mander of the tank regiment had decided to halt because the river might be strongly defended and the divisional commander was not there to press the advance onward, as Guderian's plan had ordered. Guderian was enraged. He sent men of a motorcycle battalion across the river in inflatable boats and then moved tanks across a bridge. The defenders withdrew and the Germans had a vital bridgehead for the advance.

The incident nonetheless worsened the poor relationship between Guderian and his divisional commander. Underlying this bad feeling was the fact that this man, Generalleutnant Leo Freiherr Geyr von

Schweppenburg, had seen Guderian appointed to the corps command over his head. It is especially interesting that Liddell Hart, after interrogating so many of the German generals, chose the description of Guderian that Geyr gave to sum him up.

> Sixty per cent of what the German Panzer forces became was due to him. Ambitious, brave, a heart for his soldiers who liked and trusted him; rash as a man, quick in decisions, strict with officers, real personality, therefore many enemies. Blunt, even to Hitler. As a trainer— good; thorough; progressive. If you suggest revolutionary ideas, he will say in 95% of cases: "Yes," at once.*

Tank Design

By forbidding the construction of tanks in Germany, the peace treaty of 1919 had invested this arm with considerable glamour. From then on the tank was read about, written about, and discussed behind locked doors. The taboo convinced the Germans that the tank had been a potent factor in Allied victory.

* B. H. Liddell Hart, *The Other Side of the Hill*.

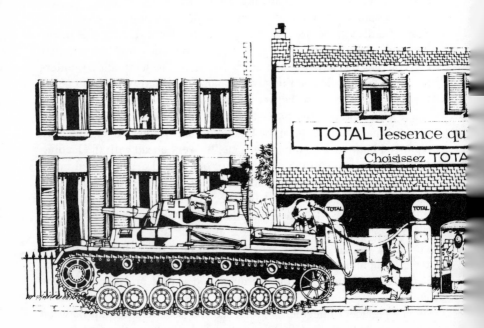

Defeat had also brought about the dismantling of Germany's heavy industry. In spite of the devious ways in which Krupp, the armaments manufacturing concern, aided since 1921 with government money and in consultation with the army, tried to circumvent the restrictions, this dismantling by the Allied Control Commission hindered German tank production far more than did prohibition. Tank manufacture provided great problems for industry. Airplanes and most other weapons could be built by all sorts of light industrial manufacturers, but heavy steel could only be worked by specialists.

A jig is a complex piece of machinery that locates and guides tools and drills during manufacturing. Typically, it took one or two years to get the jig for tank manufacture right, but then tanks could be made more rapidly. Every change in the specification, however, then brought the factories to a halt for rejigging. The kind of dilemma this brought, particularly to a country desperately short of weapons, was illustrated by a conclusion of a British War Cabinet Committee in April 1940, before the German invasion of France. In an instruction that even the official history calls "astounding," it decreed that tank production "must not be interfered with either by the incorporation of improvements to the approved types or by the production of newer models."

FIGURE 4   Since German PzKw tanks were fitted with gasoline engines, they were able to fill up at wayside gas stations in France when the spearhead of the advance outran its own supply lines. PzKw IV in front, PzKw II behind.

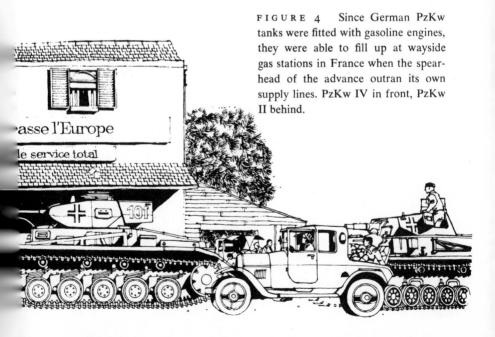

Still more astounding, neither the British General Staff nor the Ministry of Supply argued with this conclusion.

Had British tank design been sound in the first place, this instruction would not have been so devastating. In an effort to get some armored divisions into the field, tanks were being ordered straight from the drawing board and were in any case largely an assembly of already available components. The official account of the design and development of weapons says, "[We] were not avoiding the manufacture of prototypes, we were manufacturing nothing else."* Later the British did what the Germans had done so much earlier—they manufactured a considerable number of different experimental types before deciding upon a production model.

Germany, deprived of all tanks after the First World War, was provided with the chance to build a completely modern tank arm. The enormous preponderance of PzKw I and II tanks greatly simplified the supply of spare parts to the forward workshops. The German tanks had been designed about the same time (two years separated the PzKw I from the III and IV), and so many parts were interchangeable. French ordnance officers on the other hand faced a nightmare collection of different tank types, from the tiny Renault FTs left over from 1918, through some excellent modern Somuas to the incredible 81.5 ton Char 3C.

There is no such thing as a perfect tank. Basic design improvements always bring some corresponding disadvantage. For instance, speed is incompatible with heavy armor protection and yet a slow tank is more vulnerable to guns. A powerful tank (i.e., one with a high horsepower, or weight-power ratio) will be fast, but its range will be shortened. A tank with high clearance is likely to be good at surmounting obstacles, but its high profile makes it a larger target for enemy gunners.

However, most of the Allied tanks—and all the German models— weighed less than 24 tons, simply because this was the maximum weight most Western European roads and bridges could bear. Such tanks could also be carried on railway trains or be rafted across rivers. And German divisional bridging, both pontoon trestle (Type B) and box girder (Type K), was also confined to 24 tons' capacity.

German tank designers kept to the limit imposed by divisional bridging. Because tanks were usually transported by railways (tank tracks usually lasted only about 1,000 miles), they were also restricted to the continental loading width due to tunnels and oncoming traffic. In Germany this was 10 feet 4 inches, and German tanks of this period

---

* M. M. Postan, D. Hay, and J. D. Scott, *Design and Development of Weapons.*

were no wider than 9 feet 7 inches. British railways had a narrower gauge, which kept British tanks to under 8 feet 9 inches, and so were somewhat smaller. The technical problems of steering caused any limit in width to bring a corresponding limit in length. Since all tanks had a seated driver with a main armament firing over his head, the shape and size of any new tank was dictated long before a designer began his sketches.

The most important limitation was that of the turret ring. Obviously its size was limited by the width of the tank, but it was also limited by the engineering skills and machinery of the manufacturer. In the larger sizes, this delicate piece of precision machinery was very difficult to make.

The turret ring also affected what sort of armament the tank could bear. There had to be room for the gun breach and the men operating the gun, as well as for the tank commander. According to the size and quality of the turret ring, there was a limit to the shock it could sustain from recoil without damage. A tank without a turret could take a huge gun into the hull without taking recoil into account. (French tanks of the First World War had a 7.5 cm artillery piece fitted into a very primitive tractor. Later in the Second World War all the armies reverted to such combinations.) To have a fully traversing turret was an engineering luxury. It was to prevent the Germans from acquiring this special skill that the peace treaty allowed them to build only armored cars without turrets. In fact it did no more than delay them, as German industry soon mastered this vital construction.

It is often said that Guderian favored medium tanks, rejecting light "cavalry" tanks or heavy "infantry" tanks for a versatile compromise. Certainly Guderian listed his priorities as mobility, firepower, armor protection, and communication, in that order. But the tanks that Guderian asked for in the 1930s were not "medium tanks" unless compared with French 81-ton freaks or the tanks that the Russians were then building for use in a very different environment. Guderian had demanded the heaviest tanks he could get, despite any sacrifice this might mean in speed. He ordered the 20-ton PzKw III and the 23-ton PzKw IV as the main armament for his panzer divisions. All the comparable tanks—the French Somua S35, British Cruiser Mk IV, Russian BT 7, and Italian MII/39—were faster and, except for the S35, which was about the same weight, all of them were lighter too.*

The Germans were designing their tanks for adaptation to future demands, even though they could not be sure what those demands

---

* Nowadays only tanks of more than 25 tons are categorized as heavy tanks.

might be. The PzKw III was a typical example. It was designed in three sections: the lower main hull housing the engine, transmissions, and controls, onto which was fixed the front and rear superstructure. This superstructure could be changed without designing an entirely new tank. As the war continued, the PzKw III had its 3.7 cm gun replaced by a short 5 cm and then by a long 5 cm gun. Then it was redesigned to take the short 7.5 cm gun and its front armor increased in thickness from 30 mm to 50 mm without any loss of speed. The factory was unable to get the long 7.5 cm *Sturmkanone* (assault cannon, or StuK) into the tank, because the turret ring was too small, but by omitting the turret the gun could be mounted in the hull. The result was called a *Sturmgeschütz* (assault gun), or StuG III. Eventually even the very large 7.5 cm StuK 40 was to be fixed into this hull to create an anti-tank tank, or *Jagdpanzer*.

The PzKw III featured Dr. Ferdinand Porsche's latest development: torsion bar suspension. It had been tried with great success on half-track vehicles and was already fitted to the VW (*Volkswagen*) motorcar. On the tank, however, it had the advantage that very little of this suspension was exposed to gunfire.

Suspension is important to tanks for a number of reasons. As well as increasing the comfort and safety of the crew, it improves the performance, most especially at speed over rough ground. Although the theoretical pressure per square inch can be simply calculated by dividing the area of track in contact with ground by the total weight, this

FIGURE 5   The 81.5-ton French Char 3c and the tiny 7.5-ton Renault tank.

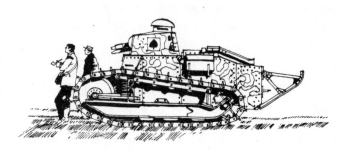

is far from what can ever be achieved. In fact, the weight will be unevenly distributed according to the number of wheels used and to the efficiency of the suspension system. As tank designs got heavier and the terrain softer—snow, sand, and mud—the suspension system became more and more important.

The failure of the tank in the First World War arose largely from its very poor speed and mechanical unreliability, though a large measure of the tank force's inability to consolidate and follow up first successes had also been due to crew fatigue. The early British tanks held eight men, including four gunners and two gear operators. They had to crouch because there was not enough room to stand upright, and every lurch was likely to bring them into contact with sharp projections or the hot engines. The temperature inside commonly exceeded 100 degrees Fahrenheit and the metal became too hot to touch. The noise was so great that the driver gave his orders to the gearmen by hammering on the engine. Dust and oil fumes added to the crew's misery, as did the heat, noise, and smoke of the guns. Small-arms fire hitting the armor outside sent metal flakes ricocheting around inside the tank or shattered the driver's glass visor, sometimes blinding him. Such discomfort and acute fatigue, added to the natural fears and tensions that accompanied all the front-line soldiers, could bring nausea, vomiting, and delirium. After a couple of days in such conditions, few crewmen could continue fighting.

Guderian, on the other hand, attached great importance to the comfort and convenience of tank crews and asked that they should be selected with the same care with which the Luftwaffe chose its aircrews. He insisted that the PzKw III and IV had crews of five so that the men were not overworked or hurried. The French and British showed little concern for the crews. French tanks virtually all had one-man turrets, inside which a commander observed ground, gave orders to his crew, watched his own and enemy units, and manually loaded, aimed, and fired its armament. Sometimes his problems were multiplied by a fixed-axis gun in the hull, which could not be aimed until the tank faced the enemy.

French crewmen felt isolated within their machines. German crews were placed close together and could cooperate in emergencies concerning guns, ammunition, driving, or injury. They were reassured by a glance at their fellows and could lip-read in the noise of battle.

German designers were also more skillful in the use of armor. While many French and virtually all the British tanks had the same armor thickness throughout, the Germans were providing extra protection where needed (particularly at the front) and using thinner armor elsewhere. Designers were also using sloped armor for added protection. High-velocity antitank missiles, always traveling more or less horizontally, had to penetrate a greater thickness of tilted metal, and some missiles would even be deflected off such sloping armor.

Construction methods also varied; instead of following the British use of joints of bolts or rivets, the Germans used electrowelding. German face-hardened steel caused uncapped shot to shatter instead of piercing the metal, so enabling many German tanks to survive even direct hits.

The first of the German tanks were hastily put together and of orthodox design, with small turret rings and simple engineering for factories with no recent experience of such work. The result was the PzKw, a thinly armored machine, 15 feet long and weighing a little under 6 tons, with room inside for only two men. The prototype was tested in February 1934, and by the end of that same year tanks were being delivered from the factory. It looked impressive enough in pre-war parades and at the Nuremberg demonstrations and was suited to elementary training. Only an obsession with sheer numerical strength, however, could justify the way in which no less than 1,500 of these curious little machines—each armed only with two machine guns—were supplied to the army. Too flimsy for battle, the PzKw I could not even survive a long journey, as the Anschluss deployment had proved.

The testing of the first prototypes of the more complex larger tanks made the army realize that deliveries would be both late and slow. There was no alternative but to order another interim machine. This PzKw II was a more reasonable compromise between the urgent needs of the expanding tank arm and something that could venture onto the battlefield. Although only marginally heavier than its predecessor, this 7.5-ton tank was given more armor in 1937 to bring it over 10 tons. Its converted 20 mm anti-aircraft gun gave it a poor armament by contemporary standards, and the overall design did not justify making 1,400 of them. Unlike the earlier tanks, the PzKw IIs did not become totally obsolete. When better tanks came along, they were simply converted for other purposes. Some were made into commanders' tanks, some gave armored protection to a selected company of each panzer division's engineers, and some were converted into self-propelled artillery pieces.

Meanwhile the little PzKw Is and IIs made up virtually the whole German tank arm. By the time that Poland was invaded, only 211 PzKw IVs had been delivered and even fewer PzKw IIIs, scarcely more than the *Panzer Lehr* (tank testing) unit needed to do its battlefield evaluation for Army Ordnance.

FIGURE 6   Torsion-bar suspension for PzKw III.

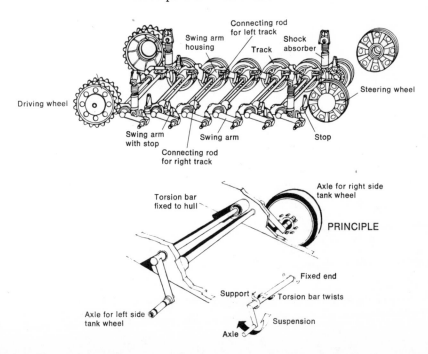

While the PzKw I and II were too flimsy and too primitive, the PzKw III and IV designs overcompensated for these failings. They were complex machines that gave too many problems to the engineering department and often had to go back to the factories for repairs beyond the skills and facilities of the army workshops. Comfortable to ride in, they were almost luxurious in design, though the armament did not provide enough hitting power to justify the high unit cost.

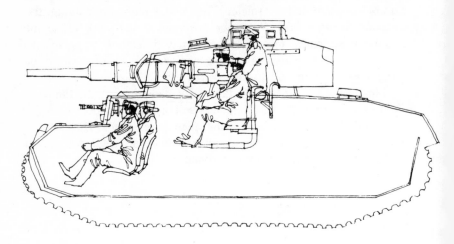

FIGURE 7   Interior of PzKw IV, showing crew positions.

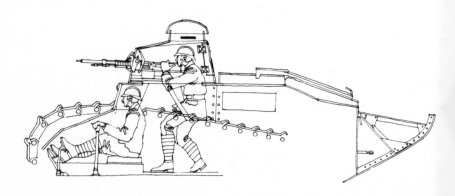

FIGURE 8   French one-man gun turret on Renault FT 17 tank.

Indeed, each machine was handmade instead of mass-produced. Both these tanks remained in production for a long time, more because of the expense and delay caused by new designs and new jigs than because their design otherwise justified it.

The scarcity of the PzKw IIIs and IVs makes it now seem very doubtful whether any attack against France in 1940 would have been contemplated without the resources the Germans gained in Czechoslovakia. And this is something against which Chamberlain's capitulation at Munich must be measured. Discounting lightweight German training tanks, no less than one third of the German armor used against France originated in Czech factories.

The two Czech tanks, called PzKw 38(t) and PzKw 35(t), each mounted a 3.72 cm gun comparable to that on the PzKw III, but these tanks were only half the weight of the German battle tanks. It is interesting, in view of Guderian's professed priority for mobility, that the first thing the Germans did was give the 38(t) another ton of armor plate, reducing its maximum speed from 35 mph to 26 mph.

Tank Armament

The effectiveness of a tank is roughly measured by the gun it carries into battle. Muzzle velocity is a very important part of this assessment. A small-bore gun with high muzzle velocity has penetrating and hitting power, long range, and great accuracy. The fast speed of its missile also makes it easier to hit moving targets. A big-bore gun with low muzzle velocity is less effective until the range decreases. In the same way, a strong man aiming a stone is more dangerous than a small child wielding a brick, unless you are close enough for the brick to tumble onto your foot.

But penetrating power is only important against hard targets, such as concrete emplacements and other tanks. A high-velocity solid missile can pass very close to a man and leave him unharmed. For what the army calls "soft" targets, a high-explosive (HE) shell is needed: one that explodes and fragments at the target. Although even the tiny 20 mm guns could be adapted to fire such HE shells, the explosion caused by them was very small. For soft targets, the soldiers wanted a big gun that could make a big explosion, even if this meant a gun with poor range and poor accuracy.

So the two German battle tanks were given entirely different armament. The PzKw IV carried the stubby 7.5 cm gun, one of the largest-bore tank weapons on the battlefield, but its muzzle velocity

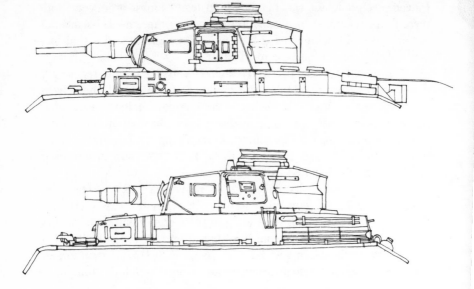

FIGURE 9   Comparison of the 7.5 cm KwK L/24 gun fitted to the PzKw IV tank with the 3.7 cm KwK L/24 gun on the early PzKw IIIs.

was only 1,263 feet per second (fps).* The short range of this weapon made it particularly unsuited to tank-versus-tank combat. But if it got as near as 500 yards to an armored target, it could penetrate 40 mm armor (and few tanks had thicker armor than this), and the missile from this 7.5 cm KwK L/24 weighed 15 pounds.†

Compare this to the 3.7 cm KwK L/45 that was fitted to the PzKw III tanks. This small-bore gun had a muzzle velocity of 2,445 fps, with all the characteristics of the high-velocity gun, but of less use against infantry or antitank batteries. Guderian had specified a 5 cm gun for this tank. This bigger high-velocity gun would be able to fire an HE shell large enough to do the same sort of job as the 7.5 cm gun on the PzKw IV. The bigger high-velocity guns were, in this sense, two-purpose weapons.

Although the high-velocity gun becomes more versatile as it gets bigger, it also becomes very much more difficult to make. The steel must be better and so must the designer's skills, and it is very much more costly. Guderian did not get the 5 cm gun for his tanks. Instead,

---

* Muzzle velocity cannot be increased simply by lengthening the barrel, of course. The charge has also to be increased to propel the missile.
† The L/24 meant that the barrel length was 24 times the diameter of the bore.

they were fitted with the barrels used for the standard German anti-tank weapon, the 3.7 cm gun.

The two lightweight Czech tanks had 3.7 cm guns rather like the Germans', so they were not suited to engaging gun emplacements or enemy tanks, or firing HE shells against soft targets.

The tank men were different from the other soldiers of the division. One crewman remembered his tank as a home:

> The need to have the tank working without fault meant that the crew were always together with a vehicle. The crew became a family and the tank a home where one was secure and rested. Rested because of track vibration; aching feet, sore back, pulled muscle were all gone after half an hour on the road. And each tank had its own smell; a combination of the odours of hot oil, petrol, steel and earth.
>
> There is also the other side of being a crewman. I have had to drive in freezing rain, the wind coming through the tank, and I could have cried because I was so cold. On these occasions there was only one way to thaw out—take it in turns to go outside on to the back of the tank, lie flat on your back on the engine plates and let the heat come through your tank-suit. Spread-eagled, one was perfectly safe and none of us ever fell off while moving along the roads.
>
> For the enemy, the tank with its steady, fast pace and covered in dust and earth looks unstoppable. There was little sound from the silenced engines, but the noise made by metal tracks on cobblestones or the steel-squeal on the roads was unlike anything previously heard and was very frightening.

Artillery

Artillery is almost as old as gunpowder, but only in the First World War did it achieve any real precision. In 1914 the French Army had virtually no artillery—its Inspector General admitted that nothing had been done about siege artillery or garrison artillery for forty years. It was a deliberate part of the French Army's philosophy of attack.

After the Western Front became static, gunners regained the sort of influence that medieval siege warfare had given them. Calibration and survey became more scientific and meteorology was introduced into the calculations. Preliminary bombardments preceded infantry attacks and became more and more complex. Tightly scheduled, they became so precise in aim that the infantry advanced close behind the "creeping barrages." All this gave artillerymen the right to be consulted about the plans of attack, and they became influential in High Command decisions.

If the First World War was a static war, in which vast batteries

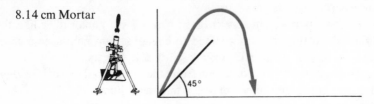

8.14 cm Mortar

MORTAR is ordnance elevating more than 45°. It is usually a portable infantry weapon, of very low velocity.

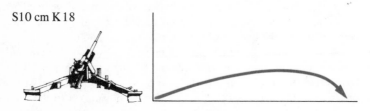

S10 cm K 18

GUN fires to an *optimum trajectory* with a fixed amount of propellant for each missile. Most heavy artillery is like this. Some guns can be used as howitzers too.

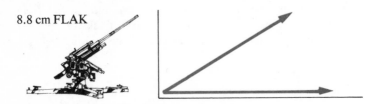

8.8 cm FLAK

HIGH-VELOCITY GUN has a *flat trajectory* needed for shooting at aircraft and for penetrating armor. The structure is strong and heavy.

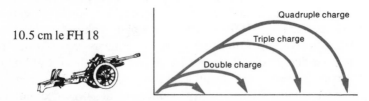

10.5 cm le FH 18

HOWITZER has varied amount of explosive to give low-velocity "plunging fire" at different ranges. Structure is less strong for these weapons, so the weight of the piece is less. Howitzers have carriages permitting high elevation.

FIGURE 10

of slow-loading, horse-drawn guns fired to hit static targets, the big question of the interwar years was not "How will such artillery manage to deploy and strike against fast-moving armored invaders?" but rather "How will any fast-moving armored invaders survive without fast-moving artillery that can keep up with them and provide them with protection?" Such questions were not expected to be anything but rhetorical. Most military experts thought it self-evident that until a very large number of heavy guns mounted on tracked vehicles (self-propelled artillery) could provide support, no force attempting a blitzkrieg would survive. This serious reservation about the blitzkrieg theories was not only that of the old die-hards; many of the tank theorists held the same point of view.

Guderian was one of the few men who had another answer. Unlike the air forces of other nations, the Luftwaffe had devoted the greater part of its resources to supporting the army. (Germany had no strategic bomber force.) The bomber, Guderian concluded, was to be the blitzkrieg's artillery.

But the Luftwaffe, in the event, did not provide the constant artillery bombardment which is often credited to it. Its bombers were assigned to the battle according to need, in that same opportunistic way that all the other weapons of blitzkrieg were used. For the immediate needs of battle, the panzer division took their artillery along with them.

All *Panzer-Artillerie* were howitzers. The howitzer is a relatively low-velocity weapon that throws a missile high into the air so that it "plunges" onto the target. To get the range wanted, the gunner varies the elevation and the propellant charge behind the missile.

Howitzers needed a minimum of time for setting up and could bring a fast rate of fire upon a short-range target. For any given size, the howitzer will have a heavier missile than a high-velocity weapon. Because the lower-velocity missile puts less stress on the mounting, the howitzer is lighter and cheaper to make. It fulfilled all the blitzkrieg requirements.

Each panzer division had three battalions of artillery. The heavy battalion had twelve big 15 cm FH 18 howitzers (three batteries, each with four guns). Lest anyone think howitzers have short barrels, let me add that these had barrels that were 14 feet long. But they could elevate to 45 degrees.

The two light artillery battalions each had twelve 10.5 cm FH 18 howitzers. These 10-foot-long barrels could elevate to 40 degrees. The guns were towed by large half-tracks which could position the

FIGURE II   12-ton Sd.Kfz.8 half-track
towing 15 cm sSH.18 heavy gun.

guns far more quickly than horses did for the infantry divisions.*
Both of them were categorized as *Haubitze*, which meant that they
could be used in high elevation as howitzers and also in lower registers.

The artillery arm was seriously criticized after the Polish fighting.
The artillery batteries had not moved forward quickly enough to give
continuing support to the attacking infantry. General von Bock, commander of Army Group North, told the artillery men to forget any
idea that the infantry must wait for them to move their guns. "The
artillery may not delay the infantry," he wrote in his diary.

More far-reaching was the report from VIII Panzerkorps about
the German artillery action against the Polish fortifications at Nikolai.
Bunkers and reinforced buildings had proved surprisingly vulnerable
to the 8.8 cm antiaircraft gun, which had been reclassified as a dual-
purpose gun.

* But not nearly as quickly as, later in the war, self-propelled artillery could be positioned. Horses took a couple of hours, half-tracks at least half an hour, but SP guns
could open fire within seconds of halting. This was because the tracks absorbed the
recoil very efficiently and no setting up was needed.

Half-track Vehicles

The weight of the artillery pieces and the way in which they had to be towed and positioned in the field were reasons enough why artillery needed tracked vehicles rather than horses. And the artillery had used tracked vehicles since long before the tank was invented. Yet, while the British Army returned to heavy-wheeled vehicles for this task, the Germans preferred the half-track.

The idea of combining wheeled front steering with tracked drive was that of M. Kegresse, a Frenchman working in the Russian Tsar's garage, who had made a vehicle for use in snow. He adapted an Austin car, using his own method of suspension. The result was later to become the Austin-Kegresse armored car, used by the Red Army and, after some were captured in 1920, by the Polish Army too. It was the suspension system of Kegresse that the Citroën company used for five half-tracks that crossed the Sahara desert in 1923.

During the 1930s, the German Army provided its panzer divisions with half-tracks. These ranged from the 5-ton *Leichter Zugkraftwagen* (light prime mover) that was used to tow antitank guns and light anti-aircraft guns, through the middle-size ones for howitzers and pontoon-bridge sections, to the huge 18-ton *Schwerer Zugkraftwagen* (heavy prime mover) that could winch a damaged tank out of the mud onto a trailer and tow it back to the repair shops.

In spite of all the expensive refinements, the half-track remained cheaper than any fully tracked vehicle because it was steered by the front wheels, like a motorcar, instead of by a complex system changing the speed of either track, as in tank steering.

FIGURE 12   Carrier
Universal No. 1 Mk1
(Bren gun carrier).

FIGURE 13
Semitrack Sd.Kfz.251
with sloping armor.

A half-track vehicle caused far less damage to the road surface and was only marginally less efficient moving cross-country than a fully tracked vehicle. But anything towed behind the half-track reduced its cross-country capability drastically. For this reason, artillery experts and tank soldiers alike agreed that guns must be put inside such vehicles. In 1940, however, virtually none of these self-propelled guns were in use.

The infantry's priority for tracked vehicles was even lower than the artillery's. Interwar theorists had never been able to agree about what such a vehicle should look like. French and British tank men had minimized the importance of infantry in the armored division: they wanted all-tank armies. Experiments with one-man tanks, which would give every man his own individual tankette, had been tried. This later led to Britain's Bren gun carrier, a lightweight, open-topped tracked vehicle that could carry four infantrymen and heavy infantry weapons across rough country. It proved too fragile for combat.

The German armored personnel carrier was adapted from artillery half-tracks and was provided with thin armor sloped on all sides to deflect hits. It was not designed as a vehicle from which to fight, though its open top enabled the infantrymen to jump out quickly. The open top, however, made it vulnerable to grenades. The large track area (it was three-quarter track) gave it excellent traction. Steering difficulties were overcome by a cleverly designed device which applied a track brake when the steering wheel was turned far enough.

These vehicles transformed the fighting quality of the armored divisions. They carried the infantry alongside the tanks, brought heavy mortars and heavy machine guns with them, and towed heavy guns in the forefront of the battle. Eventually they became a preferred vehicle of reconnaissance units too. Yet versatility created other problems. Half-tracks were required for carrying ammunition, laying cables, evacuating casualties, artillery observation, and, not least, as *Kommando-Panzerwagen* (mobile armored command cars) like the specially equipped one that Guderian used.

Despite the immense efforts of German manufacturers, armored personnel carriers were always in short supply. At the time of the Polish campaign, the only ones in use were a few given to Guderian's 3.Pz.Div. Few of the German infantry had ever seen one of these armored personnel carriers. With the average German infantry regiment (of over 3,000 men) allocated only seventy-three motor vehicles of any type, it was a lucky soldier who even got a ride on a truck.

Infantry

Paradoxically, the shock tactics of the blitzkrieg offensive were born out of the great improvements that the nineteenth century had seen in *defensive* warfare. It was Moltke who reasoned that if the defense was formidable, then tactics must be devised to provoke the enemy to attack and attack again until defeated.

From this idea came the Kesselschlacht theory—encircle the enemy so that he is forced to break out of the encirclement, then use "defensive firepower" against him. If the encirclement cannot be achieved by an outflanking movement, then the enemy front must be pierced (preferably in several places) and then encircled. This was exactly the method used against Poland in September 1939. It had been carried out almost entirely by infantry.

In 1914 the German failure had been partly due to the exhaustion of the infantry, many of them reservists no longer fit enough for grueling route marches, followed by battle. Learning from this, the German Army in Poland in 1939 used highly trained active divisions and sent reservists to other duties. It worked; Guderian, Manstein, and Halder all remarked on the strenuous efforts of the infantry.

Infantry weapons had also changed by that time. In the First World War, machine guns had usually been water-cooled models with heavy tripods and three-man crews—one to fire, one to feed the belt of ammunition, and one to bring more of it. Air cooling produced a lighter weapon that one man could carry and use. Compared to the old Maxim gun of 125 pounds, the MG 34 used by the German Army in 1939 weighed about 25 pounds. So an MG 34 was issued to each ten-man rifle squad. Each platoon had a small (50 mm) mortar and although the infantry had very conventional bolt-action rifles, these heavier weapons gave them great flexibility and fitted well to the way in which improvisation and initiative were encouraged among the rank and file.

The panzer division rifle brigade consisted of three battalions of infantry, each made up of five companies, one of which had machine-gun platoons and a heavy (81 mm) mortar platoon.

More remarkable was the way in which the infantry were given the means of providing their own artillery support. Antitank guns went to the infantry regiment (as well as to the antitank battalion), as did small artillery pieces of about the same weight (880 pounds). The gun crew could manhandle these into position. The heaviest infantry gun was a 1.5-ton howitzer—15 cm s.I.G.33—which could lob a large shell 6,000 yards.

Combat Engineers

At the heart of the blitzkrieg technique and its versatile use of heavy fire were the combat engineers. The Germans called them *Pioniere*, but they are not to be confused with manual-labor units that built roads in back areas of other armies. The Pioniere was a highly trained specialist who was likely to be at the front of the hardest fighting. But instead of the infantry's heavy weapons—antitank guns, howitzers, and mortars—the Pioniere had specialist equipment. For combat there were flamethrowers, mines, explosives in many shapes and sizes, smoke equipment, mine detectors, and barbed wire. They had inflatable boats and pontoons as well as two bridging columns per division. Combat engineers also had power saws, pile drivers, compressors, generators, emergency lighting equipment, welding gear, and a range of hand tools.

The infantry could do many simple engineering tasks for themselves. Inflatable boats were supplied down to company level, while the infantry battalion had pontoons and trestles that could be put together to make a bridge of 5 tons' capacity. One observer saw such a team under training; they bridged a river and dismantled the equipment six times in one afternoon.

FIGURE 14
River crossing with MG34 machine gun and 8.1 cm Kurzer mortar.

For a river crossing under fire, inflatable boats were used for the assault and then relegated to ferry or cable ferry use. Large inflatable boats could carry a 3.7 cm antitank gun or the small infantry howitzer. Even tanks could be rafted. Piers of pontoons or boats could be lashed together to make a bridge of 4 tons' capacity. Over this came men and weapons to enlarge a bridgehead. For the tank, a river remained a formidable obstacle. The Pioniere units searched for ways of overcoming it.

Motorcycles

Ordinary pedal bicycles had been used by all the armies in the First World War, and some were in use in the Second. But in the 1930s the German Army put many of its fighting soldiers on motorcycles. A whole battalion of a panzer division's rifle brigade was given powerful motorcycles. Soldiers rode to battle and dismounted to fight, just as in an earlier century the dragoons had used horses.

In fact, the motorcycles were quite unsuited to modern war. Riders were vulnerable to small-arms fire and to man-traps, such as deliberately spilled oil. In Poland in September 1939 the weather had remained exceptionally fine, as it did for the May 1940 fighting too.

FIGURE 15   BMW R75 motorcycle
with sidecar passing Sd.Kfz.231 armored car.

On soft ground or on bad roads the motorcycle became useless. During the summer of 1940 the German manufacturers BMW and Zundapp were both hurrying production of their massive 750 cc motorcycle combinations with engines that drove both the rear wheels of the bikes and the sidecar wheels too. Tests had shown that this radically improved the performance, but at the Volkswagen factory they were also hurrying. Professor Porsche was giving his 1936 car design a new look, changing the rear-axle reduction gear to improve traction and increasing the ground clearance to the army's requirements. This light car, the military version of the "Beetle," known as the *Kübel* (bucket), became the only passenger car to remain in production for the German Army. The motorcycle, virtually useless in battle, was relegated to communications duties.

Armored Cars

The reconnaissance forces of any army have the most dangerous job to do. They must be equipped to probe forward until they encounter enemy fire and then return to tell the story. For this reason, the reconnaissance forces need a vehicle which can retire quickly. To some extent, the motorcycle was suited to this task, and each panzer division's reconnaissance battalion had a motorcycle company. Far more suited to the task were the armored cars that gave some protection to the crew. Because country lanes are narrow, such cars usually have driving positions at both front and back, with two drivers in position and gears that can give them fast speeds in either direction.

The armored car's history predates the invention of the tank. Development of British and German cars was influenced by the fact that the British chose to armor the chassis of their touring cars, such as the Rolls-Royce Silver Ghost, while the Germans preferred to armor the chassis of larger commercial vehicles, such as those made by Büssing, Daimler, and Ehrhardt.

The British and French used their armored cars for colonial policing work, while the Germans (forbidden to have tanks) used them as the start of a modern army. They built four-wheel, six-wheel, and even eight-wheel cars, and the Germans were the first to move away from adapting old vehicles and build a completely new armored car, starting with the chassis.

By 1940 the Germans had about 600 armored cars, enough to give the reconnaissance force of each armored division about 50 of them.

Motor Trucks

At a time when the theorists were talking of all-tank armies, the Germans had a virtually all-horse army. The ordinary infantry division had 5,375 horses and 942 motor vehicles. An infantry division like this would require over 50 tons of hay and oats per day and about 20 tons of motor fuel. Motor vehicles only needed fuel when they were working, but the horses needed food every day without fail and 50 tons of hay and oats is very bulky. And horses also demanded much manpower, for they had to be fed, watered, cleaned, and exercised, and their harness and equipment cleaned and checked daily. There had to be a constant back-up of health checks and veterinary care for both healthy and sick animals.

A motorized army was more efficient and less demanding, but in 1939 there was not the slightest chance of the Germans ever having a motorized army. In fact, there was every sign that the motorized part of the army they had was falling apart.

The shortage of motor vehicles was not unconnected with the great variety of vehicles being manufactured during the 1930s. By 1938 there were 100 different types of commercial trucks in army service, 52 types of cars, and 150 different types of motorcycles. A drastic scheme—the *Schell-Programm*—had reduced this chaos, but still the German motorized columns looked like a parade of used cars and the supply of new vehicles was no more than a trickle.

At the outbreak of war in 1939 the German armed forces resorted to the desperate measure of commandeering civilian motors. They took some 16,000, but these were swallowed up immediately to replace worn-out vehicles, bring army units to their full allotments, equip new divisions, and for training. None of the civilian trucks could be kept to form a reserve, so there was no reserve. Civilian vehicles were flimsy by military standards, with only two-wheel drive, a far cry from the six-wheel (four-wheel drive) Krupp trucks that were the army's preferred equipment.

By February 1940 the situation was getting worse day by day. The Polish campaign, with its fighting, dust, and very bad roads, had caused some units to write off 50 per cent of their trucks. Replacements from the factories (many of these with only two-wheel drive and unsuited to combat conditions) were pitifully inadequate.

The army's normal peacetime loss of trucks through wear and tear was about 2,400 trucks each quarter year, but only 1,000 new vehicles were arriving each quarter. In other words, the army's supply

FIGURE 16   Opel Medium Truck, type S.

of trucks was dwindling at the rate of 1,400 trucks each quarter year *without fighting*.

General Franz Halder, from whose journal the above figures are taken, was at the time the Chief of the Army General Staff. So alarmed was he by the situation that he proposed a drastic and far-reaching "demotorization program" which would at once start procuring horses, horse-transport vehicles, and harnesses so that the German Army could begin replacing some of its motor vehicles with horses.

And yet the reports of the Polish campaign had shown repeatedly that horsedrawn units could not keep up with motorized and tank units. It also showed how dangerous things could become when they failed to do so. By now there were enough tanks from Czechoslovakia to increase the number of armored divisions. But there could be no increase in the equally vital motorized infantry divisions. On the contrary, at the end of 1940 these divisions had been reduced in size.

The Waffen-SS

It was the great shortage of trucks that suddenly made SS leader Heinrich Himmler's units of importance to the army. After the Polish campaign the few SS regimental combat groups that had battle experience were reorganized. Three SS regiments—Deutschland, Germania, and Der Führer—became the *SS-Verfügungsdivision*. The elite SS-Leibstandarte Adolf Hitler was reinforced far beyond regimental strength.

Himmler had served in the First World War without seeing combat. He had been accepted as an officer cadet, but by the time his training was completed, the war was over. He then tried to satisfy a yearning for military glory by joining veterans' clubs, rifle clubs, and a semimilitary political organization called the *Reichsflagge* (National Flag). It was in this way that he came to join the Nazis.

By ruthlessly confiscating the property of Jews and using slave labor from concentration camps in the quarries and factories owned by the SS, Himmler grew more and more powerful. The entire German police service as well as the secret police (Gestapo) and security service (SD) were all at his command. Now the Second World War brought him a chance to be the military hero he had always wanted to be. Knowing these ambitions, the army watched Himmler and his SS with dislike and distrust, feelings that were not assuaged by reports the Army High Command were receiving about atrocities committed by SS-Einsatzgruppen in conquered Poland.

Himmler was determined, however, that the SS should become the nucleus of a postwar German national police service. And he believed that only if his SS men served in the front line would they earn sufficient public esteem to do their police work properly. Yet Himmler's manpower was strictly limited, and only with the army's consent could he legally recruit men of military age. Most SS men were part-timers, called into the army just as everyone else was.

The archetypal bureaucrat, Himmler exploited the law to suit himself. He was permitted to recruit for his police service and concentration camp guards in order to keep them at normal strength. Now, although few policemen were members of the SS, he drafted 15,000 of them into his field divisions to form *SS-Polizeidivision*. He then similarly drafted concentration camp guards to form the *SS-Totenkopf-division*.* By exploiting this loophole, Himmler more or less doubled his field divisions, but the army could not prevent him calling reservists into—and recruiting for—his depleted services.

Himmler used other methods to swell his army. From his part-time *Allgemeine* (General) *SS* he called young men before they became eligible for military service. Since such recruits were in the SS before they were due to register for military service, the army had trouble finding out what was happening. From Poland and Slovakia he recruited Germans living there, in addition to any other "Germanic" foreigners who were not liable for military draft. By May 1940 there

---

* *SS-Totenkopfdivision* was quite separate from the *SS-Totenkopfverbände*, the camp guards who were officially classified as civil servants (*Beamten*). A third force called *SS-Totenkopfstandarten*, into which policemen were also drafted, handled "special tasks of a police nature" and were used in occupied Poland.

were five Americans, three Swedes, and forty-four Swiss volunteers serving with the SS.

Without asking anyone's permission, Himmler had given his Waffen-SS men field-gray uniforms exactly like those worn by the army. The generals complained, but Himmler shrugged and said that it was too late to change. Though the army tried to obstruct him, Himmler still found ways to equip his force, much SS equipment at this time being of Czech origin. Hitler was persuaded to authorize a heavy artillery battalion for each of Himmler's three formations and gave the Leibstandarte an extra battalion of light artillery. All of this artillery was motorized. (The Polizeidivision was the only SS unit not motorized; to speed things along, a regular army horse-drawn artillery regiment was temporarily attached it it.)

Suddenly Himmler's Waffen-SS looked like a formidable fighting force. His men were at the peak of physical fitness; until 1936 one filled tooth had been enough for a man to fail a medical. The Leibstandarte only recruited men under twenty-three years of age and over six feet tall. The men were more strictly disciplined than any of the rest of the armed forces. Even so, the huge German Army could still afford to dismiss the comparatively tiny force that Himmler offered, except that most of it was motorized. Himmler's field force could virtually double the motorized infantry that the German army had available at this time. Furthermore, it came complete with supply and support services, 10,000 men in the Ersatz (replacement) regiments, medical, legal, and administrative services, as well as officer training schools and training units.

The German Army had just increased its armored divisions from six to ten, with only four motorized divisions to follow them. For such an army, Himmler was offering a component that they simply could not refuse.

The Commander

Heinz Guderian was long since reconciled to the fact that he would never be able to assemble the elaborately equipped army that theorists such as Fuller and Liddell Hart had described. But Guderian was a practical man with a willingness to make things work. His knowledge and understanding of mechanized warfare exceeded that of any man in the world. His experience of staff work was long and varied, and his years of handling armored divisions gave him insights that left the paperwork of the theorists far behind. Guderian had virtually designed his tanks and sweated his way through their production problems. His job with the motorized troops had taught him about the supply and maintenance of vehicles, and in the later stages of the First World War he had worked as quartermaster behind the rapidly advancing storm troops. He also knew all about the logistic problems that had brought failure in 1914 and had commanded a military wireless station in combat conditions.

Every stage of Guderian's career had contributed something to the technique of the blitzkrieg. When finally his armored force was committed to battle, Guderian found himself fighting to capture the place of his birth. At a time when some of the German generals were wrestling with moral doubts about Hitler's war, Guderian was understandably single-minded and aggressive. Now Guderian, a Knight's Cross at his neck, was to face west and fight a battle largely of his own design.

Emphasis has already been given to the vital role that radio played in the technique of the blitzkrieg, but this importance was due entirely to the way in which German commanders were prepared to change plans minute by minute in the face of enemy opposition. It is extremely doubtful if such radio contact would have made much difference to the French or the British Army, which was trained to fight systematic set-piece battles.

British General Bernard Montgomery, in a final address to his senior officers before the battle of El Alamein, said that this was to be an army battle, carefully controlled from Army HQ, but he went to bed early that night believing, according to his memoirs, that there was nothing he could do. In fact, things went wrong and his chief of staff had to wake him up and arrange a corps commanders' conference at 3:30 A.M. This systematic approach to war was exactly what the German generals usually tried to avoid.

It is interesting in this connection to notice that according to Liddell Hart, both German and British senior commanders agreed that German soldiers were more individualistic than their opponents. General von Blumentritt went so far as to complain of this, saying the Germans' rank and file had too many ideas of their own and were not sufficiently obedient. However surprising this might be to British readers, studies of the desert fighting supported the contention that the German soldiers were better able to improvise in emergencies than their British opponents. Another finding was that British units commonly ceased fighting after losing all their officers, but Germans remained effectively organized right down to the last few NCOs.

Guderian had proved that the First World War type of tank

attacks, which simply pushed against an enemy front, could not be equated with the very fast columns traveling hundreds of miles into the rear areas, causing havoc everywhere they went and uncertainty everywhere else.

More than any other man, Guderian had opposed the idea of tying tanks to infantry (as the French had largely done) or creating all-tank units for specialized use (as in prevailing British theories). He had insisted that the armored divisions must be versatile and equipped in hardware, training, and mental attitude to tackle almost any kind of fighting. While other armies calculated the speed of any combined units as that of the slowest element, Guderian measured by that of the fastest and insisted that his divisions move as fast as possible.

Years later, in discussion with Liddell Hart, Guderian cited mobility and velocity as the primary factors of the blitzkrieg.

The Division

Military insignia, colorful uniforms, and band music have all encouraged civilians to think of armies as a collection of regiments. Soldiers, however, think in terms of battalions. It is the battalion that is the soldier's home, and men of other battalions are as strangers to him. But for generals, armies are composed of divisions.

A division is, by tradition, the smallest unit in which infantry, artillery, and cavalry (later tanks) combined with supporting services under one commander and were capable of fighting independently. Such a division was called a "general command" and the commander came to be called a "general."

It was division headquarters that organized transport, rations, maintenance, ammunition supply, medical care, religious services, hygiene and sanitation, and which provided the soldiers' pay. In addition, the division arranged for police and, if necessary, legal services, graves registration units, and mobile cinemas. Sometimes it had specially trained military government officers to administer captured territory (with all necessary paperwork including ration cards) and men with expertise concerning gas, water, and electricity supply.

A panzer division was more complicated than any other sort of division and far more versatile. The mixed nature of the panzer division extended down into the units within it. The parts of a division were to some extent self-contained and could be reassembled and tailored to the requirements of the battle. Such formations were called "battle groups" and the components were said to have "plug-in capability."

A typical battle group (used by 5.Pz.Div at this time) consisted of a rifle regiment combined with a panzer regiment, together with engineers, signals, and an artillery battalion. In this division, Rifle Regiment No. 13 was almost always chosen for use in this way since it was equipped with armored half-track vehicles and so could be committed along with the tanks. The signals battalion also had very scarce armored half-tracks. Reconnaissance units were never detached to battle groups but always remained under the direct control of divisional headquarters.

Yet an armored division was too large to be positioned easily for a surprise attack. Not only could it comprise over 3,000 motor vehicles (including the supply column), but it also had almost as many men as an infantry division (14,000 compared to 17,000).

A troop train might have little significance in an enemy intelligence report, but what secret agent could miss an armored division's tanks? One armored division transported by railway required no less than eighty trains to move it, each train with up to fifty-five wagons. This gigantic movement occupied the full capacity of a railway for four whole days and nights.

Moving an armored division by road, however, was an even more conspicuous exercise. How could a moving column of vehicles that occupied nearly 70 miles of road space and crawled along at about 2.5 miles an hour be kept hidden? (Such is the textbook calculation for perfect weather in good terrain without enemy action of any kind.) It is easy to imagine the sensation in town and village as this endless parade moved through. And what of its vulnerability to air reconnaissance and to bombers?

Even in unopposed movement, there would be wear and tear on the vehicles and most especially on the tank tracks. Tank tracks would inflict considerable damage upon the road surface too. This often caused trouble for transport following the tanks, since few German trucks had four-wheel drive. The tank was not a reliable machine, and each division needed three mobile workshops, two with 12-ton repair vehicles and one with 24-ton repair vehicles.

There were now ten panzer divisions.* The cavalry's light divisions

---

* Guderian, both in *Panzer Leader* and in his Inspector General's report dated 1944, said that only three light divisions fought in Poland. This is an error: six armored divisions and four light divisions fought there. There is also confusion about 10.Pz.Div —one source said it was newly formed *after* the Polish campaign. In fact, it was the former 4.Panzer Brigade converted to 10.Pz.Div before the war began. To be more precise, there were additional formations fighting in Poland. Some odds and ends of army and SS motorized units added up to about the equivalent of a fifth motorized

proved unsatisfactory in Poland. Too unwieldy for reconnaissance and too weak for the assault, they were now converted to panzer divisions. But it was easier to change the name on paper than to find the extra tanks needed. As a stopgap measure, Czechoslovak tanks were used, but still these modified divisions were for the most part understrength.

The Method of Blitzkrieg

At one time commanders such as Marlborough, Napoleon, and Wellington watched the progress of battle with their own eyes. They were able to modify and originate orders at a moment's notice. At the battle of Sedan in 1870, Moltke saw the battle from a hill close to the fighting. At the assault on Schellenberg in 1704, during the Blenheim campaign, six lieutenant generals had been killed.

It was the First World War that saw the military commanders moving so far back from the battlefront that they were not even in range of artillery fire. As commanders became inured to the terrible meat grinder of battle, so the quality of generalship was reduced to a formula. Seldom was a general asked to think quickly. Many were never asked to think at all.

But in the final stages of the First World War, technology started a chain reaction that we now realize led up to the blitzkrieg. Yet blitzkrieg could not exist without very close cooperation from all arms. In this respect, radiotelephony—transmitting speech, rather than Morse code—was the most crucial element in the new style of war.

Using this radio transmitter, German commanders of divisions or even of corps were enabled to stay at the very front of any action. They could make minute-by-minute decisions and bring generalship to bear upon even the smallest tactical combat. After the Polish campaign Guderian urged his panzer unit commanders to restrict their HQs to a few armored vehicles and stay much closer to the front.

In 1940 the railway system still dominated military planning, as it had since the American Civil War. But, until now, the movement of an army from its railhead had been extremely limited, partly because of the increasing size of the supply dumps required by an attacking army. In the First World War, dumps as large as half a million tons had warned an enemy exactly where the next attack

---

division. A new SS artillery regiment and an SS reconnaissance battalion were combined with an army tank regiment and the SS Deutschland regiment, a prestigious ceremonial guard unit, to make *Panzer Verband Kempf.*

would come. This limitation was also true of the German build-up for the Polish campaign, though the dangers of air reconnaissance were avoided because the invasion came without declaration of war.

Motorization and the higher tank speeds did not do away with the army's dependence upon railheads and supply dumps, but it did result in an attacking force being able to move from the railhead with greater speed and independence than had ever been known before.

In Poland these new freedoms were exploited only in a very limited way. Guderian's armor had moved deep into the Polish back areas, but these thrusts were secondary to the Kesselschlacht battles that were fought near the frontiers by horse-drawn armies. In France the world was to see something quite different. Guderian's armor, concentrated in a way it had not been before, was to shatter the French front and cause a collapse of the defenses.

The theory was well defined. Only against strong fortified positions would tank concentrations be used. They would advance in echelon—about 60 yards between each tank—and move in carefully timed waves, taking full advantage of any ground cover.

Each tank company consisted of three platoons of five tanks each, plus two tanks for the company commander (so that he had a spare tank). The company commander's tanks were equipped with two-way radios so that he could receive orders and pass them on. Each platoon commander's tank had only a one-way radio; he could hear his orders but not reply. The other tanks in the platoon had no radios and had to depend on visual signaling from their platoon commander.

Reports of enemy resistance came back to the divisional commander, who was in a tank or half-track according to the circumstances. For certain sorts of targets, he would request aid from the Luftwaffe, but otherwise he would manage to attack using his own forces. Infantry and engineers would be kept at the front of the advance, sometimes riding alongside the tanks. Armored half-tracks would carry heavy weapons and tow antitank guns. If the German tanks encountered enemy armor, they would retire through the antitank gun battery and then move round to outflank the enemy.

Once a breakthrough had been achieved, the speed of advance increased, but seldom to more than 3 mph. Air reconnaissance photographs would be dropped regularly to the mobile headquarters so that the division knew what resistance lay ahead and could change the spearhead accordingly.

Three armored cars often formed the point of the advance. One car would contain an artillery observer who could use radio to call for emergency covering fire. Motorcyclists of the reconnaissance battalion might be exploring side roads. According to their reports, other units would come forward—antitank guns to fight off enemy armor, flamethrowers to attack emplacements, or engineers to remove mines.

The *Schwerpunkt*—place of main effort—was not the place where major resistance was encountered. On the contrary, the advance elements by-passed and avoided opposition, wriggling and infiltrating wherever possible, fighting only where there was no alternative. The momentum of the attack was vital to success, and so no element would move off the roads to go cross-country without very good reason, for this would slow the advance.

Just as the tactics of the advance would keep the enemy guessing as to which way the German tanks would turn, so the German large-scale planning kept the Allied army commanders wondering. The invasion of France through the Ardennes might have turned to Paris instead of the coast and, in its later stages, there were still doubts about whether Guderian was making for Amiens or Lille.

The blitzkrieg's narrow front was always large enough to allow two or three attacking columns to advance side by side. These columns could then converge as pincers onto strong points—towns or large enemy units. Where this occurred, theory demanded that the columns diverge immediately afterward to avoid the risk of congestion on the road.

Fast armor—or at least armor faster than that of the enemy— was an essential component of the blitzkrieg. So was complete command of the air, for the attack, crammed on the road, was very vulnerable to low-flying aircraft. Air support for the blitzkrieg was needed to supplement artillery units which were often in the process of moving up—leapfrogging one over the other—when they were must urgently needed. Close air support did, in effect, protect the exposed flanks of the attacking columns.

Ideally, then, the blitzkrieg in the West needed countryside with enough roads for attackers to converge on objectives and diverge on the far side of them. The advance required at least two parallel roads stretching ahead, with some minor roads linking them. High ground commanding the advance route had to be captured. Ideally, the road system of the surrounding region had to be such as to provide difficulties for an enemy attempting to concentrate his reserves into the threatened area. The line of thrust needed to be developed so that the enemy had difficulty in deciding what each objective was.

Moving forward, even before contacting an enemy, called for

planning of great skill. A panzer division used about 1,000 gallons of fuel per mile (twice this, if moving across country). And, of course, the trucks that delivered fuel would also need fuel. Drivers also needed food and a place to park where they would not block the road. It was the usual practice to designate one supply road for each division, and this *Rollbahn* was usually the main route of that division's advance.

As needed, engineer units, with the skills and cumbersome equipment necessary to build bridges or mend roads, had to pass up the highways filled with advancing columns, so as to get to the front not a minute sooner and not a minute later than they were needed. At reasonable intervals, all of these men would go to sleep, whether given permission to do so or not. By that time, they had to occupy a section of road that was not needed by the units advancing behind them. Food and fuel had to be distributed as well as ammunition and a multitude of other supplies. The empty supply columns then needed room to pass back down the roads for more. In combat, casualty evacuation and medical units added more complexities.

Archibald Wavell, considered one of the finest of Britain's generals, stressed the importance of such planning in a lecture on generalship in 1939. He said that strategy and tactics could be apprehended in a very short time by any reasonable human intelligence. But it was the principles and practice of military movement and administration— the "logistics" of war—that was of prime importance. He went on: "I should like you always to bear in mind when you study military history or military events the importance of this administrative factor, because it is where most critics and many generals go wrong."*

Heinz Guderian was well aware of the importance of logistics. In May 1918 he had been the quartermaster of XXXVIII Reserve Corps at a time when it made an unprecedented advance of 14 miles during an offensive on the river Aisne.

But, of course, the logistics of war, like the methods of war, are subject to constant change. The broad scale of the 28-mile-wide infantry attack at Marne-Aisne in July 1918 had, by May 1940, become about a 4-mile front for the blitzkrieg at Sedan. Such changes demanded a miniaturization of planning to get enough attacking force into a narrow section of roadways. Until 1940 no one could be sure such logistics were possible.

The forward movement for such attacks is sometimes planned by

---

* From General Wavell's Lees Knowles Lecture given in 1939 at Trinity College, Cambridge, and reprinted in *The Times*.

means of large graphs. One axis represents distance along the road and the other axis is time, hour by hour. Such graphs end up as a maze of diagonal colored lines. Other graphs are prepared for such contingencies as air attack, counterattack, breakdowns, and the switching of the Schwerpunkt. The planners have to remain in constant contact with the advance forces. Sometimes the terrain demands that this be done by observers in light planes as well as by traffic police on the ground.

The nature of the ground over which the armored forces fought was critical. In Poland the tanks suffered heavy casualties when committed to street fighting. Hitler wrote a secret memorandum dated 9 October 1939 in which he took up this point. In a paper that the historian William Shirer described as one of the most impressive Hitler ever wrote, he orders that the armored divisions "are not to be lost among the maze of endless rows of houses in Belgian towns. It is not necessary for them to attack towns at all."* He stresses the importance of keeping up the momentum of the attack. He reminds the army of the need to improvise, according to circumstance, and encourages them to concentrate weapons—for example, tanks or antitank guns—in great quantities, even if this means depriving other parts of the front. In this and in many other ways Hitler's memorandum describes the blitzkrieg.

Hitler read this memo aloud to the military leaders on 10 October 1939. Up till then, Hitler seems to have regarded the armored divisions more as a propaganda device than as a decisive weapon. Now his opinion had changed.

The Air Forces

The German armed forces were as rife with arguments, rivalries, vested interests, and envy as any other armed forces. That German infantry, artillery, tank, and air force officers found a way of working in close cooperation was partly due to the Nazis, partly due to the German character but more profoundly due to the army chief General von Seeckt, who had written, "The whole future of warfare appears to me to be in the employment of mobile armies, relatively small but of high quality, and rendered distinctly more effective by the addition of aircraft . . ."

But the generals were not enthusiastic about aircraft being added to land forces. They suspected that airmen might be difficult in the

---

* William L. Shirer, *The Rise and Fall of the Third Reich.*

same way that the tank men were and similarly ready to confuse them with technicalities.

The French High Command, which already had the worst system of command in the world—many different HQs far apart, with commanders not certain where their authority ended—was able to inte-

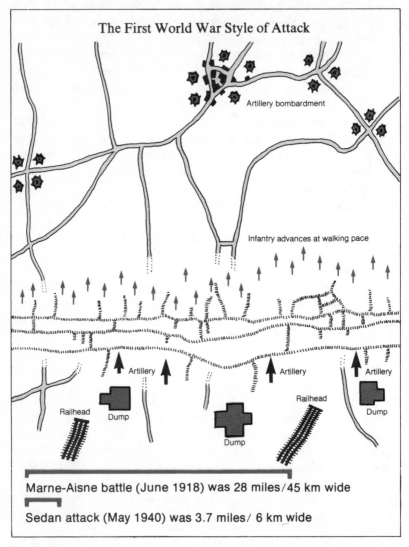

The First World War Style of Attack

Artillery bombardment

Infantry advances at walking pace

Artillery   Artillery   Artillery

Railhead   Railhead

Dump   Dump   Dump

Marne-Aisne battle (June 1918) was 28 miles/45 km wide

Sedan attack (May 1940) was 3.7 miles/ 6 km wide

MAP 9

The style of attack used in the First World War. Here only a small sector of total width is shown. It took weeks to build up supply dumps, followed by days of artillery bombardment and infantry attacking at walking pace.

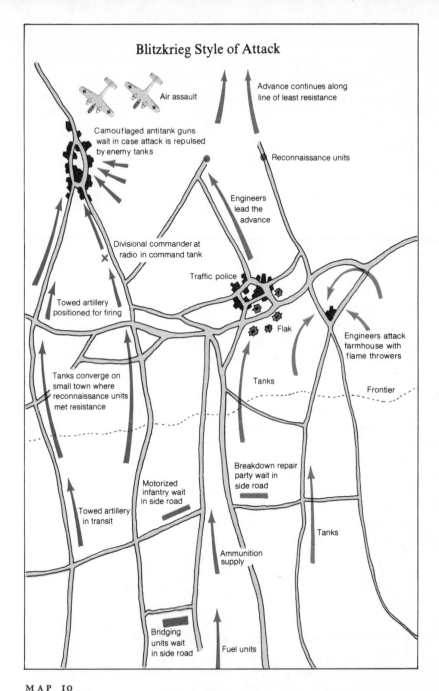

Blitzkrieg Style of Attack

Air assault

Advance continues along line of least resistance

Camouflaged antitank guns wait in case attack is repulsed by enemy tanks

Reconnaissance units

Engineers lead the advance

Divisional commander at radio in command tank

Traffic police

Towed artillery positioned for firing

Engineers attack farmhouse with flame throwers

Flak

Tanks converge on small town where reconnaissance units met resistance

Tanks

Frontier

Breakdown repair party wait in side road

Towed artillery in transit

Motorized infantry wait in side road

Tanks

Ammunition supply

Bridging units wait in side road

Fuel units

MAP 10

In the Second World War the blitzkrieg style of attack employed no preliminary bombardment; dive bombing was used instead of artillery. It was essential for attackers to have command of the air.

grate into this the worst air force command system. The chief of Air Cooperation Forces Command, General Têtu, gave the air force orders. But so did the Air High Command and also the zone commands. So, too, did the commanders of neighboring land forces. There was little or no communication between these authorities, and, like French tanks, few French aircraft were equipped with radio.

General Maurice Gamelin, the French Commander in Chief, did not believe that air forces would play an important role in any modern war. He predicted that opposing air forces would fight each other and burn themselves out in the initial clashes. Thus they would leave the real battle to the land forces. It was a remarkable example of wishful thinking, even from a man who specialized in that sort of thinking.

No doubt many German ground force commanders would have liked to comfort themselves with similar nonsense, but the system did not permit them to do so. Just as Seeckt had ordained that NCOs must be able to do the jobs of officers and officers be trained as commanders, so infantrymen had to be able to construct simple pontoon bridges and Rommel, an infantry specialist, take over an armored division. In this same spirit, the German Army learned to use the airplane.

There was much to gain. Giving senior commanders a chance to use the little Fieseler Fi 156 *Storch* (Stork) high-wing monoplanes that could land in a field, provide a bird's-eye view of battle or traffic jams, facilitate a conference at corps level, or bring them forward to the combat line was enough to convert many generals to the airplane.*

The air transport of soldiers was equally revolutionary. The Junkers Ju 52 three-motor transports could move a division halfway across Europe. In August 1936 the Germans lent General Francisco Franco twenty Ju 52 transports, which moved 9,000 soldiers from Spanish Morocco to Spain to start Franco's civil war. In Ethiopia, in 1935, the Italian Air Force had parachuted 25 tons of supplies per day to support their army column and had continued to do so for two weeks. The French, however, had virtually no air transport facilities.

Air reconnaissance was similarly vital. Before the Polish campaign began, the Germans assigned 288 aircraft to direct army control for front-line army requirements, a proportion of one squadron for each division. But the weapon that played the most dramatic part in the fighting of May 1940 in the Low Countries was the dive bomber.

---

* By 1941 every panzer division commander was provided with a Storch for his personal use.

The Dive Bomber

The ordinary method of dropping bombs from aircraft was as much a matter of luck as of skill. A bomb dropped from an aircraft continues on the same course as the airplane while dropping toward the ground. Unless the aircraft is *exactly* in line with the target, the bomb will miss to either side. In addition, since the aircraft would be traveling at 4 miles a minute, estimation of the target's distance was crucial. The wind, which might vary at lower levels and come in gusts would also affect the fall of the bomb. And this is without considering the effect of changing winds upon the track of the aircraft or of enemy action. An airplane moves slightly crabwise in wind so that it is useless for the pilot to aim the nose of the aircraft at the target.

Although bomb aimers were provided with slide rules and sights on which estimated wind strength and direction could be applied to their view of the target, level bombing remained a crude weapon, suitable for large targets but not sufficiently accurate for pinpoint targets such as strong points, ships, and bridges.

Bombs dropped from aircraft as they dived upon the target had far greater accuracy than the bombs dropped from aircraft flying straight and level. The United States Army and Navy—there was no independent air force—were both interested in this technique. It was, however, the Curtiss F8C, developed for the U.S. Marines, that first earned the name "Helldiver." It became a name for all subsequent dive bombers made by Curtiss-Wright.

It was a Curtiss dive bomber that Ernst Udet, a German air ace of the First World War, saw demonstrated in America in September 1933. It was largely due to Udet's enthusiasm for the dive bomber that German manufacturers were invited to submit prototypes for testing by the Luftwaffe.

Like all the other equipment of the blitzkrieg, the dive bomber was cheap; a small aircraft with two crewmen, its loss was calculated as a small price to pay for the elimination of a strong point that was delaying an advance.

It was the Junkers Ju 87, with its massively thick wing-roots and clumsy-looking, fixed undercarriage making it so easy to identify, which became known as the Stuka, although the word "Stuka"—derived from *Sturzkampfflugzeug*—simply meant "dive bomber." These aircraft—and the twin-engined Ju 88s that soon followed them into squadron service—were able to carry the dive-bomb attack to its extreme efficiency. Dive brakes were used to slow the speed of the

FIGURE 17   Junkers 87
Stuka dive bomber.

dive, thus putting less strain on the wing-roots during the pullout. Stuka pilots would typically dive at 70 or 80 degrees starting from an altitude of 10,000 feet and often pulling out lower than the 3,000 feet that regulations said would save them from the blast of their own bombs. Sirens were fitted to such aircraft to produce a terrifying, high-pitched scream.

If the dive bomber symbolized the blitzkrieg's air weapon, it by no means dominated it. Of nearly 2,000 bombers in the Luftwaffe's strength in September 1939, there were less than 350 Ju 87s. There were at that time nearly twice this number of aircraft earmarked for reconnaissance duties. Such a comparison reveals the way in which a blitzkrieg was designed to avoid centers of enemy resistance rather than hit them.

French Aircraft

"Slow, vulnerable and not steady enough" was the official French Air Force verdict on the Loire Nieuport LN-40 dive bomber submitted to them. It was a verdict that could also have been brought against the Junkers, which lumbered along at less than 200 mph and had only one little machine gun to defend itself. Such machines were no match for the French Air Force's excellent Dewoitine D.520, which many experts still maintain was comparable to the Supermarine Spit-

FIGURE 18   Dewoitine 520 single-seat fighter.

fire. But, by May 1940, only seventy-nine Dewoitine D.520s were in service.

The French aviation industry was still making aircraft by hand rather than mass production. It was slow and expensive and thus extremely difficult for government purchasing departments to challenge the costs. Judging from the scandals that periodically came to light during the prewar years, this latter factor was being fully exploited.

Only sixty French aircraft were made in September 1939, and this rate of manufacture was not improved. As a stopgap measure, the French government bought some American Curtiss Hawk 75A–1s. This was a cheap export version of the Curtiss P–36 Mohawk that the U.S. Army Air Corps used. It marked the Curtiss-Wright company's changeover from biplane fighters to monoplanes. It was a good fighter plane unless measured against the outstanding Messerschmitt Bf 109, which was exactly what it would be up against.

The rest of the French aircraft were as varied as their tanks. They ranged from some excellent light bombers to antiques. The mediocre Morane-Saulnier M.S.406 fighter, a rather slow machine, had been supplied with engines from the Skoda works in Czechoslovakia until 1938.

Although there were few superlative aircraft in the French *Armée de l'Air*, neither were they plentiful in the Luftwaffe or the RAF. The RAF Fairey Battle light bomber, for instance, was little more than a stretched fighter, with a crew of three. Crews displayed amazing courage, but that was not enough to overcome the limitations of this un-

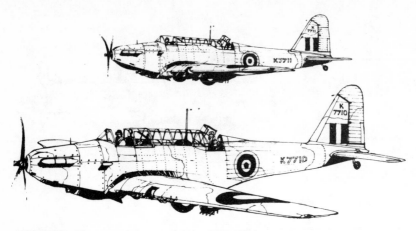

FIGURE 19
2/3 seat Fairey
Battle bomber, capable
of 257 mph.

wieldy machine. The tactics of air armies—like those of land armies—consisted in bringing superior weapons to bear upon vulnerable ones. Fighters were the trump card of the air battle, but their range and flight duration were short and they could not be everywhere. Looking at the rival air forces of the Western Front as they were at the beginning of 1940, it was reasonable for one to assume that the burden and special difficulties of being an attacker might well even out any disparity in the equipment of the French and German armed forces. If one threw into the scales the RAF contingents, with their Hawker Hurricane fighters and medium bombers and the air forces of Belgium and the Netherlands, German air power looked marginally inferior to what it faced.

Anti-aircraft Guns

There was another factor in German air power, a weapon that would totally change the fortunes of the bomber, especially the low-level and medium-level bombers. By supplementing the defensive role of the fighter arm, it would even release fighter aircraft to other duties and so expand German control of the air. This weapon was the anti-aircraft gun, or what the Germans called *Flak*, short for *Fliegerabwehrkanone*.

The primary components of the ground attack were tanks and aircraft. To shoot at either, a gunner needed a gun with a high rate of fire, long range, flat trajectory, and hard "punch"—in other words high muzzle velocity. The howitzer had been given to every arm that could make do with it, so that these expensive guns were available to shoot at aircraft and tanks.

The German divisions' flak guns from 20 mm to 10.5 cm all had muzzle velocities approaching 3,000 feet per second. But unlike Allied guns, they were supplied with armor-piercing (solid shot) as well as high-explosive shells. Large numbers of the German guns were dual-

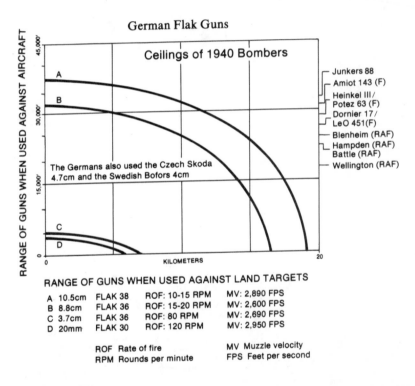

German Flak Guns

Ceilings of 1940 Bombers

RANGE OF GUNS WHEN USED AGAINST AIRCRAFT

A
B

The Germans also used the Czech Skoda 4.7cm and the Swedish Bofors 4cm

C
D

KILOMETERS

Junkers 88
Amiot 143 (F)
Heinkel III /
Potez 63 (F)
Dornier 17 /
LeO 451(F)
Blenheim (RAF)
Hampden (RAF)
Battle (RAF)
Wellington (RAF)

RANGE OF GUNS WHEN USED AGAINST LAND TARGETS

			ROF	MV
A	10.5cm	FLAK 38	ROF: 10-15 RPM	MV: 2,890 FPS
B	8.8cm	FLAK 36	ROF: 15-20 RPM	MV: 2,600 FPS
C	3.7cm	FLAK 36	ROF: 80 RPM	MV: 2,690 FPS
D	20mm	FLAK 30	ROF: 120 RPM	MV: 2,950 FPS

ROF Rate of fire   MV Muzzle velocity
RPM Rounds per minute   FPS Feet per second

FIGURE 20

Diagram shows maximum ceiling against aircraft and maximum range when used against ground targets. Note the similarity of rate of fire (ROF) and gap in defenses in the medium-altitude band. All these guns were supplied with armor-piercing (AP) ammunition as well as high explosives (HE). This graph shows *maximum ranges;* the *effective range* is considerably less. A postwar analysis showed that all bomber forces, at this period, attacked most often in the 16,000–20,000-foot band.

F I G U R E 21   German 8.8 cm anti-aircraft gun.

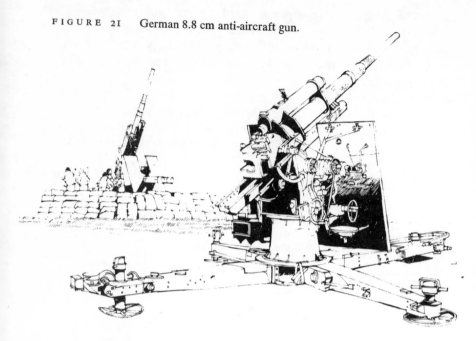

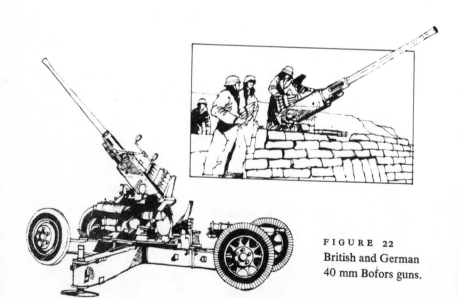

F I G U R E 22
British and German
40 mm Bofors guns.

purpose weapons, and in keeping with the German passion for mobility, designers had managed to keep the guns' structural strength while making them light in weight. The German 8.8 cm gun weighed 4.92 tons compared with the almost identical British 3.7 inch that weighed 10.3 tons. Even the 4 cm Bofors gun, which both armies had bought from Sweden, weighed twice as much in the British version as in the German.

The problem of defending motorized columns and all the other mobile units had not been faced by the French High Command. Gamelin's absurd theory, that airplanes would fight only airplanes in any future battles, had been accepted by most French experts, and when Edouard Daladier, the French Premier, asked about the French Army's lack of antiaircraft guns, this was the official answer he was given.

By 1939 France had five antiaircraft regiments while the Germans had seventy-two. And the French were particularly short of the smaller weapons—in the 20 mm to 40 mm class—needed to combat low-level attacks upon bridges or small targets.

The morale of the French Air Force was excellent in 1940. Its air-crew training was longer than that of the German Air Force, and it had been built round a cadre of First World War fliers who were second to none. The French aircraft industry, whatever its failings, was the foundation upon which all the world's aviation had been built. The Luftwaffe, on the other hand, had officially existed only five years and had hurried most of its designs into the air. But by May 1940 the Germans' great advantage was in the percentage of senior air crews who had experienced modern war in the fighting in Spain, Poland, and Norway. They knew the techniques of the fighter-bomber, the effectiveness of small-caliber antiaircraft fire, how a bomber formation could be "bounced," and the value of flying in open pairs rather than in tight Vs. The fliers of the *Armée de l'Air* knew nothing of these things. Had they known of them, perhaps their morale would not have been quite so high.

French Tanks

France narrowly missed being the first country to produce a tank. The Holt tractors, used to move British artillery pieces, had prompted a French Army colonel, J.-E. Estienne, to propose an armored version that could be used to advance guns in support of an infantry attack. Work on this project was done quite separately from the British tank, and neither army was informed of the work being started by its ally.

The first French machines were primitive. One of the famous

French "75" artillery pieces was put inside a steel box and the whole thing mounted on a Holt tractor chassis. Appropriately the result was named *artillerie d'assaut*. Early models, available just after the British tanks, were intended to support infantry from behind rather than lead it. They suffered even more mechanical failures than British tanks. Their curious boat-prow front caused them to get stuck in shell holes and prevented them from surmounting any serious obstacle.

On discovering that the British were working on something rather more sophisticated, Estienne agreed to concentrate on a smaller, lighter French design. The result was the much more effective Renault FT, a tiny two-man tank with the first proper gun turret. Its size and weight limited it to ground that had not been churned up by artillery fire (which limited all the tanks), but it gained some tactical successes.

The Renault FT was mechanically reliable, and after the First World War ended the French eventually had 3,000 of them. This surplus resulted in their becoming virtually the sole armament of the French tank units of the postwar period. Some were still in use during the Second World War.

French tank men demanding newer tanks were told that machine-gun and rifle fire had not improved enough to make the old tanks obsolete. When the tank men indicated the improvement in high-velocity antitank guns, their opponents used this to prove that *all* tanks were obsolete.

The name *artillerie d'assaut* was unsuited to the two-man Renaults and, in keeping with their top speed of 5 mph, these tanks were given to the infantry department.

German rearmament made France look again at the lack of modern equipment. In 1935 a new production program started, and the new tanks were superb ones. By 1939 the French Army had the best tanks in Europe, far more sophisticated than anything the British or Germans could field. The 4.7 cm gun on the medium and heavy tanks was the best weapon of its kind used by any army at the time. And by 1940 France was not short of tanks. The French Army's collapse was not due to poor equipment but to inadequate skills.

French Armored Divisions

In prewar France Colonel Charles de Gaulle had emerged as the best-known advocate of tank warfare. In 1933 he published his book *Vers l'armée de métier* (Toward a Professional Army). Even the title was enough to provoke anger in many of his fellow soldiers at a time when the army was asking that the length of compulsory military service be

extended. Socialists and Communists were alarmed at what they immediately interpreted as a proposal for a small elite force that would have
political power. The top brass saw it as criticism of their faultless skills
and ordered that all future articles or lectures by serving officers must
be approved by them before publication. This successfully quashed all
discussion.

The book set out a proposal that France should have an armored
mobile force of professional soldiers who would protect the country
from invasion during that hazardous period when the reserves and
conscripts were being called into the army. It established de Gaulle's
position as a man who wanted an armored force but suggested no new
ways of using it. The air force was given no role other than laying
smoke screens for the mobile forces, but great emphasis was given to
the need for heavy artillery. It was evident that de Gaulle failed to
understand the way in which the Luftwaffe was to be the artillery of
the blitzkrieg. After his experiences with the German Stukas in 1940,
de Gaulle modified later editions of his book.

Liddell Hart gave the book faint praise. He pointed out that de
Gaulle had not served with tanks, so his view was "rather hazy" and
his proposed armored force too large to maneuver. German tank experts gave the book passing attention, and in France the first edition
sold only 750 copies and had no effect on official opinion. Few French
politicians were prepared to support the cost of the armored force described in the book when the Maginot Line had cost the taxpayers so
much. Where would we put such a force, asked some sarcastic critics
of de Gaulle, in front of the Maginot Line or behind it?

During the 1930s French cavalrymen had realized that there would
be no combat role for the horse in modern war. Already using armored
cars, the cavalry was given tanks and put together a "light mechanized
division." This DLM (*division légère mécanique*) combined a brigade
of tanks with a brigade of motorized infantry and added a regiment of
artillery, a regiment of armored cars, and some motorcycles. Together
with an engineer battalion, signals, and various support units, this was
the world's first armored division.

By 1940 there were three DLMs. Their weakness was the obsession among Anglo-French commanders that tanks must either be
"cavalry tanks" or "infantry tanks." The DLM had been formed from
cavalry regiments. So, even though the DLM had most of France's
finest tanks—Somua S35s and Hotchkiss H39s—its function was
henceforward to be restricted to what the High Command persisted in
thinking of as "cavalry tasks," even though cavalry had not been used
in the previous war. The DLMs were assigned to reconnaissance and

Table 1

Tanks and armament in 1939*

	Max. speed (mph)	Weight (tons)	Number available	Name
FRANCE	25	20	260	Somua S35
	12.5	9.8	950	Renault R35
	17.5	32	311	Char B1 *bis*
	17.5	11.5	545	Hotchkiss H35
	22.5	12	276	Hotchkiss H39
BRITAIN	15	26.5	75	Infantry Tank A12 Mk. II Matilda
	18	14	126	A10
	30	14	30	A13
GERMANY	16	9	1,095	PzKw II
	25	19.3	388	PzKw III
	26	9.7	410	PzKw 38(t) (Czech)
	25	10.5		PzKw 35(t) (Czech)
	18.5	17.3	278	PzKw IV

* Tanks equipped only with machine guns not included.

Number in crew	Guns			Remarks
	Cal. main gun (cm)	Length/ Cal. ratio	Muzzle velocity (fps)	
3	4.7	34	2,200	Perhaps the best tank in Europe.
2	3.7	21	1,273	
4	7.5	17.1	725	Steering system ahead of any in any of tanks forces, including German.
	4.7	34	2,200	
2	3.7	21	1,273	
2	3.7	33	2,300	Up-gunned H 35 but with double the power. No radio.
4	4.0	50	2,600	All these tanks had the same 2-pounder gun. It had almost the highest muzzle velocity on the field, but the missiles often shattered on German face-hardened steel.
5	4.0	50	2,600	
4	4.0	50	2,600	
3	2.0	71	2,625	
5	3.7	45	2,445	
4	3.72	47.8		Similar gun to that of PzKw III, but tank is only half the total weight.
4	3.72	40		
5	7.5	24	1,263	Large gun but poor velocity.

"scouting," providing what outdated textbooks called a "forward protective screen." It was another way of saying, "Spread thinly in front of the invading spearheads." Deployed like this, their destruction was inevitable.

By the time the Second World War began, French tank resources were at least equal to those of the Germans in both quality and quantity. Even General Gamelin was later to admit that the French tank force was better equipped to deal with German tanks than the Germans were to deal with the French ones. But French tanks were not properly organized. They were in tank battalions assigned to infantry units or kept in a general reserve. Only in 1939 did the French Army form its first real armored division (*division cuirassée*). In an overreaction to the years of delay and in keeping with the "all-tank army" theories, the division was given a very high ratio of tanks. It was a long way from the "miniature army" ideas of Guderian. At the time of the German attack, French armored divisions were virtually untrained and lack of coordination with other elements was made worse by a grave shortage of tank radios.

The French Army

It is certainly difficult to lay blame anywhere but on the French military men themselves for the chronic shortages, of time as well as of vital equipment. It is not true to say that France's armed forces were underequipped because of the taxpayer's meanness, nor that the cost of the Maginot Line deprived France of an army good enough to defend her.

The Maginot Line was completed in 1934 at a cost of £30 million at the contemporary rate of exchange. Yet in 1933, 1934, and 1935, an average of 47 per cent of the total armaments credits available was left unspent by the military.

The following year, 1936, German rearmament prompted the French War Minister to ask General Gamelin, Chief of the General Staff, to submit a four-year plan for rearmament. Gamelin asked for 9 billion francs. The War Minister increased it to 14 billion. The French parliament in turn increased this by 20 per cent to allow for devaluation of the franc. In 1938 another 12 billion francs were allotted to the military program and, as 1939 began, yet another 11 billion francs. One French military historian, Colonel A. Goutard, says of this period, "The army was never refused any money."

The money had been made available to the French War Ministry, but the armed forces were pitifully short of weapons they would soon

Table 2

The vehicles of a typical German infantry division until 1943*

	Motor vehicles	Horse vehicles
Divisional Headquarters: administration, supply, police, medical, veterinary, post	253	245
Reconnaissance battalion	30	3
Signals battalion	103	7
Antitank battalion	114	none
Artillery regiment	105	229
Engineer battalion	87	19
Three infantry regiments: each with 3,250 men, 683 horses, 6 small infantry guns, 2 large ones, 12 antitank guns, all needing towing	73	210
TOTALS: 17,000 men, 5,375 horses	942	1,133

* After 1943 the number of motor vehicles was decreased and horse vehicles increased.

A division of this size would normally require every day 53 tons of hay and oats, 54 tons of food (including cooking fuel), 20 tons of petrol, 1 ton of lubricants, 10 tons of ordnance stores, and 12 tons of various other stores. It would also require ammunition and baggage.

need. At the outbreak of war, the French Army did not have any anti-tank mines at all and there were very few antitank or antiaircraft guns.

The French Army was short of antiaircraft guns because the army had not asked for them. Few tanks and even fewer bombing aircraft were fitted with radio, which lessened their effectiveness in the sort of war they were about to fight. The army's Commander in Chief had not even bothered to equip his own HQ with radio.

There was a grave shortage of antitank guns in the French Army, but in the period up to May 1940, the French were still *exporting* such guns. Eight hundred and thirty 2.5 cm antitank guns and 500 artillery pieces, with ammunition, were exported on the eve of the German attack. Of the last 500 Renault R35 tanks manufactured up to May 1940, nearly half went for export. Even after the German victory in Poland, France's Inspector General of Tanks rejected any suggestion that such a blitzkrieg could defeat France. He repeated his contention that the tank was solely an infantry-support weapon.

The reason that tank units would remain a subordinate arm, argued the experts, was the excellence of the modern antitank gun and the antitank mine. This was also the popular argument against forming any armored divisions, or what the *Revue d'Infanterie* as late as 1939 still derisively called a "cavalcade of tanks." At this time, France had no armored divisions (apart from the tank-equipped cavalry divisions), no antitank mines, and precious few antitank guns either.

Even today it is still argued that the armored division is only useful as a weapon of aggression. But the armored division proved to be the best sort of force with which to counter an armored attack.

Generaloberst Wilhelm Ritter von Leeb, German army group commander in both the Polish and Western campaigns, was one of the world's foremost authorities on defensive warfare. In 1936 he wrote an article and later a book on the subject (*Die Abwehr*). "Operative defense," he wrote, "must meet the threat of offensive by using the same weapons and the same means." It echoed what Colonel de Gaulle had already written in his book, but the French Army would not believe it.

PART FOUR

The Battle
for the River Meuse

"The frontiers of nations are either large rivers, or chains of mountains, or deserts. Of all these obstacles to the march of an army, deserts are the most difficult to surmount; mountains come next; and large rivers hold only the third rank."

—NAPOLEON. Military Maxims, Part One, No. 1

Unlike the Polish campaign, the German thrust through the Ardennes in Belgium to the Channel coast of France in May 1940 was accomplished by a concentrated armored and motorized army and remains the only true example of blitzkrieg in the history of warfare.

For the first time, tanks shattered an enemy front by shock action, and then, instead of following the small encirclements prescribed by the Kesselschlacht theory, plunged deep into the heart of France. No effort was wasted putting a bullet into the "brain" represented by military staffs or capturing Allied army headquarters. Instead, Guderian sped westward, simply severing communications and frightening the whole population to such an extent that all resistance to him was undermined and the frailty of his own extended force was never truly tested. Blitzkrieg theory was entirely vindicated. In one terrible Whitsun

---

AUTHOR'S NOTE. It may be helpful for readers to have here an easy reference to the German High Command in 1939/1940

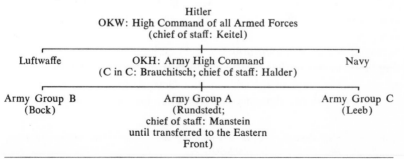

Hitler
OKW: High Command of all Armed Forces
(chief of staff: Keitel)

| Luftwaffe | OKH: Army High Command (C in C: Brauchitsch; chief of staff: Halder) | Navy |

| Army Group B (Bock) | Army Group A (Rundstedt; chief of staff: Manstein until transferred to the Eastern Front) | Army Group C (Leeb) |

holiday weekend, the shape of Europe and the history of the world was changed.*

Blitzkrieg: The Way to Victory

The Ardennes woodlands gave the Germans a chance to move secretly through country hitherto regarded as impassable for armor. The flat land beyond it was the tank commander's dream. In ideal weather Guderian's highly trained armored force used equipment designed to the scale of Western Europe. Never again in the Second World War were such factors to provide another chance for blitzkrieg.

What the Germans called *"Fall Gelb"* (PLAN YELLOW) began on Friday, 10 May. Surprise attacks by armored divisions and air force units were mounted on the neutral countries of Holland, Belgium, and Luxembourg. Within three weeks the force's most southerly prongs were to reach the Channel coast and encircle the Allied armies which had been concentrated in the north. Demoralized and cut off from supplies and any effective command, the French and British could fight only defensively.

During June, PLAN RED was put into operation. Now the German armies redeployed and fought southward. On 10 June Italy declared war on France and invaded the Riviera to secure some pickings from the carcass. Two days later the French government declared Paris an open city and moved to Bordeaux. The French Premier resigned and the French President, Albert Lebrun, asked an elderly First World War hero, Marshal Henri Philippe Pétain, to form a government. On 17 June Pétain asked the Germans for an armistice. On 22 June he accepted the German terms and fighting ended.

The fighting in June is usually called the "Battle of France," but for the far more crucial campaign in May there is no accepted name. One historian, J. F. C. Fuller, called it "the second battle of Sedan," and it is tempting to compare the May fighting with the crushing defeat that the French suffered there in 1870. In that earlier battle the Germans wrested from France the hegemony of Europe and lined themselves up for an eventual military and commercial confrontation with England. In the earlier battle, it had been the inadequacy of French command, as much as the efficiency of German staff work, which had resulted in the encirclement of the French. That German victory had

---

* It is quite clear from the records that the Germans did not choose the date in order to take advantage of the holiday weekend.

been gained through the initiative of Prussian commanders, by the industrial technology that backed them, and by bombardment.

In all those respects, May 1940 was indeed "the second battle of Sedan." Yet the title denies to the German attack the very essence of its theory. For it was not one that would succeed or fail according to the resistance met at any one defensive position; it was a plan that spontaneously set up its objectives, by-passed resistance, and reinforced success. Such a victory should not bear the name of a fortress town.

It was a battle of movement, one that depended upon a breakthrough at Sedan to start it off. It was the river Meuse that settled the fate of the German attack, from Holland—where it is called the Maas —to Sedan, where the main thrust came. Even the most enthusiastic blitzkrieg theorists had reservations about a fortified river obstacle as formidable as this. Guderian himself, when his troops practiced with their inflatable boats, cautioned them not to be overconfident about the task ahead. But once over the river, there could be no doubt about the ultimate victory of the panzer divisions.

The German Plan

When war began in September 1939, the German Army plan for an attack on France was the one that had failed in 1914. The armies would wheel through the Low Countries rather like a gigantic door, the hinge in Luxembourg, the outer edge the Channel coast. If this door could be slammed down upon Paris, well and good; otherwise a mighty battle would be fought on the great plain of Flanders, which has for centuries been Europe's favorite battlefield.

For such a movement, the units on the outer edge—which would have so much farther to travel around the rim—would need to consist of motorized soldiers; slower horse-drawn units would be positioned nearer to the hinge.

The Allies guessed that the Germans would adopt such a plan and, having decided to advance to meet the enemy and do battle in Belgium, also allotted their motorized formations to the outer rim of their front line. Although both sides were in accord as to what sort of war it was to be, few generals on either side believed that such strategy would come to fruition. The German High Command reported that their army was not strong enough to carry it through. Only after the victory in Poland did the prospect begin to look more feasible. When Hitler ordered the German Army to be enlarged to 130 divisions and the number of armored divisions increased from six to ten, the German generals looked toward France with new confidence. On the same afternoon that Poland capitulated, 27 September 1939, Hitler ordered his army to prepare an operational plan.

Arbeitsstab Rundstedt, the team which had produced the successful attack against Poland, was not consulted. This time the task was given to planners of the OKH headed by Halder, Director of Operations of the Army General Staff. By 10 October, Hitler had produced a fifty-eight page memorandum describing in some detail the way in which armored forces should attack on both sides of Liège. With this to inspire them, the OKH produced an equally mediocre plan for an envelopment of Ghent. Both of these ideas aimed for only modest gains which, at best, would merely separate the British Expeditionary Force from the French armies and secure for the Germans some forward air bases.

"Manstein's Plan"

On 21 October General Erich von Manstein, Chief of Staff of Army Group A, obtained a copy of the orders laying out PLAN YELLOW while passing through Berlin on his way to set up Army Group A headquarters at Koblenz. He found little to admire in it. If General von Bock's Army Group B swung through the Low Countries to come into frontal conflict with the Allied armies on the flat land of Belgium,

---

MAP II

(a) The German Fourth Army occupied Luxembourg before the coordinated attack. This plan can be likened to a door, hinged on Luxembourg and swinging through Belgium and northern France. The original plan was for a larger door which could slam down on Paris, but in the event it was modified. Thus the exposed flank of the German First Army became vulnerable to a counterattack from Paris. A vital weakness of this operation was the German failure to supply its fast-moving armies.

(b) Superficially resembling the 1914 attack, this plan lacked its boldness. Even the generals who evolved this plan hoped for no more than a clash of armies that would push the Allies back as far as the Somme. Such an advance would have provided air and naval bases close to England.

(c) This plan was both audacious and subtle. While the Allied armies hurried to meet Army Group B, the bulk of the German armored divisions would race through the undefended rear areas to the sea. The Somme would provide a defense line in case of counterattacks from Paris.

NOTE.   These maps are diagrammatic and do not take into account the units in reserve.

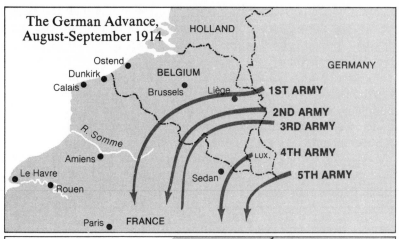

The German Advance, August-September 1914

HOLLAND
GERMANY
BELGIUM
Ostend
Dunkirk
Calais
Brussels
Liège
1ST ARMY
2ND ARMY
3RD ARMY
R. Somme
Amiens
LUX.
4TH ARMY
Le Havre
Rouen
Sedan
5TH ARMY
Paris
FRANCE

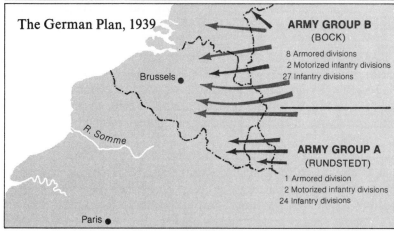

The German Plan, 1939

ARMY GROUP B
(BOCK)
8 Armored divisions
2 Motorized infantry divisions
27 Infantry divisions
Brussels
R. Somme
ARMY GROUP A
(RUNDSTEDT)
1 Armored division
2 Motorized infantry divisions
24 Infantry divisions
Paris

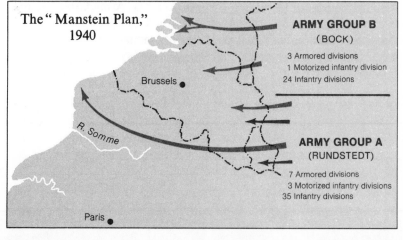

The "Manstein Plan," 1940

ARMY GROUP B
(BOCK)
3 Armored divisions
1 Motorized infantry division
24 Infantry divisions
Brussels
R. Somme
ARMY GROUP A
(RUNDSTEDT)
7 Armored divisions
3 Motorized infantry divisions
35 Infantry divisions
Paris

the clash would be followed by a war of attrition like that of 1914–1918. It was the sort of war that Germany had little hope of winning. Manstein even predicted where the new trench line would come—along the river Somme.

"I found it humiliating, to say the least, that our generation could do nothing better than repeat an old recipe," Manstein wrote, with a chilling professionalism, in *Lost Victories*.

The German General Staff, prodded by Hitler into preparing hasty plans for a battle they could not hope to win, lacking sufficient motor transport to overcome the supply problems of 1914, facing a French Army that was already mobilized, had produced a plan for "partial victory." It was not expected to conquer France, only to grab a large section of the Channel coast as a basis for future operations in a long war.

Although Manstein was not a tank specialist, he could see that Holland was a difficult area for tank operations. There were too many water obstacles there, and the dikes could be opened to bog down the armor in a sea of mud. Moreover, these regions through which the northern armies were to wheel had become more and more built up in the preceding twenty years. These strung-out urban regions, their suburbs almost touching, were in effect a massive tank obstacle, no less efficient than the ones that had been built along the front of the Maginot Line.*

None of the German tank soldiers had had time enough to forget that as recently as September, 4.Pz.Div had lost 57 out of 120 tanks in one day's fighting against the Poles. And it had happened in just such a built-up area: the suburbs of Warsaw.

Manstein began to sketch out a dramatic new route for the panzer divisions. If most of the armor was transferred to Army Group A and was able to thread its way through the Ardennes Forest and over the Meuse, it would be in the flat open sort of country that the tank men liked. That sort of country continued all the way to Paris or to the Channel.

Manstein had added another vital dimension to the plan. The invaders would not be able to prevent mobilization by overrunning the mobilization centers, for France was already mobilized. Yet fast-moving German forces could cut right through the areas in which the French Army would have to redeploy in order to mount a counter-offensive, and this he took into account.

---

* It was a conclusion heartily endorsed by Allied tank armies going the other way in 1944.

From the beginning, Manstein thought in terms of long armored thrusts that would take the panzer and motorized forces far ahead of the horse-drawn support. It was in this respect that Manstein, Guderian, and eventually Hitler saw it differently from the rest of the army chiefs.

The army's order for PLAN YELLOW was dated 19 October 1939. Its basic strategy was Hitler's, but he studied it with little enthusiasm. On 25 October he asked questions about cutting the enemy off "south of Namur" but was told that such an attack was impossible.

On 29 October the plan was amended to leave Holland neutral. Hitler believed he could persuade the Dutch to stay out of the war, even if he did go through the Dutch town of Maastricht to attack Belgium. The next day Hitler confided in General Jodl, his operations chief at OKW, a "brainwave" he had had for concentrating an attack on the Arlon Gap and through the Ardennes Forest to strike at Sedan. Only one man in Germany could be sure as to the feasibility of getting tanks along the narrow, twisting roads of the Ardennes, and that was Heinz Guderian. General Keitel consulted Guderian on Hitler's behalf.* Remembering the terrain from the First World War, Guderian thought it would be possible to move and supply his armored and motorized forces through this sort of hilly countryside.

Meanwhile, the OKH plan had brought a forthright response from Army Group A. Rundstedt, the commander of Army Group A, wrote a long letter to his Commander in Chief, Brauchitsch, explaining why he felt the plan could not achieve a decisive victory. A second document added detailed suggestions (from Manstein) to move the weight of the attack from Bock's Army Group B in the north to Rundstedt's forces drawn up east of the Ardennes in the south. This correspondence was dismissed at OKH, where it was whispered that here was simply a further manifestation of the bad feelings between Rundstedt and his northern neighbor Bock, and the new proposals no more than a device for gaining greater power, importance, and glory for Army Group A. Manstein's suggestions were simply filed away and forgotten. Franz Halder confided in his diary that Manstein's memorandum should not reach Hitler's attention. Yet it was in essence Manstein's plan that eventually changed the shape of Europe and found a permanent place in the history books.

On 3 November Brauchitsch visited Army Group A headquarters at Koblenz, where Manstein personally expounded his ideas in detail.

---

* Kenneth Macksey, in *Guderian*, describes this meeting with Keitel. Guderian makes no mention of it in his memoirs, however, and refers to a meeting with Manstein about such a plan as if it was the first time the subject had been broached.

Brauchitsch was not impressed, and said that, anyway, there was no question of making major changes to the OKH plan at this stage. However, he did promise Army Group A two motorized regiments and an armored division from the reserves. Such small additions contributed little to the capability of the armies in the south. Undismayed, Manstein continued to bombard OKH with memos about his own plan.

There was indeed good reason for Brauchitsch to believe that the attack would be launched long before there was any chance of putting into effect changes to PLAN YELLOW. Already the code word for troop assemblies had been issued several times, only to be canceled again in the light of weather forecasts. In fact, the offensive was to be postponed twenty-nine times before it finally took place.

It was during one such delay, due to bad weather on 11 November, that Hitler, still fingering the Ardennes Forest on his operations map, suddenly ordered Guderian's XIX Panzerkorps (two panzer divisions and a motorized infantry division) to be moved to join Army Group A and given Sedan as its objective. At that time the move was intended as little more than a diversionary feint, the main weight of the attack remaining the responsibility of Bock and his Army Group B in the north.

When Guderian arrived at Koblenz to take up his new position, Manstein immediately tackled him about the problems of moving tanks through the Ardennes Forest. Until this meeting Manstein had simply *assumed* that it would be possible, whereas Hitler had already discovered what Guderian, his most knowledgeable exponent of tank warfare, felt about negotiating the difficult terrain of the Ardennes and had personally directed Guderian's XIX Panzerkorps there on the strength of it. Yet even the addition of Guderian's corps did not greatly change the overall thrust power of Army Group A, and Guderian himself reckoned that there was still not enough armored force in the south to break through the French defenses along that stretch of the river Meuse. Furthermore, the order to attack Sedan itself added new problems.

By then, Hitler was reminding his generals that they must be ready to reinforce Guderian should the need arise and that the whole army effort must be switched behind Army Group A if that sector seemed to be achieving the best results. If Hitler's instinct was drawing him to Sedan, he still did not recognize the full impact of a plan like Manstein's that envisaged a grand sweep through the Ardennes to the French coast, so severing the Allied armies in two. To Manstein, such a bold stroke depended entirely on speed and momentum; Hitler did not understand that time lost in bringing up reserves or switching divisions from another army group would prove fatal.

Hitler talked to Rundstedt and Guderian on 27 November, in order to find out at first hand what was happening in the forward areas. Once again, the Führer was beginning to take a close interest in every detail of the planning, right down to regimental level, as he had before the Polish campaign. Then his military assistant was sent to Koblenz and returned with more news of Manstein's proposals. At last, one of Manstein's memos filtered through to Hitler himself.

The Forced Landing

During the autumn and winter of 1939–1940 the order for the PLAN YELLOW attack came and was canceled again and again. On 10 January 1940, with a weather forecast that promised temperatures cold enough to make the ground firm for the mobile forces and skies clear enough for the Luftwaffe, Hitler gave the order to attack on 17 January. Yet the uncertainties of putting this second-rate plan into action during the winter months were illustrated by an aircraft accident that took place on the very day that Hitler was talking to his chiefs of staff in the Chancellery.

The trouble began in the officers' mess at an air fleet base in Münster. Over glasses of beer a staff officer, a major, complained of the uncomfortable train journey that he faced in order to be at the next day's staff meeting in Cologne. His companion, an aviator in the previous war and now also a major, offered to fly him there in a Messerschmitt Bf 108 communications aircraft. Strong winds, bad icing, a landscape whitened by frost all militated against the pilot, and soon the two majors were completely lost. The staff officer was in contravention of the standing order that no secret papers must be carried by aircraft. In his briefcase there were the air fleet's operation orders for an airborne division at Cologne.

After searching for some familiar landmark without success, the aircraft ran out of fuel and was forced to land in a field near Malines, on the wrong side of the Belgian border. Realizing that they would be interned, the Germans attempted to burn the documents but neither man smoked and they had to borrow a lighter from a Belgian farmer. The papers were beginning to burn as the gendarmes arrived. The two German officers were then held captive in a hut where they made another abortive attempt to destroy the papers, this time by pushing them into the stove.

In spite of all this—or perhaps because of it—the Belgian High Command and the Allied commanders to whom the operation orders were passed were convinced that the antics of the two men were all part of an elaborate deception scheme. What purpose such a scheme could have had is not easy to guess.

It is tempting to see this incident as the reason for the German changeover to the Manstein plan, but this was not the way it happened. "Heads rolled" because of the forced landing, but no significant changes of strategy were mentioned at the Commander in Chief's conference at Bad Godesberg on 25 January. Army Group B, under Bock, retained most of the mobile formations; Army Group A could not hope to get farther than the Meuse.

Rundstedt perhaps hoped to use the forced-landing fiasco as a way of converting the Commander in Chief to the new ideas when he sent a message on 12 January. Outspoken to the point of being insubordinate, he insisted that the Manstein plan should be shown to Hitler. Again the request was refused.

By the end of January 1940 the OKH had decided to settle the matter of the Manstein plan once and for all. Manstein was ordered to assume command of an infantry corps on the other side of Germany. (There was a Panzerkorps command in the West open at the same time, but this was given to General Georg-Hans Reinhardt, an officer junior to Manstein.)

Luncheon with Hitler

During February war games were staged to test Manstein's ideas. One game used aerial photographs and went into exacting detail about road capacities, parking, refueling, and air defense during the approach march. Vigorous air attacks by the Allies were programmed into the game. Halder, Brauchitsch's chief of staff, was impressed with the results.

He concluded that such an attack could succeed if far more weight of armor was given to Army Group A. But he was concerned about the effect of enemy air attacks and worried lest the panzer divisions of the spearhead should outrun the motorized infantry behind them. He was worried, too, about the difficulties of getting tanks across the river Meuse in the face of enemy fire. All in all, Halder was beginning to believe that Manstein could be right, although he was convinced that the armored forces must halt at the Meuse and wait for infantry and artillery to arrive. He suggested a crossing on the ninth or tenth day of the campaign.

Both Guderian and General Gustav von Wietersheim, commander of the XIV Motorized Corps following the armored divisions, were horrified. They explained that the loss of momentum would be fatal to such an operation and expressed a lack of confidence in the leadership. Halder argued. Manstein was not present, having already departed to his new job. Rundstedt, until now a strong supporter of all Manstein's ideas, equivocated. The meeting ended with bad feeling on all sides.

It was on Saturday, 17 February 1940, that Manstein lunched with Hitler. It was a practice of the Führer to have informal meetings with newly appointed generals, and three other such corps commanders were fellow guests. Also present was Erwin Rommel, who had taken command of 7.Pz.Div just one week previously. It was a mark of special favor that Rommel should be at the table with officers so senior to him. After the lunch Manstein was taken into Hitler's study and encouraged to elaborate on his ideas for the coming battle in the West.

Four days previously Hitler had criticized the OKH plan with such fury that two colonels had been assigned to prepare a detailed study based on the Führer's complaints. Now Hitler listened to Manstein with evident approval. This plan was bold and "miraculous," and such projects always appealed to him. Manstein's cool professional reasoning endorsed intuitions that Hitler had long felt about the chances of an advance through the Ardennes Forest and an assault on Sedan. It also promised the blitzkrieg he needed rather than the war of attrition that he dreaded.

The generals at OKH had been shortsighted about the Manstein plan, but they recognized quickly enough the turn of the wind. The following morning, Halder presented himself before Hitler with a new plan. It was a complete reversal of everything the OKH had been offering. Not only was it in accord with Manstein's ideas, it was even more drastic than anything he had dared to propose. No credit, however, was given to its true author. Instead, it was claimed that this was all their own work. "Now we have reverted to the original scheme," claimed Halder vaguely. The army did not recall Manstein from his infantry corps in far-off Liegnitz.

German cryptologists had broken the French military codes in October 1939, and the radio traffic confirmed that Sedan was the weak joint of two second-class divisions. To strike at this junction, Army Group A was given what was actually a small armored army called Panzergruppe Kleist. (It consisted of five panzer divisions: Panzerkorps Guderian plus Panzerkorps Reinhardt. They were followed by

Armeekorps Wietersheim, comprising three divisions of motorized infantry: 1.Div, 29.Div, and 13.Div.)

In addition to Panzergruppe Kleist, two panzer divisions (Panzerkorps Hoth) had been assigned to the command of the Fourth Army
(Kluge), which was also in Army Group A. Only three panzer divisions remained in Army Group B, under Bock.

The uncertain weather of that 1939–1940 winter had played a part
in the planning as it would have played a part in a battle. For had the
attack been made according to the earliest PLAN YELLOW, it would
almost certainly have come to a stalemate in mud. Now the offensive
was to be launched in the fine spring weather of May. The actual day
was the tenth of that month, and here again luck was on the side of
the attacker. By May the action in Norway was obviously an Allied
disaster of some magnitude. In France Paul Reynaud, a clear-sighted
and energetic man who had been calling for reform of the army for
several years, had been Prime Minister for only six weeks. Reynaud
had never had much faith in General Gamelin, the French Commander
in Chief, and the Norwegian fiasco prompted a furious row in the War
Cabinet, which Reynaud interpreted as resignation on the part of his
entire Cabinet. He said that he would announce it as such the following day, 10 May.

For Britain, the timing of the German invasion was just as fateful.
On 9 May, Chamberlain, still at that time Prime Minister, was suffering widespread unpopularity, not only for the Norwegian defeats but
also for the inappropriate complacency shown concerning them. After
a revolt of backbenchers on the day before, he was now forced to ask
the Opposition leaders for support. They declined, leaving him politically bankrupt. On the morning of 10 May, as news of the German
attacks in the West came over the radio, Chamberlain faced open
rebellion in his Cabinet and, a sick and broken man, offered his resignation. That evening Winston Churchill was asked to form a government, comprising both Socialists and Conservatives. Prime Minister
Churchill declared himself Minister of Defence, without defining the
role of that new office.

Codeword DANZIG, 10 May 1940

In the First World War, the importance of air reconnaissance had
eventually been recognized. The greater number of fliers lost in that
war were shot down because of the British High Command's determination that airmen should watch for concentrations of men and ma-
tériel at the railheads. Had Allied fliers shown such curiosity about

German deployment in the spring of 1940, they would have seen Kleist's armored units, which were backed up into a traffic jam stretching back more than 100 miles behind the frontier.

Reconnaissance aircraft might have seen the eight military bridges across the Rhine that had been reported back to Swiss intelligence and had enabled the Swiss to guess that an attack was to be made in the region of Sedan. One French bomber pilot, returning from a night mission over Düsseldorf where, in accord with the Allied air policy since war began, he had dropped nothing more dangerous than propaganda leaflets, did report a 60-mile column of vehicles, all with headlights on, making for the Ardennes. It seemed too fanciful to be believed, and no action was taken, even after the reports were confirmed by other French fliers.

At 9 P.M. on 9 May 1940 the code word DANZIG went out to the alerted units. The grotesque traffic jam had begun to move. That night, Hitler boarded his private train to set up a HQ at Münstereifel, 25 miles southwest of Bonn. In keeping with the Führer's melodramatic taste, it was called *Felsennest* (eyrie).

1. The Northernmost Attack: Holland

For many generations the Dutch had known no enemy but the ocean. Their soldiers had fought only in colonial wars and the occasional riot in the homeland. The Dutch had benefited economically from their neutrality in the First World War and were convinced that Hitler too would pass them by. They were almost right. On 29 October 1939 the invasion of the Netherlands had been dropped from PLAN YELLOW, but the Luftwaffe objected. The German airmen, lacking any long-range bombing units, insisted that they would need forward airfields there for the ensuing war against England. Holland was then included once more in the invasion plan.

The German Eighteenth Army was smaller than the Dutch Army that it faced. It had only one panzer division, and this was the weakest of all the armored units. If the lightweight PzKw I and PzKw II tanks are discounted, it had only thirty-eight tanks. But this northern army was supported by almost the entire German airborne force.

German Airborne Forces

Confusion has arisen about this campaign because of the way in which the English word "airborne" has been used to describe both paratroops and air-transported infantry.

Hermann Göring, in accordance with the empire building that was fundamental to the Nazi regime, had gathered into his Luftwaffe many associated units, including the paratroops. Numerically the most important were the antiaircraft gunners, who comprised nearly two thirds of the Luftwaffe. Although the army had managed to retain command of some of its antiaircraft crews, all parachute troops were transferred to Luftwaffe command in 1939.

The paratroops were a highly trained, carefully selected force of about 4,000 men. Many of them would have been given higher rank in some other infantry unit. For this reason it was the normal procedure to preserve them by pulling them out of combat as soon as other troops were available. For the invasion of Holland, the 1. Parachute Regiment was part of General Kurt Student's 7. Flieger Division.

Also participating in the invasion was the army's 22. Air Landing Division. Often described as airborne troops, these were, in fact, about 12,000 infantrymen who had been shown how to pack themselves and their equipment into transport aircraft and get out quickly once the aircraft were on the ground. Although the paratroops were an elite fighting force, the weight and bulk of their parachutes reduced the amount of heavy weapons they could take with them. In this respect the air-transported infantry were sometimes more formidable in battle.

The airborne and paratroop units used in the Netherlands in May 1940 were all part of a plan which centered upon a takeover of the government. They were to capture Den Haag (The Hague), take control of the War Ministry and other government offices, and detain the royal family. Possibly with such a regal audience in mind, the commander of the 22. Air Landing Division took his full-dress uniform and horse with him.

The attack on the three airfields outside Den Haag went disastrously wrong for the attackers. The airfields proved difficult to find on the flat landscape in the early morning light. Many paratroops were dropped at the wrong place. The Junkers Ju 52 three-engine transports, packed with infantry, met with fierce opposition at the airfields. At Ypenburg, eleven of a flight of thirteen transport aircraft went down in flames. Smoke reduced visibility, and many of the transports ran into obstacles strategically placed by the Dutch defenders. At Valkenburg so many

Defense of Holland

- Ⓐ Airborne attack
- ▬ Grebbe line
- ▬ ▬ East Front. Country behind this is called "Vesting Holland"
- ➤ Advance of French 7th Army
- ▪▪▶ Withdrawal of French 7th Army
- ▨ The provinces of North Holland, South Holland, and Utrecht that formed a defensive region.

Groningen

Ijsselmeer   Meppel

Amsterdam

HOLLAND

Den Haag

R. Lek

Arnhem

Rotterdam

18

R. Waal

9. PZ. DIVISION
SS INFANTRY

Gennep

Breda

Tilburg

FRENCH 7TH ARMY

GERMANY

BELGIUM

R. Maas

MAP 12

German paratroops, followed by air-transported infantry, tried to capture Den Haag, the seat of government and military command, but, in the chaos of force-landed aircraft, failed. Surviving elements were ordered to move on Rotterdam. French 7th Army units reached Breda on 11 May and split to move east and west, then later retreated. The bridge at Gennep was captured by a ruse when German soldiers wore Dutch uniforms.

of the first wave of transports were wrecked that there was nowhere for the second wave to land. They had to turn away.

The commanding general of the Den Haag operation was to land at Ypenburg. His pilot saw so many wrecks that he flew on to Ockenburg. Still he could not find a landing place. The air was filled with Junkers transports trying to find space enough to touch down, while on the airfields the first wave of attackers were fighting for their lives. Finally the general landed in a field. He used his radio to warn the headquarters of 2. Luftflotte (Air Fleet) that the plan had gone wrong. They ordered him to abandon the idea of capturing Den Haag. Surviving elements were to move southeast and support the attack on Rotterdam.

The attempt to capture the Dutch capital by airborne assault had failed, but that same morning an airborne attack on the small town of Arnhem was a complete success. In the extreme north, other infantry divisions were pushing through Friesland to the IJsselmeer.

But Rotterdam was the key to the defense of the whole country. The most important task of the German Eighteenth Army was to sever the Dutch armies from the other Allied armies now heading north to link with them. Vital to even the first few miles of the panzer division's drive westward was the bridge over the Maas at Gennep on the Dutch-German border.

The Gennep Bridge

Hitler's personal interest in the detailed planning is shown by the meeting he held at the Reich chancellery in November 1939. He instructed the Abwehr (military intelligence) to prepare plans for seizing the bridges over the Maas before the Dutch had a chance to demolish them. The nature of the task and its timing indicated that it could only be accomplished by men dressed in Dutch uniforms.

Meanwhile, the Dutch Foreign Minister revealed that Dutch uniforms were being smuggled into Germany. A German agent was arrested in Belgium with Belgian uniforms. Although the authorities in Belgium and Holland were not suspicious enough to issue any special orders to their frontier guards, the general public got the idea right away. A Flemish newspaper even published a cartoon in which Göring was seen admiring himself in the uniform of a Brussels tram conductor.

The plans were very elaborate and included code words and countersigns, sealed envelopes, and the instant recruitment of German locomotive crews who were given Wehrmacht armbands, steel helmets, gas masks, and identity cards and suddenly found themselves in the very forefront of the German attack.

Only at Gennep did the scheme work. Two trains—one armored followed by a troop train—went over the bridge into the fortified Peel Line. Soldiers from the train then attacked the blockhouses from the rear, while more Germans came over the border.

Some Brandenburgers (the army battalion usually assigned to Abwehr operations) worked closely with about thirty Dutch Fascists to prepare details of the raid.* Two men, dressed as Dutch military policemen, crossed the bridge on foot escorting men they said were German prisoners. (Whether any of these escorts were Dutch is still argued.) The men in Dutch uniforms spoke enough Dutch to allay the fears of the frontier guards. While they were talking, the grotesque-looking armored train—preceded by two flatcars mounted with machine guns—started to move. The Dutch defenders were overpowered and the bridge captured intact. The Brandenburg unit commander was awarded one of the first Knight's Crosses of the war.

However, after that things did not go as smoothly as planned. The Dutch in the fortifications put up enough resistance for the Germans to call for heavy artillery. When it came, the horses drawing the guns got their hoofs caught in the planking used to cover the rails on the bridge. There was a whole day of fighting before the road was clear.

Over the bridge then moved the largely Austrian 9.Pz.Div and its Austrian commander, Dr. Ritter von Hubicki. It was supported by motorized infantry of the SS-Verfügungsdivision. Although under the army's tactical instructions, the Waffen-SS were fast becoming a separate military force of the sort that the army had once feared the SA would become.

The panzer division and its motorized SS infantry moved west along the southern side of a complex of three rivers. The Maas (Meuse), the Waal (Rhine), and the Lek, which flows to Rotterdam, together made a barrier behind which the Dutch were expected to withdraw when they formed *Vesting Holland* (Fortress Holland). Their great cities were immediately to the north of these rivers, and the shape of the IJsselmeer would give defenders a good chance of holding off an attack indefinitely along the narrow front that would remain. For a narrow front nullifies the advantage of strength; two strong men can hold off a battalion of infantry if they are fighting in an office corridor.

---

* Admiral Wilhelm Canaris, chief of the Abwehr, established Bau-Lehr-Bataillon *z.b.V.* 800 early in 1939 from men with special skills including foreign languages. The Brandenburgers later became a regiment and finally the Brandenburg Division.

The Moerdijk Bridges

A battalion of paratroops had been dropped to capture the very long bridges at Moerdijk, about 16 miles south of Rotterdam. Two companies were dropped south of the bridges and two on the north. Long before any advance elements of 9.Pz.Div could reach Moerdijk, motorized elements of the French Seventh Army, advancing northward to contact the Dutch, had reached Breda, no more than 10 miles south of the bridges. Instead of striking at the paratroops holding the bridges, the French split their forces to head both east and west.

As early as 500 B.C. Sun Tzu had warned against dividing a force in the presence of the enemy, but the French did not divide their force because they were unfamiliar with the writings of Sun Tzu. They were prompted by the same motives that had kept the British Expeditionary Force training in France practicing bayonet charges and digging trenches. The style of the 1914–1918 war was so deeply embedded in Anglo-French military thinking that the French were unable to regard this as anything but a salient that must be "contained" and "sealed off." Actually, it was the final move of an armored invasion which, at Moerdijk, had succeeded in slicing the Netherlands in two, isolating the greater part of the country from the Anglo-French and Belgian armies.

The French were attacked by the Luftwaffe, and the part of the force moving east without tanks blundered into advance elements of 9. Pz.Div and had to fall back before the German advance. The panzer division brushed them aside to reach the paratroops who still held the intact bridges at Moerdijk. These bridges—a road and railway bridge side by side—spanned a stretch of water a mile wide at the only place the Germans could cross. When the panzer division reached Moerdijk the most hazardous part of the German route was secure.

Another infantry unit—the motorized SS-Leibstandarte Adolf Hitler—which had "got itself stuck" in the central offensive was redeployed. It was now put in to follow the route of 9.Pz.Div. In the face of this determined force, the French moved back along the route to Roosendaal and Antwerp. With them went the last chance of reinforcing Fortress Holland. Advance elements of 9.Pz.Div reached the small force of paratroops who were holding the Moerdijk bridges and moved on northward toward Rotterdam.

The Dordrecht bridge was also intact and in the hands of the paratroops by the time the panzer division got there. Now they were almost in sight of Rotterdam, the capture of which would provide a foothold in Fortress Holland.

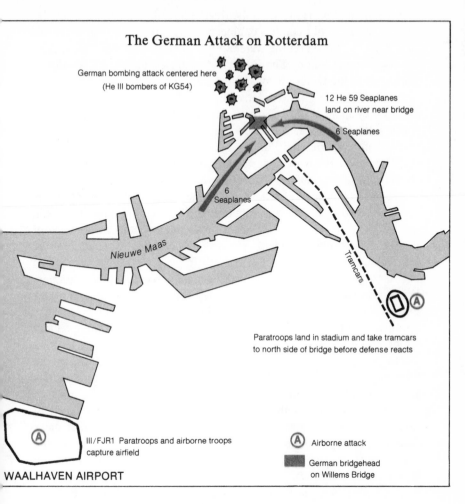

The German Attack on Rotterdam

German bombing attack centered here
(He III bombers of KG54)

12 He 59 Seaplanes
land on river near bridge

6 Seaplanes

6 Seaplanes

Nieuwe Maas

Tramcars

Paratroops land in stadium and take tramcars
to north side of bridge before defense reacts

Ⓐ III/FJR1 Paratroops and airborne troops
capture airfield

WAALHAVEN AIRPORT

Ⓐ Airborne attack

German bridgehead
on Willems Bridge

MAP 13

Rotterdam

The German campaign of May 1940 shows a preoccupation with tricks and novelties. The most ambitious of them was the attempt to seize the Willems bridge in the heart of Rotterdam in the first few hours of the invasion.

It was five o'clock in the morning when twelve rather antiquated

Heinkel float planes landed on the river. This suicidal mission consisted of 150 infantry and combat engineers. The aircraft, six on each side of the bridge, taxied on the water so that the soldiers could use inflatable boats to get ashore. Soon they had managed to take up position at both ends of the twin railway and road bridges.

The Dutch might well have dislodged this force. In fact, some Dutch accounts speak of Germans from seaplanes withdrawing to the south side of the river. But at the crucial moment in the fighting, German reinforcements arrived.

The new arrivals were paratroops which had been dropped at the Rotterdam sports stadium near the river on the south side of the city. These men, from the 1. Parachute Regiment, commandeered tramcars and came rattling up the road and over the bridge to join the soldiers in the bridgehead. Although the Dutch also put into the battle some of their toughest fighting men—marines—the Germans could not be dislodged.

As the morning wore on, fighting became fiercer and more complex. Dutch ships—trawlers, mine sweepers, a patrol boat, and a motor torpedo boat—began firing at pointblank range. In turn, these ships became the target not only for the German guns south of the river but for bombing attacks.

In desperate folly, the Dutch sent the destroyer *Van Galen* up the river to shell the airfield at Waalhaven. Attacked by German bombers and unable to turn in the narrow river she sank.

The Dutch also bombed the Germans at the airfield but failed to stop the troop transports landing there. By the end of the first day's fighting the Germans held all the southern side of the town. On the bridgehead, paratroops still clung to their tiny patch of ground and the bridge remained intact.

On the second day the Germans gained command of the air. Constant bombing attacks had a terrible effect on the Dutch troops who, as Dutch official sources later admitted, were not well trained or well armed. German airborne soldiers and paratroops in the region to the north of Rotterdam failed to gain their first objectives, but they created confusion among the defenders, who couldn't decide the whereabouts or the strength of the German pockets. The use of Dutch uniforms at Gennep and other border-crossing places had given rise to rumors of German soldiers dressed as everything from traffic cops to nuns. A great deal of time and energy was devoted to chasing and checking up on innocent civilians.

In spite of the fighting at Waalhaven airfield, German soldiers were being landed there and in spite of terrible casualties were getting to Willems bridge.

It was the evening of 13 May when the first men of 9.Pz.Div arrived in Rotterdam. The Austrian commander was no longer in contact with the men on the north side of the bridge. Already the German Eighteenth Army commander was pressing for results. And he in turn was being pressed from above.

Civilians, under a white flag, had talked to soldiers on both sides of the bridge and, by the morning of 14 May, messages about a surrender were being exchanged. Meanwhile an air bombardment was scheduled for 3 P.M. and tanks were being moved into position for an attempt to storm the bridge half an hour later.

The Dutch commander at Rotterdam was in no hurry. He still held virtually the whole city of Rotterdam and his forces outnumbered the German attackers. The Dutch supreme commander told him to play for time. By 2:15 P.M. the Dutch were asking that German messages be rewritten to include the name, rank, and signature of the German commander. The German signals section at Waalhaven airfield sent a message to the Luftwaffe asking that the bombers be recalled to give more time. The German commander rewrote the surrender demand in his own handwriting and said that a decision must be in his hands by 6 P.M. The message was timed 2:55 P.M.

The sound of Heinkel bombers was heard as an officer crossed the bridge with the German note. The aircraft had wound in their trailing radio antennae and did not hear the recall message, though air crews had been told to turn away to secondary targets if they saw red flares.

The antiaircraft fire was fierce, and most of the aircraft failed to see the signals. By the time the bombing started, even the German commanding general was firing a signal pistol. In one Heinkel a *Gruppe* commander spotted a red light after he had let his bombs go. By quick action, he sent a radio message to the other Heinkels behind him. Of 100 aircraft in the attack, 43 turned away and bombed alternative targets. The rest put their high-explosive bombs down close to the northern bridgehead. There were no incendiaries in the bomb loads.

Usually high explosive does not start fires to any great extent, but a margarine warehouse caught fire and the burning fat spread the flames. The water mains were empty and Rotterdam had only a part-time fire brigade using antiquated two-wheel hand pumps. This citizen fire brigade, which had successfully handled domestic outbreaks, was not suited for fires of this size and was not properly equipped to pump water from the river. The fire destroyed 1.1 square miles of central

Rotterdam, 78,000 people were made homeless, and 980 died. Rumors about the bombing spread through the country, culminating in an official announcement that 30,000 died in a "fiendish assault." Within six hours of the attack, the Dutch supreme commander announced the surrender of his army virtually intact. German fire equipment was brought from as far away as the Ruhr before the flames were completely extinguished.

There is no doubt that the bombing of Rotterdam was a result of the hurry-up policy. There was pressure from the top to conclude the fighting in the Netherlands so that the armor and the motorized infantry could be pushed into the fighting farther south. There is nothing, however, to support the allegation that the city was bombed on the explicit orders of Hitler or Göring. The bombing was accurate and centered on the military defenders at the bridgehead. It was not contrary to the conventions of war. But for a great and gracious city that had lived at peace with its neighbors for centuries, Rotterdam paid a high price for the German redeployment.

2. The Attack on Belgium

While the northernmost panzer division struck at Rotterdam, the two panzer divisions allotted to the Sixth Army were cutting across the narrow strip of Holland that dangles between Germany and Belgium. These divisions of General Erich Hoepner's XVI Panzerkorps were heading for the pleasant town of Maastricht, for this junction of road, river, and canal is one of the strategic prizes of this region. Here were the roads to Brussels and Antwerp and this is where the Albert Canal met the river Maas.

It was the river Maas that 9.Pz.Div crossed at Gennep on 10 May to invade the Netherlands and recrossed at the Moerdijk bridges on the way to Rotterdam. It was this same river—its name now the Meuse—that the southernmost panzer divisions were to cross at Sedan and others at Monthermé and Dinant.

Only at Maastricht does the river link up with a complex of canals and roads. And only here, on the Belgian border, was the water defended by what, in 1940, was regarded as the most formidable of modern fortesses.

The fort of Eben Emael, built in 1932 to stem the German advance of 1914, was completed largely by German subcontractors. It is shaped like a wedge of pie, with a radius of 990 yards and a width of 770 yards. Along one side of it runs the Albert Canal, which also marks Belgium's frontier with Holland. Cutting the canal left a sheer rampart along the water. Into this hill were built tunnels and air shafts, with casemates and cupolas. Eight machine guns were its only defense against air attack.

If this segment of pie had been sitting on an empty plate, it would have commanded all the surrounding landscape, but too much of the complete "pie" of surrounding landscape remains. To the southwest, the roof of the fort is level with the adjoining fields and defense depends on a 7-yard-deep antitank ditch. On the other side of the canal the land was originally level with the fortress top. (I use the past tense, because the land is at the time of writing being changed by a new building project.) The fort still remains there, behind notices forbidding trespassing. It is a spooky place, the howling of guard dogs echoing in the underground tunnels. The Belgian Army energetically guards this scene of humiliation, but the intrepid trespasser will find gun positions overgrown with weeds and the fortress top under the plow of a farmer who has found a way over the "antitank ditch."

Eben Emael was never the obstacle that the Belgians thought it was and that the map makes it appear. It did not command the surrounding landscape. It did not even properly command the neighboring bridges over the canal, nor even Maastricht town.

Assaulting Eben Emael and the nearby bridges by means of glider troops was Hitler's idea. The men had been trained on Czech fortifications in the newly acquired Sudetenland, and on Polish installations too. Perhaps because the idea was Hitler's, training was intensive. Secrecy was so rigidly enforced that the men of "Assault Detachment Koch" did not learn each other's names until after the attack. During training two men were sentenced to death for trifling lapses in security.

On 11 May the gliders were towed behind Junkers Ju 52 transport aircraft. A glider could be landed more precisely than parachute troops; an experienced pilot could land in a circle 44 yards across. Furthermore, the towing ropes could be disconnected well before the target was reached so that the approach was completely silent. However, tests showed that gliders should not be used in poor visibility. The earliest possible safe landing would be at sunrise minus thirty minutes. Because of Hitler's personal interest in this project, the entire German assault in the West was delayed from 3 A.M. to sunrise minus thirty (5:30 A.M.).

To capture the Albert Canal bridges nearby, paratroops of the 1. Parachute Regiment were used, but for the fort itself the men were the most highly trained of any soldiers in the battle. They were

Fallschirm-Pioniere, combat engineers trained to be part of the paratroop force. In this case, however, they were transported in gliders piloted by specially chosen men with prewar experience. There were plenty of them, for glider clubs had been supported by the German government in lieu of the air force that was forbidden by the peace treaty. One of the glider pilots used the unmistakable shape of the water junction to find the fort. They landed on its roof with commend-

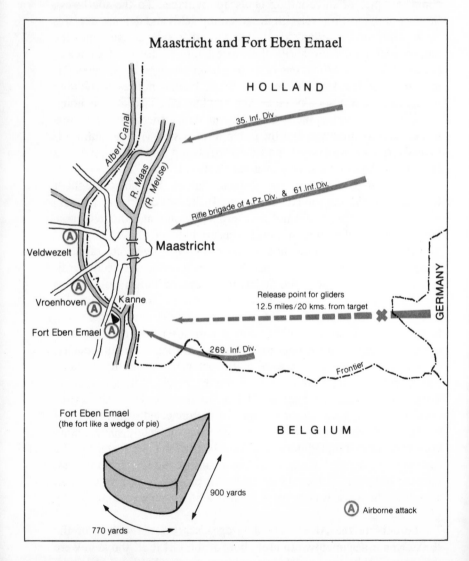

Maastricht and Fort Eben Emael

HOLLAND

35. Inf. Div.

Albert Canal

R. Maas (R. Meuse)

Rifle brigade of 4. Pz. Div. & 61. Inf. Div.

Maastricht

Veldwezelt

Vroenhoven   Kanne

Fort Eben Emael

Release point for gliders
12.5 miles / 20 kms. from target

GERMANY

269. Inf. Div.

Frontier

Fort Eben Emael
(the fort like a wedge of pie)

BELGIUM

900 yards

770 yards

Ⓐ Airborne attack

MAP 14

able accuracy. Knowing that every minute counted, German troops fought hard to cripple the rooftop gun emplacements and periscopes before the Belgian defenders realized that war had begun. For the first time in war, the "hollow charge" was used.

The theory of hollow charges had been known for many years. It was not an invention so much as a discovery made by mining engineers who noticed that the brand name, incised into blocks of explosives, could sometimes be seen marked upon the rock face where it exploded. It was soon found that deeper incisions in the explosive could direct a "jet" of force, and if a liner of steel was inside the hollow part, it melted to become a jet of molten metal that enabled a 110-pound charge to penetrate 9 inches of high-quality steel. One can compare the difference between a bullet thrown into an open fire and its resulting pop with the force of a bullet directed down the barrel of a gun.

The obsessive secrecy that surrounded all the training included smoke screens, high walls, total isolation of the men, even to the extent of not allowing them to see the effect of the hollow charge on steel. It is safe to assume that without the development of the hollow-charge weapon there would have been no glider attack on the Eben Emael fort.

In view of all the warnings that the Belgians had had about an intended German invasion, it is surprising that the army had not even put mines or barbed wire across the fort. The garrison had never had infantry training and there were no trenches round the casemates.

The gun ports and any other openings were attacked with flamethrowers. Then the terrified Belgians waited while the attackers fixed charges to the steel cupolas, to the gun slots of the casemates, and even in the barrels of the big guns. More explosive was thrown into the ventilating system, and finally some 110-pound charges were dropped down the staircase shafts to explode with truly terrible crashes that shook the whole fortress.

The glider attacks upon the Albert Canal bridges nearby were successful enough to preserve a route for the invaders. The assault upon the fortress was a more limited victory. Although the Germans got into the entrances of the fort and the upper galleries, they did not take possession of it because they in turn were attacked by artillery fire and Belgian infantry. But the glider-borne Fallschirm-Pioniere had rendered the fortress completely ineffective until more combat engineers of Reichenau's Sixth Army had advanced to join them.

Fears of the unknown, the fact that the attack began long before the Germans declared war, and the claustrophobia that is always present among men underground all contributed to the German success.

But had the Belgian garrison, about 750 men, come out of the fort, there is little doubt that they could have overcome the eighty-five Germans on the roof. Whether this would have held up the westward advance is more doubtful.

Hitler's scheme to disable the fort dated from the time when the main German effort was to be behind Bock's Army Group B. Manstein's plan reduced the importance of the Eben Emael attack to no more than a dramatic sideshow. But certainly the fall of the fort was a great psychological blow to the whole Belgian nation and possibly contributed to the Belgian decision to capitulate.

When the shooting ended, Hitler was photographed with the men who had won medals at Eben Emael. The brawny Pioniere wore battle smocks and the special paratroop helmets instead of the *Waffenrock* parade uniforms that most newly decorated soldiers drew from stores before an audience with the Führer. Goebbels's propaganda did nothing to deny the rumors about a secret new gas that had put the defenders of Eben Emael to sleep while the fort was captured. In Belgium there began stories about German immigrant workers who stayed in the caves where endive was grown until the moment came to take the fort by means of secret passages. This story can still be heard in local bars when the good Belgian beer is flowing. It is published every few years by excited writers who believe they have found the true secret of Belgium's fall.

The attack on the fort was born of the same static warfare mentality that transfixed the men who built it. The invaders could have moved past it with no great danger or delay. Blitzkrieg would conquer or die long before barge traffic on the canal could affect the fortunes of either side. The roads out of Maastricht to Brussels and Antwerp were important only insofar as they attracted attention away from the vital thrust at Sedan. Had such forts been used to house powerful fighting units that threatened to sally out and menace the German communications, they would have been a real obstacle. But in 1940 the fortress and defense works of Europe were manned by so-called fortress divisions. It was a clever title for troops not young enough or fit enough to fight, drill, or march along with the first-line infantry. It was a way of describing a unit without heavy infantry weapons, antiaircraft guns, or any transport, locked up in a concrete prison with some antiquated siege artillery.

In Brussels, at 8:30 on the morning of 10 May 1940—some three hours after the invasion had begun—the German ambassador went to see the Belgian Foreign Minister and began reading aloud: "I am instructed by the government of the German Reich to make the following declaration: in order to forestall the invasion of Belgium, Holland, and Luxembourg, for which Great Britain and France have been making preparations clearly aimed at Germany . . ."

The Belgian Foreign Minister interrupted him. "Hand me the document," he said. "I should like to spare you so painful a task."

3. Army Group A: Rundstedt's Attack

Thus armored spearheads of Bock's Army Group B were slicing into Holland and Belgium exactly as planned. And, as anticipated by the German planners, the Anglo-French armies were hurrying north to meet them. But the success or failure of Manstein's plan would depend on what happened to the much larger and better equipped armored forces—and the motorized infantry supporting them—of Rundstedt's Army Group A.

Guderian had told Hitler that his panzer corps could advance through the Ardennes Forest, a region without railways or any wide roads, but he well knew the difficulties involved. Now Rundstedt's Army Group was about to find out just how difficult it was to be.

The first stage of the Panzergruppe Kleist's advance, which began 10 May, was more a matter of traffic control than of fighting. The roads they used in Luxembourg and the Ardennes were narrow twisting lanes, through dense woods, between steep slopes and over humpbacked bridges. The area is deeply cut by streams which are at some places unfordable. A breakdown of one large vehicle would have been enough to bring the invasion to a halt.

Ahead of the reconnaissance armored cars came "tourists" in civilian clothes. They were passed through the Luxembourg frontier by unsuspecting guards. Actually the civilians were soldiers of the Brandenburger battalion trained to spot and disconnect demolition devices placed on bridges and in narrow cuttings. Combat engineers came close behind to remove more complex obstacles. Guderian's 1.Pz.Div crossed Luxembourg without opposition until, that evening of the first day, they reached the roadblocks and minefields that marked the Belgian border, where they worked all night to clear the obstructions.

A detachment of the Grossdeutschland Regiment had been landed by twenty-five Fieseler Fi 156 Storch light aircraft at Esch-sur-Alzette on the Franco-Luxembourg border. This curious idea of Göring's was intended as a way of demoralizing and confusing the defense, but the

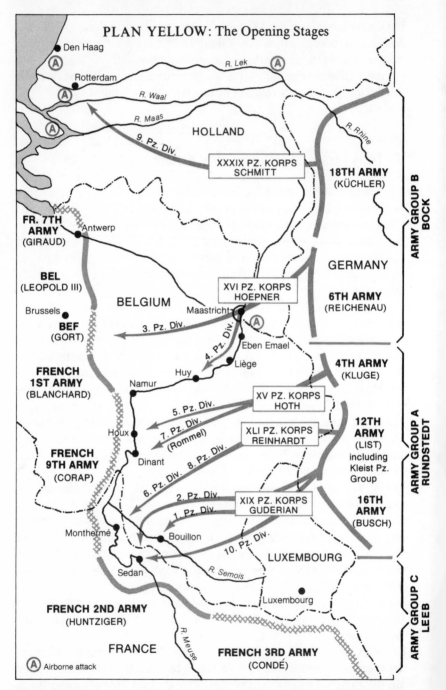

PLAN YELLOW: The Opening Stages

Den Haag

R. Lek

Rotterdam

R. Waal

R. Maas

HOLLAND

9. Pz. Div.

XXXIX PZ. KORPS
SCHMITT

R. Rhine

18TH ARMY
(KÜCHLER)

ARMY GROUP B BOCK

FR. 7TH
ARMY
(GIRAUD)

Antwerp

BEL
(LEOPOLD III)

BELGIUM

Brussels

BEF
(GORT)

GERMANY

XVI PZ. KORPS
HOEPNER

Maastricht

6TH ARMY
(REICHENAU)

3. Pz. Div.

4. Pz. Div.

Eben Emael

FRENCH
1ST ARMY
(BLANCHARD)

Huy

Namur

Liège

4TH ARMY
(KLUGE)

5. Pz. Div.

XV PZ. KORPS
HOTH

7. Pz. Div.
(Rommel)

Houx

FRENCH
9TH ARMY
(CORAP)

Dinant

XLI PZ. KORPS
REINHARDT

12TH
ARMY
(LIST)
including
Kleist Pz.
Group

ARMY GROUP A RUNDSTEDT

6. Pz. Div. 8. Pz. Div.

2. Pz. Div.

1. Pz. Div.

XIX PZ. KORPS
GUDERIAN

16TH
ARMY
(BUSCH)

Monthermé

Bouillon

10. Pz. Div.

LUXEMBOURG

Sedan

R. Semois

Luxembourg

ARMY GROUP C LEEB

FRENCH 2ND ARMY
(HUNTZIGER)

R. Meuse

FRANCE

FRENCH 3RD ARMY
(CONDÉ)

Ⓐ Airborne attack

MAP 15

Belgian defense line was farther to the west and these airborne soldiers had little to do except wait for Guderian's tanks. Another such operation, on a larger scale, in the Belgian Ardennes was similarly futile.

On the morning of 11 May Guderian's armor moved across the southern tip of Belgium. Units of the Belgian *Chasseurs Ardennais* and motorized French infantry were unable to slow the advance.

More serious than this skirmish with the French and Belgians were the consequences of an order given by General Ewald von Kleist, who had been given command of Guderian's XIX Panzerkorps as well as Rienhardt's XLI Panzerkorps and the motorized infantry following them. Kleist had been appointed to this job largely because the High Command calculated that his natural caution would provide a counterweight to what they thought of as Guderian's impetuosity. Now Kleist gave an example of the caution that had secured for him his job.

Guderian was ordered to put his 10.Pz.Div along his left flank to guard against attacks by the French. To make room for it, Guderian had to move the axis of 1.Pz.Div slightly northward just as the division was about to cross the river Semois. It was a complicated change to make at such a time. As might have been expected, the move tangled it into the advance route of 2.Pz.Div on the right, whose units in turn became mixed with those of Reinhardt's 6.Pz.Div. It might have been enough to cripple the entire invasion had the Allied air forces attacked the traffic jams, but that did not happen and slowly the vehicles started moving again.

The Germans had chosen their moment well. In that first week of May, General Gamelin had restored normal leave to the French Army and General Gaston Billotte told his corps commanders not to worry about shortages of weapons because "nothing will happen before 1941." The place of attack was also a surprise. The French command were stunned to hear that German tanks were rolling through the "impassable" Ardennes Forest. At first they convinced themselves that it was a small diversionary force and that the main attack was the one they had sent their armies to fight up in the north. But by the following day—11 May—Gamelin began to realize that here, in the region of the Ardennes, was the Schwerpunkt of the German assault.

Even so, the French command did not panic. They calculated the German advance in terms of French logistic achievement. The Germans would have to halt at the river Meuse. There they would regroup, bring up the artillery, and prepare for the river crossing. Gamelin ordered eleven French divisions to move to aid the threatened sector. He gave them top railway priority. It meant that the first elements of French support would arrive at the Meuse on 14 May, the last of them by 21 May. But by 13 May, the invaders, using road transport, were already at the Meuse and preparing to cross.

It was soon apparent that the Germans, notably Guderian and Rundstedt, were not keeping to the normal methods of war or logistics. Outrunning the infantry of General Wilhelm List's Twelfth Army, Guderian's spearheads were moving forward as fast as they could go. Rolling through villages, smiling tank men waved to amazed civilians from open turrets.

Each division transported its own fuel, ammunition, and food. Army supply services were used only in emergencies. Each division had, in addition, a pool of mechanics and spare tanks complete with fresh crews. After the breakthrough, the Germans carried three days' rations with them. Sometimes they even fueled their armor and transports by breaking the locks off roadside filling station pumps. Teams of mechanics pressed enemy civilian trucks or transport into service if they could be put into working order or plundered them for spare parts. Such measures enabled the supply services to devote their maximum efforts to ammunition replenishment. Air supply was not needed.

German hopes, and French hopes too, centered on the Meuse. The river provided a natural barrier, its defiles and difficulties artfully utilized by defense works that had been built along it. All through their training and their planning the Germans thought of the Meuse crossing as the most hazardous moment. Once the German spearheads were over the river and through the defense works on the west bank it was clear to the German planners—although not so apparent to the Allied commanders—that only a stroke of military genius could save the Allied armies to the north of the attack line. No evidence of genius emerged.

The Panzer Divisions Reach the River Meuse

On 15 March in the year 1813, the Emperor Napoleon had sent a dispatch to Eugene, his stepson. It contained advice about defending the line of a river. He wrote: "Nothing is more dangerous than seriously to attempt to defend a river by holding the bank opposed to the enemy; for directly he forces a crossing, as he always succeeds in doing, he finds his adversary extended in a thin defensive order, and, therefore, incapable of concentrating his forces."

Rommel in Dinant Sector

The first of Rundstedt's armored columns to reach the Meuse was the one that did not go through that complex of forests that is generally called the Ardennes. The 7.Pz.Div commanded by General Rommel skirted the forest's northern edge.

The 7.Pz.Div had been what the German tank forces called a "light division," but this experiment had proved unsuccessful. Now Czech tanks had been added to the division to make it up to normal Panzer-division configuration. In fact its strength in the better tanks made it one of the most powerful tank divisions on the field. Not only was the division thus re-formed, but its commander, who was newly appointed, had never before commanded a tank unit.

At the age of forty-eight, Rommel had had to learn the complexities of his new command in scarcely three months. Now he was to be put to the test. Rommel was an outsider, lacking the sort of military ante-cedents that so many of the Prussian generals enjoyed and lacking the staff training and staff experience that might have compensated for his being the son of a schoolmaster.

Rommel's devotion to Hitler and his enthusiasm for the Nazis made his fellow generals uneasy. Having heard the Führer flay his senior commanders on 23 November, Rommel noted that it was no more than they deserved. Even more disturbing for his fellow generals was Rommel's publicity seeking. From his neck there usually hung a Leica camera given to him by Josef Goebbels, the Minister of Propaganda. Often the camera was handed to a subordinate so that Rommel could be included in the picture. Soon his photographs would be used to portray blitzkrieg from the victors' point of view and make Rommel the most famous general in Germany. Eventually he would become the most famous general in the world.

Whitsunday, 12 May

Late in the afternoon of Whitsunday, motorcyclists, at the very front of Rommel's division, reached the Meuse near Dinant. The Dinant bridge had already been blown up and so had the railway bridge near Houx. The next bridge, at Yvoir, 2 miles north, was destroyed by a Belgian officer who was killed doing it. He exploded the charge as a German tank was on the bridge. Tank, bridge, and men fell into the river.

The men of Rommel's motorcycle battalion moved along the riverbank and found a weir at Houx. It was then an ancient one, narrow and made of stone but strong enough to support the soldiers. They went across the weir to a small wooded island and found it unoccupied, but when they attempted to cross the next weir they came under fire from men of the French 66th Regiment who were on the west bank of the river. The Frenchmen had been ordered to guard the riverbank until reinforcements arrived. The Germans waited. Being motorcycle troops they had no heavy equipment and no heavy weapons other than the air-cooled MG 34 machine guns.

This valley of the Meuse north of Dinant could become a trap for the advancing Germans. They looked across the river to the steep cliffs on the other side. That cliff top—the heights of Wastia—commanded the whole line of the river. Beyond it the countryside rolled gently away to the next major objective at Philippeville.

After dark the motorcyclists made another attempt to get from Houx island to the other bank. Now things were easier. French reinforcements had arrived but were not as tenacious as the men they had relieved. Instead of coming right down to the riverbank, they contented themselves with firing from the hillside. By the small hours of Monday morning some of the Germans were on the far bank of the Meuse. Carefully they made their way uphill through the woodland to where French infantry of the 39th Regiment were positioned.

Surprised in the darkness, the French withdrew after a short fight. The Germans positioned the only heavy weapons they had—machine guns—and waited for the dawn of 13 May.

And so the first Germans were across the Meuse. The French Ninth Army under General Corap had failed to hold the line of the Meuse as the French High Command believed it would hold it. Corap was a sixty-two-year-old veteran of France's colonial wars in North Africa. Now his Ninth Army was spread more thinly than any other army along the front. His seven divisions, including two in reserve, were attempting to hold 75 miles of front at a time when military textbooks decreed one division was needed to defend just over 6 miles. Those textbooks were not written by men who anticipated the impact of blitzkrieg. Nor did the textbooks take into account the long march that so many men of Ninth Army had had to make from the Franco-Belgian border. Some French soldiers had marched 75 miles immediately before going into action. Only one of the Ninth Army's divisions was motorized. Most of them were short of transport and the fortress division was not entitled to any. Apart from the motorized division, the entire army was made up of reservists. There were shortages of antitank guns; two divisions had none at all. The army was similarly short of anti-aircraft guns.

The French policy of spreading artillery and tanks in small units throughout the army had resulted here in leaving only a company of tanks for an attack against the motorcyclists holding the west bank. They were to attack the Germans the next morning—13 May—at 8 A.M.

Monday, 13 May, Dinant

But Rommel was not working office hours. He did not wait until 8 A.M. As dawn broke, his infantry of the 6. Rifle Regiment were trying to force a crossing at Bouvignes and getting badly shot up by French artillery and small-arms fire as fast as they put their inflatable boats into the river. They persevered in the face of casualties. By the time Rommel himself arrived at the riverbank, one company was already across.

Noting the absence of smoke that would screen his men from the enemy fire, Rommel ordered some houses to be set ablaze so that smoke would pour down the valley. The crossing attempts continued. Rommel ordered tanks and artillery support and then went back for a meeting with Kluge, the commander of the Fourth Army, and with his panzer corps commander, Hoth, both of whom had arrived at Rommel's HQ to watch the progress of the battle.

Both Kluge and Hoth were at fault for requiring Rommel's presence at headquarters. In such critical circumstances the divisional commander must be left to get on with his job or the higher ranks should go to the place where he is.

By the time Rommel had returned to Dinant, the crossing attempt had come to a complete standstill. Punctured rubber boats lined both sides of the river, and his officers had ceased to urge their men out from the cover behind which they sheltered from fierce French fire.

Partly due to the effect that the presence of the divisional commander had upon the men, and more especially upon the junior officers who led them, a few Germans managed to get across the river.

The cumbrous communications system of the French Army was already playing a part in the battle. The telephone was subject to delays and even the corps commanders had no clear picture of what was happening. The French counterattack, planned for 8 A.M. that morning, was canceled. At the battlefront it became apparent that only a sharp riposte would dislodge the Germans, for although they had no tanks or artillery across the river, infantry were filtering along the bank. By 10 A.M. Bouvignes was in German hands. At noon the German foothold was about 3 miles wide and 2 miles deep. By now the artillery support that Rommel had requested was beginning to arrive. So were some of the PzKw IV tanks, with 7.5 cm guns, that could fire back at the French positions.

Rommel's lengthy and frequent visits to the front enabled him to make instant decisions about tactics, forcing subordinate commanders to show similar energy and initiative with their units and inspiring lower ranks to extraordinary feats. His operations staff remained in the rear, and he kept in contact with them by means of radio and twice-daily conferences with his IA, the operations officer. Said one German officer:

> In all the war in France from frontier to Channel, Rommel never saw his Chief of Staff personally. Never! He only had with him, next to the tank of my regimental commander, two armoured reconnaissance cars with long-range radio. The one car was in contact with all the troops of his own division. The other car was for contact with the corps, the Army and often to the air force.*

Rommel was criticized by his seniors for spending too much time at the front, but he had never commanded a panzer division before and needed to see the problems of the advance at close hand.

Now Rommel went even further. He took command of the second battalion of his 7. Rifle Regiment, urging them forward to get their boats into the water. Climbing into one of the boats, he personally led the assault on the far bank.

It was while Rommel was on the west bank of the Meuse that some French tanks were sighted. Without tanks or antitank guns, the Germans had no alternative but to engage them with small-arms fire. Rommel ordered even flare pistols to be fired at them. Perhaps believing the flares to be the sighting rounds for an artillery battery, the French tanks moved away.

A cable ferry had been built under covering fire provided by the guns of the PzKw IV tanks. The engineers moved twenty antitank guns to the west bank by noon of 13 May. Rommel, having returned from the far bank, told his engineers to convert the 8-ton pontoon into a 16-ton unit to ferry light tanks and armored cars across. The very first trip took Rommel himself across the Meuse for a second time, together

---

* Taken from the transcript of a lecture (now in the Imperial War Museum, London) given in 1970 by Colonel Hans-Ulrich Schroeder to British officers during a reconstruction of the battle.

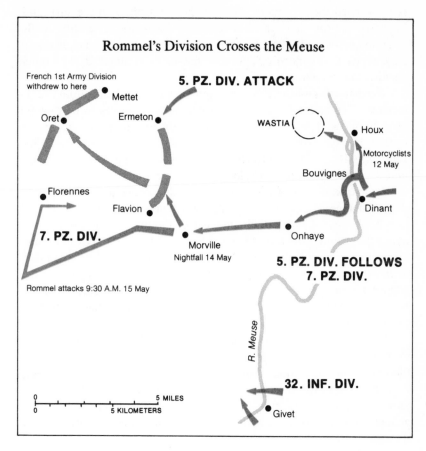

Rommel's Division Crosses the Meuse

French 1st Army Division withdrew to here

Mettet

Oret

Ermeton

5. PZ. DIV. ATTACK

WASTIA

Houx

Motorcyclists 12 May

Bouvignes

Florennes

Flavion

Dinant

7. PZ. DIV.

Onhaye

Morville
Nightfall 14 May

5. PZ. DIV. FOLLOWS
7. PZ. DIV.

Rommel attacks 9:30 A.M. 15 May

R. Meuse

32. INF. DIV.

0   5 MILES
0   5 KILOMETERS

Givet

MAP 16

with his eight-wheel armored car. But it was a slow business, for here the river was 120 yards wide, twice the width of the river at Guderian's Sedan sector.

The cable ferry was under constant fire and at least one tank went to the bottom of the river. When darkness fell, the engineers were able to work with less interference, and by dawn of the next day, 14 May, Rommel had moved fifteen tanks to the west side of the river. Local people told me that access ramps at the marble quarry were used to get the tanks up to the heights by the quickest possible route. And several local people remembered seeing the tank that had toppled into the water.

It was the Germans who had got up to the heights of Wastia that most worried the defenders. This plateau controlled all the surrounding terrain. From here there was a view down the steep cliffs to the river and across to the eastern bank, along which the German attackers were arrayed. The morning operation having been canceled, the French decided that a counterattack would begin at 1 P.M.

German triumphs in this campaign have caused their military recklessness to be hailed as genius, their dangerous gambles to be thought of as miracles. The great columns of armor and transport, trailing as frail as threads across the French rear, were in theory protected by the Luftwaffe. But in fact the Luftwaffe commanders interpreted their role in as foolhardy a manner as did the panzer generals.

To overwhelm the enemy air forces and to concentrate dive bombers and fighters enough to pulverize the defenders, it had been decided to concentrate the Luftwaffe in one sector at a time. As the French prepared the counterattack on the heights of Wastia, the bulk of German air power was over Sedan far to the south. But such was the inadequacy of the French Air Force that the small covering force assigned to the Dinant sector on 13 May dive-bombed the French infantry and the reconnaissance with enough vigor to delay the counterattack a further five hours to 6 P.M.

Motorized infantry and tanks to the north of Wastia were ordered to dislodge the Germans from those heights, but before they moved, the operation was retimed for the following day, 14 May. However, French tanks to the south of the Germans did go into battle. As twilight came, French armor attacked the German motorcyclists and gained possession of the high ground that dominated the bridgehead, the river, and the crossing places.

But the French supporting infantry failed to arrive, and without them the tanks could not properly consolidate their gains. After dark the tank crews fell prey to the fears that all unprotected tank forces have at night in the presence of enemy infantry. So the French tanks withdrew to their starting place and let the Germans reoccupy the vitally important high ground.

The bridging unit of Rommel's division was now provided with a perfect opportunity to start work, except that all its bridging tackle had already been used on the first day of the advance. With that ruthlessness he was already displaying in battle, and secure in the personal support of Hitler, Rommel simply helped himself to the bridging tackle of his neighboring 5.Pz.Div. He brushed aside protests from the commander of that division, General Max von Hartlieb, and said that he was going to make sure that his division was first across the Meuse.

Tuesday, 14 May, Dinant

By dawn, Rommel's bridge was across the Meuse at the small village of Bouvignes. Several tanks had already been rafted across the river, but now a continuous column of tanks, armored cars, and artillery was moving westward. The 5.Pz.Div had no alternative but to wait at the Meuse while Rommel's men crossed. This provided Rommel with an opportunity to take command of some of the 5.Pz.Div heavier tanks and add them to his own tank forces. By now protests from the 5.Pz.Div commander were arriving at Berlin, but little could be done about it. With amazing arrogance, Rommel complained at the way in which his neighboring armored division failed to keep up with his own advance.

These tanks did not move up to the heights of Wastia where, since dawn, the French had been counterattacking the German positions. Neither did the armor swing round to dislodge the French holding the river line farther south. Instead, the tanks moved directly on to attack Onhaye village, the key to the westward advance.

Rommel's determination to be in the forefront of the battle was even more evident. He left his armored signals vehicle and took command of a PzKw III. About thirty tanks were across the river by the time Rommel responded to a call for help from German forces attacking Onhaye. Rommel's tank was hit twice and Rommel was cut by a splinter from the shattered glass of the periscope. The driver went full speed for the nearest cover, crashed through the bushes, and plunged down a steep slope on the far side. The tank ended up in full sight of the enemy, tilted too steeply to bring the gun to bear. At that moment a tank commander told Rommel over the radio that his arm had been shot off, the tank ahead of Rommel's was also hit, and so was the armored signals vehicle following behind. Rommel abandoned the tank. It was a serious situation, and it confirmed Rommel's theory that his division should open fire at woodland and villages as a way of discovering whether enemy guns or infantry were there. It was sound tactical thinking, but it inevitably increased the number of civilian casualties.

Rommel was particularly fond of tricks and ruses which he claimed were likely to bring success with fewer casualties on both sides. However, it seems unfortunate that Rommel's instruction that his men should open fire without discovering whether enemy forces were present came at a time when his favorite trick was to have his tank crews wave white flags. One oncoming convoy of trucks encountered by his tanks was shot to pieces by the time is was discovered that they were in fact ambulances.

Rommel's advance on Tuesday went far beyond Onhaye. It was his success, together with news of other German bridgeheads, which persuaded the French High Command to abandon the defense line of the river Meuse at this place and move back as far as the railway line behind Philippeville. The French generals were beginning to believe reports that thousands of German tanks were west of the Meuse, and their fears were fomented by the energetic way that Rommel put into the fight 100 per cent of his available resources. So far Rommel had encountered only the tanks that the French had thinly distributed among the infantry, but by the evening of 14 May, the French 1st Armored Division, which had begun moving its tracked vehicles three days earlier, was assembling them, together with the wheeled vehicles, just a few minutes' walk from where Rommel's vanguard were resting and refueling.

Reinhardt Reaches the Meuse at Monthermé

If some of Rommel's success was due to the way in which his roads to the Meuse skirted the northern edge of the Ardennes Forest, then some of Reinhardt's troubles were due to the route right through the heart of it. Here too there was the added complication that the forest continued ahead of him far to the west of the river Meuse.

Reinhardt's approach roads could not be compared with the wide flat roads which Hoth's XV Panzerkorps had used. Here the roads were narrow and meandering as they wound their way over steep wooded hills. At Monthermé the forest dropped steeply down to where the Meuse looped around a piece of land that the Germans came to call "the breadroll." There was time enough to find names for local landmarks, for here the Germans ran into fierce resistance and were halted for three days. The Luftwaffe failed to appear and the French 102nd Fortress Division—one of the few regular army divisions in Corap's Ninth Army—met every attempt to force a way over the partly destroyed bridge with devastating fire from the hillsides.

At 4 P.M. on 13 May, riflemen of the 6.Pz.Div got across the river at the Place de la Mairie in Monthermé by using inflatable boats. The metal girder bridge had fallen into the shallow river, and soon men began to scramble over that too. After dark, inflatable boats and wooden planks were lashed together and strapped to the buckled girders, enabling infantry to cross without getting their feet wet.

Overlooked on all sides, the Germans at the river came under fierce fire from the machine guns of French colonial troops, who fought for France with more determination than most other units. German infantry—brainwashed with Nazi stories of racial superiority—found this situation an unpleasant surprise. No matter how hard they tried, they could not get a foothold in Bois de Roma at the base of the peninsula, and until they did, there could be no chance of getting tanks across the Meuse.

The difficulties that the planners had foreseen for Reinhardt's forces in this hilly wooded terrain had persuaded them to assign only one panzer division to this crossing. Reinhardt's other armored division—8.Pz.Div—was to cross farther south at Nouzonville.

The traffic jams on these approach roads (resulting from Kleist's order that Guderian change the axis of his attack) had already caused great confusion. Very little of 8.Pz.Div had got to the Meuse at Nouzonville, and neither of its two motorized divisions was yet there. Instead, an infantry division was trying to make the crossing assisted by a few tanks from 8.Pz.Div. The inadequacy of the attacking force, and the fierce resistance of the French along the opposite riverbank, made the task almost impossible.

Stuck at both his crossing places, Reinhardt was advised by his subordinates to reinforce the 6.Pz.Div bridgehead for a strong southward thrust that would threaten the French rear at Nouzonville. Reinhardt refused. He knew that his success or failure would be measured by movement westward. He wanted 6.Pz.Div kept intact and concentrated for a breakout, which would by-pass the Nouzonville defenders and leave them to wither away.*

Meanwhile, Reinhardt's advance forces in the bridgehead and approach road were suffering heavy casualties, while his *Feldgendarmerie* (Military Police) units tried to untangle miles of traffic jams.

Guderian at Sedan: The Most Vital Attack

In the southern part of the Ardennes, the roads were not only narrow, meandering, and steep, but few in number. The supply columns for

---

* Some of these details are taken from correspondence (now lodged in the Imperial War Museum, London) between Reinhardt, Halder, and the head of Army Archives when, later in the war, a bitter argument arose about whether Reinhardt's corps had only been able to cross the Meuse because of the crossing made beforehand by III Armeekorps at Nouzonville and Mézières. The dispute became more and more complex because, on paper, Reinhardt's corps had been made subordinate to III Armeekorps (Haasegruppe) for a short time during the battle. The bridge at Montcy was discovered and captured intact, which led to more arguments about the crossing.

Guderian's 2.Pz.Div were already entangled with those of Reinhardt's supply units on 12 May, and the engineers and artillery that Guderian desperately needed for his crossing at Sedan were held up somewhere on the road. Furthermore, 2.Pz.Div itself had got so entangled crossing the river Semois that it had to be disentangled by an officer in a light aircraft overhead. Indeed, so cramped were vehicular movements on these forest roads that the infantry moved through the woods in order to keep the roads as clear as possible for wheeled and tracked units.

It was not difficult for the French to guess that the Germans would swing south to strike at Sedan, even if for no better reason than that, in 1870, the French Army had here suffered the greatest defeat of modern times—and at German hands.

Gamelin, the French Commander in Chief, had ordered that the town of Sedan must be defended at all costs. In fact it was not defended at all. The fortress regiment stationed there simply disappeared long before the panzer columns reached the town.

If the town was difficult to defend, even more so was the adjacent loop of water, short-circuited at its neck. On the other hand, by withdrawing from the town and this "island" the French could use the Meuse as a natural defense line, for the land rose along the south bank; the German-held northern bank was open, flat, and in places marshy.

To the west of the town the French 55th Infantry Division, a B-class unit (mostly reserves), manned concrete blockhouses along the river. Like its neighbors, this division had about a quarter of its full complement of 2.5 cm antitank guns, although in storage depots at this time there were 520 such guns, enough to equip ten divisions. These were the same weapons that the French had been selling abroad by the hundred. There was a similar shortage of antiaircraft guns. However, 55th Infantry Division did have double the normal number of artillery pieces, and most of the corps artillery too, making twenty-eight guns per mile for its five-mile-wide front.

In billets behind this defense line there was another B-class infantry division, the 71st. It was less effective than the 55th. On 10 May, because of leave and sickness, 7,000 of its 17,000 men were not available to fight. Those remaining were hurried forward at the news of the German attack and squeezed between the two units already there. This led to some confusion about who manned what, but eventually it was sorted out.

This was the decisive moment for Guderian. During training, great emphasis had been given to the tactics of crossing the Meuse under fire. A section of the Moselle River, in the western Rhineland, had been chosen in order to reproduce the terrain for exercises, and Guderian's most bitter arguments with his superiors had come when they suggested a delay at the river Meuse. But the Meuse advance had gone less smoothly than he had hoped, not because of enemy action but simply because of the traffic jams. His 1.Pz.Div and 10.Pz.Div were already at the river, but 2.Pz.Div was delayed. This was one of the best-equipped divisions, as well as having with it an extra battalion of artillery which would be sorely needed for the attack.

Guderian, shaken no doubt by a narrow escape when a bomb hit his headquarters in the Hotel Panorama on the heights above Bouillon, now showed a most uncharacteristic failure of nerve. He decided to wait until his whole armored corps had arrived at the Meuse. Ironically it was Kleist—the man who had been appointed panzer group commander to limit Guderian's impetuosity—who now ordered that the attack should go ahead with all possible speed, in spite of the absence of the 2.Pz.Div and its extra artillery, and despite Guderian's cautions. In order to start the crossing attempt by 4 P.M. the following day, 13 May, Walther Nehring, Guderian's chief of staff, resorted to the use of the war-games orders, amending just the times and dates.

Monday, 13 May, Sedan

Partly because of his missing artillery, and partly because he wanted to bring maximum firepower to the front, Guderian placed his tanks and 8.8 cm flak guns to fire across the river, which, at some places, was no more than 66 yards wide. The French gun positions, deep-set into the thick concrete of the pillboxes, gave adequate protection against most bombs and plunging fire. But gunners using high-velocity missiles, with their very flat trajectory, could get lucky shots right into the emplacements. Since the success of such shooting against Polish fortifications at Nikolai, the German gunners had practiced this technique.

The Sedan sector that day was granted the major part of the Luftwaffe's resources, which was a considerable force. In spite of urgent pleas that the French air force oppose this, the defenders were told that they could expect no air support until the next day. The French army commander was not dismayed or angry. He commented that it was as well that the men had a "baptism of fire." No such baptism was to be given to the Germans. The 55th Infantry Division, defending the line of the Meuse to the west of Sedan and on the receiving end of a terrible German bombardment from all calibers of gun and relays of dive bombers, was now ordered to ration its use of shells.

Fixed-position artillery bombardment, using map references to familiar targets, was an aspect of warfare at which the French Army excelled. As Guderian closed his men to the river for the assault, French artillery observers reported concentrations of hundreds of tanks, in sight and in range. The rationing of shells remained in force, for the French commander still believed that the assault could not take place for several days as the Germans would need to concentrate more artillery.

That the Germans were short of artillery was evident to the defenders, but only slowly did they realize that the bombing plane was to be its substitute. The value of the bombing plane was still a matter of dispute among theorists, and even its staunchest advocates could not with any certainty predict the role it would play. It was not the bomber's destructive power against assigned targets which made it a decisive weapon, but rather the by-product of destroyed transport and communications that had paralyzed the Polish Army and was now about to paralyze the French chain of command. A second by-product was no less important. In keeping with German theories of frightening the enemy, Stuka bombers, their wings strengthened to withstand the strain of pulling out of a steep dive, were equipped with screaming devices on both airframes and bombs. The shrill threat of such attacks made the defenders run for cover. Men taking cover do not observe, train guns, or shoot. If they take cover often enough for the process to become continuous, they lose the will to fight altogether.

The contribution that the dive bomber made to German victory cannot be too strongly emphasized. One British officer described the effect of dive bombing on soldiers of the BEF fighting alongside the French after an attack that did no more than wound ten men and destroy three trucks: "The chaps were absolutely shattered. I think afterwards the officers and a few sergeants got up and tried to get things moving but the chaps just sat about in a complete daze, and one had to almost kick them to get them moving to the next positions . . . on this first occasion the effect was truly fantastic"*

It was to make use of this effect that Nehring, Guderian's chief of staff, suggested a technique of air attack that, while adding nothing to the bomber's destructive power, was to make a vital contribution

---

* Taken from the transcript of a lecture given by Major I. R. English, now in the Imperial War Museum, London.

to German victory. He wanted dive bombers sent in in relays, rather than in one massive onslaught, and to make diving passes over their targets even after their bombs were gone and to continue to do so until the next relay of aircraft arrived.

In air support, in firepower, and in the quality of its leadership, the German attack at Sedan was very different from the more opportunistic attacks to the north. It was this massive armored thrust that would strike deep under the Allied armies moving to the north. And, although the philosophy of blitzkrieg was the reinforcement of success, the nature of the Ardennes roads ruled out any chance of switching this attack to some lucky crossing downriver.

At Sedan, where the defenses on French soil had been better prepared, the attack was similarly detailed. The three crossing places were dictated by the terrain and German assault troops had trained on similar ground and were provided with aerial photos and excellent maps of the French defense line, detailed down to individual blockhouses. Not that those pictures could have comforted the men of 10.Pz.Div infantry and engineers who waded knee-deep through flooded meadows before reaching the edge of the river where their rubber boats could be launched, for the French on the forested hill of Marfée were ideally situated to decimate the attackers.

The 10.Pz.Div infantry on the left flank suffered heavy casualties, but the fact that they reached the French emplacements alive, captured them, and continued as far as the Marfée heights was as much a tribute to the Luftwaffe as to the assault troops. Sealed into their pillboxes like the Belgians in Fort Eben Emael, the French were vulnerable to determined infantry attack. For there is no weapon or vehicle of war that is not vulnerable to some other device or warrior. Just as the French tanks at Wastia had withdrawn rather than remain after dark without infantry support, so did the French pillboxes at Sedan require the "interval troops" to protect them. Winkling action at close range by infantry with explosives, hand grenades, and flame-throwers can knock out even the strongest emplacement, smashing the periscopes and blocking the gun slots and air intakes. Here at Sedan the "interval troops" assigned to protect the French emplacements were not in position; they were taking cover from the interminable bombing runs of the Luftwaffe.

Guderian's XIX Panzerkorps was assigned to the most vital region of the whole German invasion, and 1.Pz.Div was at the most vital sector of Guderian's attack. This division, its personnel Saxon and Thüringen, had fought well in central Poland, and for its present task

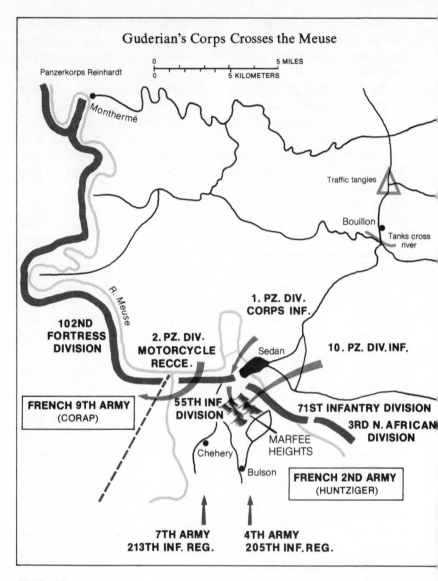

Guderian's Corps Crosses the Meuse

0 _____ 5 MILES
0 _____ 5 KILOMETERS

Panzerkorps Reinhardt

Monthermé

Traffic tangles

Bouillon

Tanks cross river

R. Meuse

1. PZ. DIV. CORPS INF.

102ND FORTRESS DIVISION

2. PZ. DIV. MOTORCYCLE RECCE.

Sedan

10. PZ. DIV. INF.

FRENCH 9TH ARMY (CORAP)

55TH INF. DIVISION

71ST INFANTRY DIVISION

3RD N. AFRICAN DIVISION

MARFEE HEIGHTS

Chehery

Bulson

FRENCH 2ND ARMY (HUNTZIGER)

7TH ARMY 213TH INF. REG.

4TH ARMY 205TH INF. REG.

MAP 17

it was reinforced with artillery battalions from the panzer divisions on either side of it as well as by the corps artillery and some extra combat Pioniere too. At the very front of the division's attack there was the most prestigious unit of the German army—Grossdeutschland.

The *Infanterie-Regiment Grossdeutschland* had until June 1939 been *Wachregiment Berlin*. This ceremonial unit supplied guards of honor in the capital and for Hitler's bodyguard, and each province in Germany sent its best soldiers to serve in it for a few months. Each company retained its regional character, and by tradition the home province provided it with the beer, sausages, and cheese of that locality. Now the regiment had been renamed and put on a permanent basis, but its prestige was retained. (The Grossdeutschland Regiment was not an SS formation and was in no way connected with the *SS-Regiment Deutschland*, one of the earliest SS field formations.)

Grossdeutschland had been given only rear-area duties during the Polish campaign. But now, its training finally completed, it was positioned at the point of the most important attack of the whole campaign in the west. They crossed the Meuse at the western edge of Sedan. Their sector was about 88 yards wide, and they advanced across open ground to Glaire village, while every weapon the Germans could find, from 2 cm flak to the howitzers of the reinforced artillery batteries, hit the French positions. The ferocity of the German assault supported the advance units as they spread out through the village of Glaire with its vegetable gardens, ramshackle tool sheds, and barns where the concrete pillboxes were hidden to the railway and beyond that to the main road.

Without a pause the infantry ran, ducked, and dodged across the flat land and across the road and finally up the green slopes beyond. By 7:30 P.M. on 13 May, infantry of Grossdeutschland were on the Marfée heights, together with infantry of 1.Pz.Div, which had followed them. As it began to get dark, they were joined by men of 10.Pz.Div, who had fought their way over the swampy land to the southeast of Sedan. It was the classic pincer tactic.

Today Glaire is still a flat area of vegetable gardens and ramshackle buildings and the rubbish dump of Sedan. The hazards of what must have seemed a long, long walk across this area to the west of Sedan are still obvious to anyone who turns off the highway and wanders down to the Meuse and along it to the big factory on the northeast bank where, that afternoon even as the first assault began, engineers were busy assembling the sections of a pontoon bridge. The flat land that endangered the infantry also exposed the bridging units to the same sort of fire. Yet almost any risk was worthwhile, for here at Glaire was the axis of the Sedan attack. It was this bridge which would carry almost the whole XIX Panzerkorps across the Meuse, as well as the motorized infantry following them.

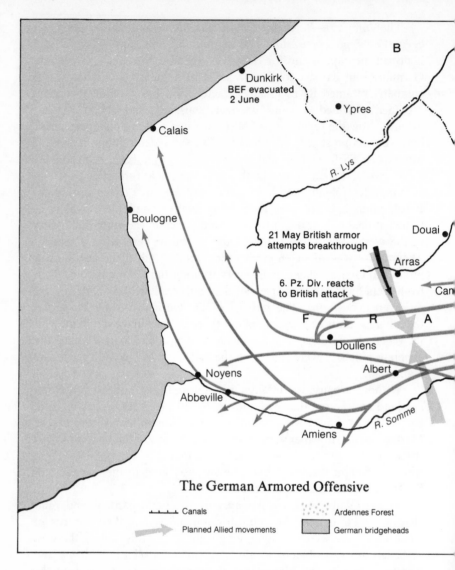

The German Armored Offensive

⊦——⊦——⊦ Canals   ∷∷∷ Ardennes Forest

→ Planned Allied movements   ▓ German bridgeheads

MAP 18

The German engineers more than fulfilled expectations: the first ferry was assembled within thirty-eight minutes. By midnight, a pontoon bridge of 16-ton capacity was across the Meuse at Glaire.

The right-hand prong of Guderian's three-division attack was led by 2.Pz.Div, Guderian's old division. It had taken part in the annexation of Austria under his command and had stayed there so long that

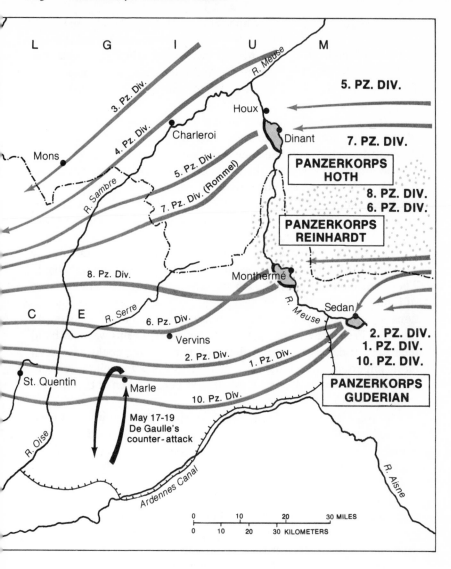

it had earned the nickname of the "Vienna Division," and by now many of its men were Austrian recruits. Deprived of its artillery and snarled up in traffic jams around Bouillon, 2.Pz.Div began arriving at its jumping-off point only as zero hour approached that afternoon of 13 May. It was sent straight into battle.

Like its neighboring assault forces, 2.Pz.Div found itself in flat exposed country, facing gun emplacements on ground that rose steeply on the south bank of the river. But 2.Pz.Div was not ordered to move toward the high ground of Marfée woods for which the other two divisions were heading. This right-hand attack was to go only to the top of the low hills that faced it and then swing due west, trying to find a way between the French 55th Infantry Division that faced them and the 102nd Fortress Division that continued the defense line of the Meuse in the northwest. For those two divisions were each part of a different French Army, and such a place of junction is always vulnerable to attack. In this case, the weakness was compounded by the fact that General Corap had put a weak division on the extreme flank of his Ninth Army, while General Charles Huntziger had put a division of reservists on the adjoining flank of his Second Army. It was a formula for disaster and 2.Pz.Div was its catalyst.

The immense effort of the Grossdeutschland and 1.Pz.Div on the central sector of this front helped the 2.Pz.Div units on the right flank. They gained a hold at a place where some of the French defenses were still unfinished. Noticing wooden scaffolding, where even the foundations had not been poured, one German soldier remarked, "Astonishing these Frenchmen! They have had now nearly twenty years to build their lines of defense . . ." For that German, nothing could have been more important than building defenses. For the French there were many other things to do, which might have been a token of their higher aspirations rather than lower ones.

As noted above, the French 55th Infantry Division was a B-class unit. Of its 450 officers only twenty were regulars. Considering how many of them were elderly civilians, they fought well against the finest soldiers Germany could muster and what Guderian had promised would be "almost the whole German air force."

During 13 May, the screaming of the Stukas, the broken communications, the low morale, and the lack of infantry protection for the blockhouses all contributed to the gains the Germans made on the south side of the river. It was at ten minutes past five in the afternoon, when the German assault had been going on for a little over an hour, that a message from 55th Infantry Division reported that they had lost contact with the infantry on their left. A gap had opened between the French Ninth and Second armies, and it was never to be closed.

Yet it was not in this gap between the French armies that the first stone was dislodged in the landslide of disaster. It was an artillery battery commander, in the village of Chaumont, who, at half past six on that fine summer's evening, reported that German tanks had got as far as the heights of Marfée. It was quite untrue, but anyone inclined to dismiss the report as hysterical had to think again when from Bulson, a little way to the south of Chaumont, an artillery colonel reported—also prematurely—to his corps artillery commander that fighting was so near his command post that he must withdraw or be encircled. The corps artillery commander—himself about 5 miles away from the fighting—decided that it would be prudent to pull back his own command post. None of these artillery officers got verification of the reports.

The 55th Infantry Division command post was just south of Bulson. Its divisional commander had just ordered a battalion to support the defenders of the Marfée heights and was beginning to reestablish communications with his neighbors, when down the road came "a wave of terrified fugitives." There were gunners and infantry, officers mixed with men, some on foot, some with transport, some insisting that they had orders to withdraw and others just running for their lives. All agreed that there were German tanks at Bulson.

This was the greatest tank victory in all the records of warfare. Several times tanks had gained a victory without firing a shot, but now they had routed an enemy without even going into action. For Guderian had not yet managed to get his tanks across the Meuse. Any tanks the panicking soldiers had seen were French tanks. It was ironic that the panic had begun among artillerymen—the primary antitank weapon—of a division that had double its normal artillery complement. And they were men of an army that had instructed them throughout their military careers that tanks had no independent value and no function but the support of infantry. The tank, like the Stuka, was more fatal to morale than to men, as neither of these weapons caused significant battlefield casualties, the tank no more than 5 per cent of them. It was the *idea* of the tank that was so effective, and that is why the lightweight PzKw I and PzKw II tanks could prove as effective on the field as the heavier models.

Faced with a torrent of soldiers hurrying from the fighting, a French general and his staff blocked the road with trucks to halt them. But the mob was not even slowed. Some did not stop until they reached Rheims, 60 miles away. And every man who fled had his story ready. Combining the pleasures of delivering bad news with a zeal for conversion, they told of tanks and Stukas by the thousand, and their numbers grew as the story was repeated.

Now even the divisional commander sought permission to move his command post to the rear. Still without any proper verification, the corps commander agreed. And so it was that the 55th Infantry Division changed from an effective fighting force to a routed mob.

Front-line infantry who doubted that the artillerymen had already fled had only to listen to the lessening of the fire from them. Officers who doubted that there was a general withdrawal had only to send a messenger to the command posts and find them abandoned.

It says a great deal for the courage and morale of France's 213th Infantry Regiment that they continued to make their way toward the front through the tidal wave of the routed 55th. Even so, the consensus of opinion about German tanks "just up the road" caused them to halt when darkness fell. And so it was with the other infantry regiment and two battalions of tanks that made up the corps reserve. All of them had been put under the 55th division commander, General Lafontaine, for the purposes of counterattack. The dawn attack which he had ordered for 14 May was to be in two prongs with tanks in front of infantry for each prong. Coming up as fast as they could were the strategic reserves: the 3rd Armored Division and the 3rd Motorized Division. The 71st Infantry Division, to the right of the routed 55th, were holding firm. A bombing attack upon the German positions was requested for that night.

In spite of the rumors, Guderian had not managed to get any tanks, artillery, or even antitank guns across the river by the time darkness fell on 13 May. The bridgehead was little more than 5 miles wide and 5 miles deep, and a small tank unit could have wiped it out with comparative ease.

It was the time factor that surprised and defeated the French. Not only did the French deploy slowly, but they did not believe that the Germans could move any faster. Even the "impassable" nature of the Ardennes was a conclusion based on the difficulties of advancing heavy artillery through that region, a factor the Germans were able to ignore by substituting bombing aircraft. And nowhere during the battle did the Germans make such good use of time, and the French squander it, as at Sedan during the night of 13/14 May.

Tuesday, 14 May, Sedan

During the hours of darkness Oberstleutnant Hermann Balck, an old friend of Guderian and commander of the 1. Rifle Regiment of 1.Pz.Div, pushed his infantry another 3 miles to the village of Chéhéry, which greatly expanded the bridgehead.* This left plenty of room for the engineers to complete a pontoon bridge across the Meuse at Glaire,

---

* This town is mistakenly called Chémery in *Panzer Leader*, by Heinz Guderian. Chémery is another town a few miles farther south.

where 1.Pz.Div infantry had attacked. As dawn broke, some tanks had already crossed, but without lights it was slow work and the tanks could not be sent south one by one. It took until 6 A.M. to get a whole tank brigade across the river. Had the French counterattack gone in as planned at 4 A.M., Balck's infantry, as far south as Chéhéry, would probably have been overrun. But the French attack was postponed to 7 A.M. Meanwhile more German tanks were moving across the bridge.

The French combined some infantry and light tanks and sent them north to find the Germans who were in fact on that same road. Over-confident, the tanks of the 1.Pz.Div had begun refueling without making adequate reconnaissance southward. The French attackers knocked out two German tanks and severely wounded a colonel of the tank regiment.

The response to this dangerous situation shows what determined infantry can accomplish against tanks. German combat engineers, led by their colonel, who died in the action, moved against the French tanks using hollow charges to break the tracks. Some heavy anti-aircraft guns were always near the front of the advance, and two of these 8.8 cm guns were also put into their defensive operation.

The French had started their attack at about 7 A.M. Within one and a half hours 1.Pz.Div deployed enough force to attack with a ferocity that sent the French sprawling. Well over half of the French tanks were knocked out and the infantry regiment's commander was taken prisoner.

Although more French armor was waiting behind the fighting, the counterattack stalled, fell back, and as it did so, the adjoining left flank of the French 71st Infantry Division retreated with it.

The cumbersome chain of French army command, the damage the Stukas had wrought upon the communications, and the fact that so many commanders had moved their command posts to the rear still could not account for the cheerfully inaccurate reports that were being exchanged by French senior commanders. Huntziger, commander of the Second Army, chose this moment to tell Gamelin that the counter-attack had gone in at 4:30 A.M. and that "the breach at Sedan is sealed off."

On the other side of the fighting front, Guderian knew otherwise. He had been in one of the early assault boats across the Meuse while Huntziger was considering whether to move his Second Army HQ from Senuc all the way back to Verdun. Before departing, Huntziger sent to his superiors another totally inaccurate account of the battle, in-cluding a claim to be holding the Marfée heights from which his soldiers had been driven the previous evening.

Guderian now had to make a decision of such vital importance that it was more a strategic than a tactical one. His three armored divisions had ripped a large gap in the French defenses. To what extent should he consolidate and guard that crossing place? Should he fight the big reserves, which anyone could guess must be moving northward to the gap? Should he batter at the broken edges of the armies on his flanks and thus "roll up" those defenders? Guderian did none of these things. He paused only to make sure the somewhat mauled Grossdeutschland Regiment and 10.Pz.Div were in possession of the high ground at Stonne, a few miles due south of his crossing place. Guderian took 1.Pz.Div and 2.Pz.Div, and disregarding all the theories of war, moved due west, away from the battle areas, across the flat open land of the Aisne and the Somme. Had he known just how close the French 3rd Armored Division and 3rd Motorized Infantry were to his bridgehead, he might have made some other decision.*

4. The Defense: France's Three Armored Divisions

The French 3rd Armored Division

The French 3rd Armored Division had been formed only six weeks before it went into battle. It lacked antitank guns, radios, repair units, engineers, and artillery, and it was below strength in tanks. However, it was still a powerful unit, its Hotchkiss H39 tanks giving it considerably more strike power than the stripped-down German panzer divisions that were operating farther north.

It was training at Rheims when the German attack started on 10 May. Since it took all orders about two days to arrive from GHQ, it did not receive orders to move to Sedan until 12 May. The division arrived there by dawn on 14 May, but there was a delay while its fuel tankers caught up with it. By noon, however, the division was refueled and moving north along the route taken by the ill-fated counterattack launched by the corps reserve. The men of the 3rd Armored Division were in high spirits and looking forward to hitting the Germans hard.

By three o'clock that afternoon of 14 May, as Guderian began his exposed movement westward with only the Grossdeutschland infantry regiment to protect his flank, the French 3rd Armored Division, in

---

* "Yes—at once attack," wrote General Nehring in my manuscript at this place.

company with the French 3rd Motorized Infantry Division, was closing in upon him. Guderian's two panzer divisions were vulnerable, being astraddle three water courses: the Meuse, the Ardennes Canal, and the river Bar, which ran close beside the canal. Cadets have been thrown out of military academies for a military decision such as Guderian had made. But Guderian put all his trust in the motorized infantry which was following him, the XIV Motorized Corps of General von Wietersheim. Technically it was the army commander's job to worry about Guderian's flank and rear. There could be no doubt about the calculated risk that was involved in this decision.

But that was not the way it looked to the French. General J. A. Flavigny, who commanded the 21st Corps of armor and motorized units, was not confident. Only thirty minutes before zero hour he postponed the attack until the next day. General Huntziger, commander of the Second Army, was moving his headquarters back to Verdun and so was not in a position to overrule this cancellation. Flavigny then gave up the idea of counterattacking. He dispersed the French armor along a 12-mile sector, assigning two or three tanks to each road.

After the war Flavigny gave his reasons for the cancellation: it was because the counterattack "was bound to fail." He added, "I wished to avoid disaster." General Flavigny's place in history is assured if he helps us remember that bloodthirsty generals are not the only commanders of whom men should go in fear.

Flavigny did not know that Guderian's divisions were moving west and, although both RAF and French bombers attacked the bridge over which the German armor was streaming, no aircraft reported the German movement. Nor were any hits made on the bridge.

Huntziger told his superiors that the counterattack had been canceled for technical reasons, adding that the roads were all now sealed off. He was told that the 3rd Armored Division was given to him for a counterattack. It must therefore counterattack—and "energetically." Huntziger decided to do nothing about this until a confirmation of the order arrived.

At 7 A.M. on 15 May Flavigny was finally ordered to attack. Flavigny took no action until 11:30 A.M. for, having dispersed all the tanks, he decided that it would take at least twenty-four hours to concentrate them again, and blamed General Antoine Brocard, the armored division commander, for not assembling it quickly enough. Huntziger obligingly relieved the tank division commander of his job. Having settled the question of who was to blame for all the delays in the counterattack, the attack itself was forgotten. Huntziger now put the armor and motorized troops with the rest of his shattered army and formed the kind of defense line his generation so revered. It was Huntziger's chief of staff who later told an investigating committee that this proved to be "a defensive success."

With only a small proportion of his army, which included the armored division, ever having seen combat, Huntziger's was the greatest failure of the whole campaign (though later he was promoted and became War Minister). The understrength units that Guderian had left to guard his flank proved entirely adequate. Once the Germans crossed the Meuse and headed west, Huntziger's army was the one best placed to move against them. In fact it did not halt them, harry them, or even inconvenience them.

The French 1st Armored Division Encounters Rommel

At Sedan the French 3rd Armored Division had been defeated by its own commanders, who nonetheless claimed "a defensive success." Opposite Rommel's 7.Pz.Div's crossing place by the evening of 14 May there was the French 1st Armored Division, under General Bruneau. That evening, as Rommel's armor rested only a stone's throw away in Morville, the French were lined up for refueling between the villages of Flavion and Ermeton.

The French tanks, intended for infantry support, were designed with fuel tanks that gave them enough range for an infantry advance of 1914–1918 war dimensions. Thus French armored divisions needed frequent refueling. Catering to this, they used specially designed tanker vehicles. Theoretically this seemed an excellent facility, but in practice it was far slower and less convenient than the German system of refueling by means of small steel containers, later nicknamed "Jerricans" by British troops, which could be brought by hand, wheelbarrow, truck, or tank and enabled tanks to take fuel as required and go back into action at short notice.

By 9:30 the next morning, 15 May, the French 1st Armored Division's artillery had already begun its move to new positions, but the tanks had not finished refueling. It was at that moment that Rommel's 7.Pz.Div and Hartlieb's 5.Pz.Div fell upon it in the classic two-prong attack of the blitzkrieg. Under heavy Stuka attack and with part of Rommel's division coming round behind them through Florennes, the French armor got no assistance from the Ninth Army's artillery or infantry units and no support from the French Air Force.

In the early afternoon, battered and outflanked, the French began to pull back to new positions along the small roads that link the villages

27. General Gamelin, Commander in Chief of the French Army, conducting King George VI on a tour of the Maginot Line defenses in December 1939.

28. Meanwhile Hitler harries his top generals—Keitel, Halder, and Brauchitsch (all three later made field marshals)—for ways and means of realizing his ambitions in the West through PLAN YELLOW.

29. General von Bock, commander of Army Group B.

30. Rotterdam: one of the German seaplanes that brought infantry to Willems bridge.

31. Inflatable boats used by the German Army to improvise a crossing over the destroyed bridge at the Dutch town of Maastricht.

32. German infantry making contact with the parachute troops near Rotterdam.

33. Rotterdam: a Dutch soldier with white flag discussing the cease-fire just before the German bombing attack.

34. LEFT: General von Reichenau.

35. ABOVE: A hollow charge.

36. Fort Eben Emael, Belgium. German gliders landed on its roof.

37. Bouillon, Belgium, where the bend in the river Semois provided a ford for Guderian's tanks, which moved up the old ramps conveniently placed for them, to get quickly to the road. This photograph was taken by the author from the Hotel Panorama, used as Guderian's headquarters.

38. General Heinz Guderian.

39. Monthermé, where steep wooded hills gave French colonial troops an opportunity to hold up Reinhardt's advance across the Meuse.

40. Sedan, France. Infantry of the 10. Panzer Division advanced in mid-May 1940 to cross the river Meuse and capture the heights of Marfée (arrow). This photo was taken by the author at the same time of year as the attack took place.

41. Bouvignes, Belgium. German cable ferry taking Rommel's tanks across the Meuse. This photograph now hangs in the Auberge de Bouvignes and was lent to the author for this book by the proprietor, Paul Leyman.

42. Bouvignes village. Rommel seized the equipment for this 18-ton bridge and started a bitter argument. Notice the way the pontoons are fitted with outboard motors to hold the bridge against the flow of the river.

43. LEFT: General Reinhardt. 44. CENTER: General Rommel (right) with his corps commander, General Hoth. 45. RIGHT: General von Kleist.

46. A German communications aircraft circles over a column of Rommel's armored division, where a tank has toppled over a steep embankment. This photograph was taken with Rommel's own Leica camera.

of Florennes, Oret, and Mettet. By now, one unit of thirty-six heavy tanks had only three left. Many tanks, lacking fuel, had been destroyed by their own crews. That evening, the 1st Armored Division began a general retreat. When it got as far as the French frontier there were only 17 tanks remaining of the original 175.

Already Rommel was on the move again westward. He left the French armor for 5.Pz.Div to finish off and passed right through the new defense line to which the Ninth Army had decided to withdraw, even before the French were there to begin forming it.

The Defense: Command Decisions

On the morning of 15 May Churchill was awakened by a phone call from the French Prime Minister, Paul Reynaud, who said: "We are beaten, we have lost the battle." This cry of despair was out of character with the aggressive little man with the dyed hair and the overbearing mistress. "Mickey Mouse," as his enemies called him, had been one of the few Frenchmen interested in preparing his country for war.

Churchill was alarmed by such despondency when the battle was less than a week old. He flew to Paris the next day. The Dutch Army had already capitulated virtually intact. Gloom pervaded the Anglo-French conference. Sixteen French generals had already been dismissed for failing in their duty. Corap had been replaced. General Huntziger had ordered that French soldiers precipitately surrendering blockhouses must be fired upon.

A hole had been punched through the French line, between the armies of Huntziger and Corap, and the Germans were streaming through it. Gamelin—the French Commander in Chief—admitted that the long corridor which the Germans had formed, with a need for flank guards along its whole length, was a vulnerable target. He gave a hopeless shrug of his shoulders and said, "Inferiority of numbers, inferiority of equipment, inferiority of method."

However, the French High Command maintained their calm optimism. The vocabulary of the First World War was being given a new airing. The Meuse had been crossed, but the enemy was being "held" and "contained." The "situation is improving" and the enemy "sealed off."

Even during that terrible day of 15 May, the French GHQ was not alarmed. But reports were getting shorter and fewer as communications failed and commanders froze into indecision. The High Command began imagining attacks upon the Maginot Line and still had not even begun to understand the German strategy. Gamelin's report for 15 May did not dwell upon inferiorities. On the contrary, he detected "a lessening of enemy action, which was particularly violent on the 14th May." The front was "re-establishing itself."

In fact, the action had not lessened. It had quickened. Rommel pushed his men on even during the night. He described the scene: "Our artillery was dropping heavy harassing fire on villages and the road far ahead of the regiment . . . civilians and French troops, their faces distorted with terror, lay huddled in the ditches . . . we drove through the villages of Sars Poteries and Beugnies with guns blazing . . ." The blitzkrieg spared no time separating terrified civilians from active opposition.

It was Rommel's declared policy to shoot first and ask questions afterward. He wrote: "I have found again and again that in encounter actions, the day goes to the side that is the first to plaster its opponent with fire. The man who lies low and awaits developments usually comes off second best. Motorcyclists at the head of the column must keep their machine guns at the ready and open fire the instant an enemy shot is heard. This applies even when the exact position of the enemy is unknown, in which case the fire must simply be sprayed over enemy-held territory"*

Wednesday, 15 May: Breakout at Monthermé

Of the three Meuse crossings only Reinhardt's XLI Panzerkorps was still held up at the river on 15 May. Here the French 41st Corps, under General E. A. Libaud, had pinned the Germans down in spite of everything the Luftwaffe threw at them. Yet in the wooded valley the German bridge remained intact and the forces in the bridgehead were getting more and more powerful.

For men of the French 102nd Fortress Division, the German pressure was becoming too strong. A fortress division was without transport and therefore a prey to added fears. Before dawn on the morning of 15 May combat engineers of 6.Pz.Div, using flamethrowers and with artillery support, renewed efforts and got through the bunker line of French defenses. The French began to withdraw, but, lacking transport, had to abandon many of their heavy weapons. German motorcyclists and tanks began to move across the bridge. Elated by this first sign of success, after such a long time bottled up in the bridgehead, the Germans hit the withdrawal with enough force to scatter it

* From *The Rommel Papers*, edited by B. H. Liddell Hart.

and turn it into a rout. A French truck, bringing the antitank mines for which the soldiers had been pleading, was hit by a German tank gun and blown to pieces.

At Nouzonville, to the south, the Germans were still held up at the river line. Reinhardt refused to let the 6.Pz.Div help them, realizing that the breakthrough alone must force the French back. That afternoon the infantry at Nouzonville was also across the river. Working feverishly the engineers got a 16-ton bridge completed that night.

While the 6.Pz.Div and its supporting infantry moved across the bridge at Monthermé, 8.Pz.Div was lined up for the Nouzonville bridge. Traffic jams here brought tanks and trucks to a standstill. Although the panzer units had priority for the crossing, infantrymen filtered past the stalled vehicles and moved over the river westward along roads assigned to the tanks.

At Montcy an intact bridge was discovered and more infantry moved over that. By now a whole infantry division had nosed in sideways at the Nouzonville bridge. Foot soldiers added to the chaos, which also extended to the far side of the river. They blocked the roads, hindering panzer units and supply columns trying to reach the advance elements of 6.Pz.Div, which, by nightfall, were far west of the Meuse and separated from the rest of the corps.

The French 2nd Armored Division Encounters Reinhardt

By the evening of 15 May, advance elements of Reinhardt's 6.Pz.Div had more than made up for three days' waiting at the Meuse; they were farther west than any other German units, having raced a record-breaking 40 miles in one day, something few armored units could achieve in a peacetime exercise. Now they were to encounter one of the most formidable units that the French Army had in the field.

The men of France's 2nd Armored Division had also endured three anxious days. Its tanks had been loaded onto trains and separated from the division's wheeled elements. On the morning of 14 May the divisional commander, General A. C. Bruché, had admitted that he was not sure where all the different components of his division were. A change of orders on 15 May placed the division under a new army commander and ordered it to Signy-l'Abbaye. To join it, the tanks would have to make their own way from the railway station at Hirson.

It was the fate of the French 2nd Armored Division that Reinhardt's 6.Pz.Div was heading for Signy too. The Germans blundered right through the middle of the division, knocking it out piece by piece.

Gun batteries were overrun while they were still on the road, and the French tanks were surprised as they moved from the railway station. By the morning of 16 May the 2nd Armored Division was split in two and scattered across the countryside, lacking divisional HQ communication with High Command and any supplies. The divisional commander spent the next day wandering about, trying to locate his various elements before the Germans destroyed them.

Meanwhile Reinhardt's panzer columns continued westward. By 16 May the gap in the French defenses was over 40 miles wide.

Beyond Sedan

Even Gamelin now realized that the situation was desperate. Soldiers were arriving from the front at his HQ and the staff were taking the maps from the walls. Gamelin's chief of staff ordered that an old 7.5 cm gun in the courtyard be pointed in the general direction of Germany. Bitterly one colonel remarked, "In 1814 it was 'the Cossacks are coming,' in 1870 it was 'the Uhlans are coming' and now 'the Panzers are coming.' "

On 17 May more French armor made an attempt to counterattack at Montcornet. It was a hastily assembled collection of armored bits and pieces, amounting to about three battalions, under the command of Colonel de Gaulle. Although it fought bravely, it was cut up by air attack before it could come to grips with the enemy armor. It retired and tried again, with no better result.

The German Army High Command (OKH) feared for the vulnerability of those armored columns which had pushed on so far west. On 16 May, General von Kleist ordered Guderian to halt. Guderian ignored his superior's order. Reluctantly, Kleist's chief of staff agreed that Panzerkorps Guderian would have to move forward in order to make room in the Meuse bridgehead for the infantry—Armeekorps Wiersheim—that was following the panzer divisions. On this pretext, Guderian resumed the headlong advance.

The next day Kleist flew to Guderian's advance airstrip and demanded an explanation for his disobedience. By this time Guderian's corps HQ was outside Montcornet and his vanguard at Marle. Guderian became so angry at Kleist's unequivocal halt order he asked to be relieved of his command. Shaken by this unexpected display of temperament, Rundstedt—commander of the whole of Army Group A—sent General Wilhelm List, commander of the Twelfth Army, to explain to Guderian that the order had come from OKH. List and Guderian exchanged some complex double-talk about the necessity for "reconnaissance in force" and, on the strength of this, Guderian advanced again. This time, however, Guderian laid down a wire so that his chief of staff could keep in touch with his advance HQ and yet deny the wireless intercept units of OKH the opportunity to get a bearing on him and report his position. By the end of that day, 17 May, his 10.Pz.Div was across the river Oise near Moy. They were 70 miles beyond Sedan, replaced there by Wietersheim's motorized infantry.

On 19 May, Guderian's 1.Pz.Div crossed the Somme near Peronne. Many French senior officers had arrived in Peronne to find out what was happening. They were captured.

All this time Guderian, on the south side of the offensive, had depended upon the Aisne, Serre, and Somme rivers to protect his left flank. He had rightly believed that the French would not mount a full-scale counterattack until they were sure of his exact position. He kept moving.

It was Guderian's theory that no panzer column need stop because it was out of fuel: "if they become tired, they lack fuel," he said and refused to accept such excuses for a halt. When 2.Pz.Div reached Albert, it captured a British artillery battery, drawn up on the barrack square and equipped only with training ammunition. Some wanted to stop here, but Guderian ordered them on. They reached Abbeville before nightfall.

That evening Guderian watched approvingly as his flak batteries shot at, and hit, a German airplane that was attacking his personal lodging. The crew parachuted to safety. Guderian reprimanded them severely for their mistake but later gave them each a glass of champagne.

It was a time to celebrate. With his panzer units at Abbeville, the trap was sprung. From now on the French armies fighting north of that line and the BEF with them could receive from their bases in France no more fuel, food, spare parts, or, worst of all, ammunition. It seemed inevitable that the encircled armies, including a quarter of a million of Britain's best soldiers with their modern equipment, would be forced to surrender to the German command.

5. The Battle in the Air

It was appropriate that Guderian should toast his fliers in French champagne. The German air force had protected his panzer forces during the time when they were closed up and vulnerable. Artfully the Luftwaffe had kept to an absolute minimum its air attacks against the Allied armies moving into Belgium and Holland. This had ensured that they would all be well to the north by the time Panzergruppe Kleist reached the Channel coast. Throughout the battle, the Dornier Do 17s had provided a continuous picture of Allied attempts to concentrate and deploy for a counterattack, while Henschel Hs 126 spotter planes passed to the divisional commanders news of the tactical moves of the enemy. Even more important, the bomber force had provided the sort of artillery support that theorists had said would be possible.

There was nothing for the Allied air forces to celebrate. Between 1 September 1939 and 1 May 1940 the French air force had lost 914 aircraft, only 63 of them as a result of combat, the remainder through accidents. Luftwaffe losses during the same period (in which it had waged war in Poland and Scandinavia, as well as in the West) totaled 937 combat aircraft.

While the Luftwaffe helped the German Army to flatten Poland, politicians in France and Britain were ordering their air forces to confine their activities to taking aerial photographs and dropping propaganda leaflets. It was an attitude which never really changed. On the night of 4/5 June 1940, after three weeks under German attack, the French air force bombed the factories of Badische Anilin at Ludwigshafen and left the sky red with flames. But the following day French air force HQ said there must be no more attacks like this in case the Germans retaliated. A few days later a combined Allied air raid against Italian targets was canceled after the French air force component was withdrawn and, when the RAF aircraft were about to take off, vehicles were used to block the runways.

Friday, 10 May

On the day that the German attack on the West began, the RAF Commander in Chief requested permission from the French High Command to begin bombing attacks on the enemy columns advancing through Luxembourg. When no such permission arrived, he decided at midday to order an attack anyway. The first wave of Fairey Battle light bombers was ordered to attack the German columns.

The Fairey Battle was an attempt to get a fast light bomber by stretching the fuselage of a monoplane fighter and putting three people in it. The same engine that made the Hawker Hurricane a first-class fighter inevitably made the heavier Battle a slow, underpowered freak with short range and small bomb load. Lacking the range to operate from England, they were sent to the forward airfields in France. Even on their way to active service, one was lost in the Channel because of engine failure. Before the first month of war had passed, the Battles abandoned their trips along the Franco-German border when Messerschmitt Bf 109s bounced a flight of five, shot down four, and damaged the fifth so badly that it could not be repaired.

So on 10 May, heading for the columns in Luxembourg, the Battle crews could have been in no doubt about what they faced, especially since they were promised little or no fighter protection. They went in very low—at about 250 feet—using bombs with eleven seconds' delay so that they were not caught in their own blast. The German panzer division put up intense fire from everything that could be brought to bear. Three of the first eight Fairey Battles were shot down.

A second mission dispatched that afternoon was met by similarly intense small-arms fire. Of the thirty-two Fairey Battles that were sent out that day, thirteen were lost and not one aircraft returned undamaged. The effect upon the German columns was "negligible," says the official history.

The effectiveness of infantry rifles and machine guns against low-flying aircraft was one of the great surprises of 1940. The German infantry machine guns had high rates of fire, and so did the French Chatellerault and the British Bren gun. Even without light antiaircraft guns, the Allied infantry could have been making the skies above them as dangerous for low-flying aircraft as the German columns did for Allied planes.

During that first day of the attack, the French made no attempt to bomb the German columns coming through the Ardennes. Nor did they bomb them on the second day when one RAF attack was mounted by eight Fairey Battles. Only one pilot returned to describe the intense ground fire.

Saturday, 11 May

It was still the northerly thrust, at Maastricht, that was occupying the attention of the French High Command on the second day of the battle. Gamelin believed that, providing French aircraft did not hit built-up areas, it might be possible to prevent the air war escalating into the bombing of large towns in France and Germany. At 8 A.M. on 11 May he reminded his air force commanders that only fighters and reconnaissance aircraft should be used. Three hours later Gamelin was sanctioning attacks upon the German columns.

The Belgian Air Force had already attacked Maastricht and the

Albert Canal bridges, but ten out of fifteen Belgian planes had been lost. These Belgian aircraft were also Fairey Battles, carrying only tiny 110-pound bombs, which were unlikely to do the sort of damage that would halt the German invasion. The RAF sent bombers—Bristol Blenheim IVs this time—and five out of six of these were destroyed by flak.

On the same day another Blenheim squadron was all but wiped out. The Luftwaffe bombing squadrons were working their way down the list of airfields to be raided. That morning it was to be Vaux, an airfield near Rheims, now being used by the RAF. Dornier Do 17s came in very low and found the Blenheims fueled and bombed-up, waiting for orders. They were lined up as if for inspection. The Dorniers destroyed them at leisure. One bomber pilot made an extra circuit of the target so that his radio operator could film the destruction with his amateur ciné camera. That footage was rushed to Hitler's HQ to show him what the Luftwaffe was doing to win the war.

Whitsunday, 12 May

The Allies still concentrated their attention, and their air forces, upon the northern sectors. The Maastricht bridges and the road to Tongres were where Hoepner's XVI Panzerkorps looked as though it was making a desperate attempt to capture Brussels and might succeed. On Whitsunday morning the French called for an RAF raid on that stretch of road. Nine Blenheims attacked; seven were shot down by German fighters.

The French air force's Groupe 1/54 also attacked that day. It was their first action in the battle. Since the German breakthrough they had moved from airfield to airfield. Suddenly they were found to be short of bomb-release equipment. Only by collecting supplies from the manufacturers were they able to mount the attack by noon. Eighteen Breguet bombers went in very low, but the German columns' light flak shot down eight of them. That evening a formation of French Lioré et Olivier LeO 45 bombers again attacked the columns but kept to about 2,500 feet and so avoided most of the 20 mm and small-arms fire. All the bombers were damaged, but they all returned to base.

Lessons were being learned but were not being learned fast enough. Right from the beginning of the battle, the value of low-level attacks was as obvious to the Allied air forces as it was to the Luftwaffe. Then why had the French so neglected the 20 mm and 40 mm antiaircraft gun, particularly when the useful Swedish Bofors was

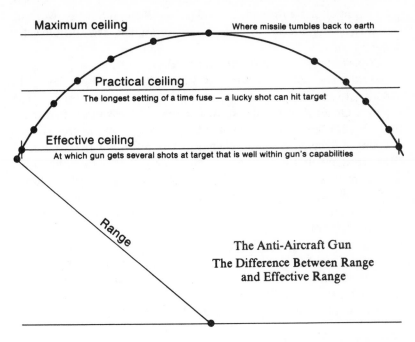

Maximum ceiling   Where missile tumbles back to earth

Practical ceiling

The longest setting of a time fuse — a lucky shot can hit target

Effective ceiling

At which gun gets several shots at target that is well within gun's capabilities

Range

The Anti-Aircraft Gun
**The Difference Between Range
and Effective Range**

FIGURE 23   Note that only at the lower ceiling—and below it—does the plane remain in range long enough to be seen, aimed at, and hit.

available to all comers? Both the Germans and the British already had it. Why did the air forces continue to send bombers into raids without providing them with close fighter escort? And why was the element of time still being squandered by Allied commanders?

Realizing now what sort of defense the Germans were likely to have on the Albert Canal bridges near Maastricht, the RAF commander requested No. 12 Squadron to send six volunteer crews to attack the Vroenhoven and Veldwezelt bridges. Since all the crews of "the dirty dozen" squadron volunteered, they continued to go by the duty roster. Although Hurricanes flew "protective patrols" there was no attempt to provide close escort for the Fairey Battles. One plane going in almost at ground level, with its bombs on eleven seconds' delay, managed to knock a section out of the metal bridge at Veldwezelt.

An RAF survivor from the burning wreckage of one Battle was told by a German, "You British are mad. We capture the bridge early

Friday morning. You give us all Friday and Saturday to get our flak guns up in circles all round the bridge, and then on Sunday, when all is ready, you come along with three aircraft and try and blow the thing up."

None of the six Fairey Battles survived.

By the end of Whitsunday, 12 May—after only three days—the RAF's Advanced Air Striking Force had lost 63 of its original 135 aircraft. On Friday it had lost 40 per cent of the sorties it flew. On Saturday 100 per cent. On Sunday 62 per cent. These figures take no account of damage suffered by almost every returning aircraft. On 13 May the Blenheims did not fly and the Fairey Battles flew only once.

There was at least one indication of what the Allied air forces might have achieved if used with more skill. The French air force's *Cigognes* (Storks) unit—which became famous in the First World War when its pilots included the ace Georges Guynemer—was flying Curtiss Hawk 75 fighters, which were not the best fighters the French had. They found twelve Junkers Ju 87 Stuka bombers returning from Sedan and shot down all of them without loss to themselves. They then found the second wave and shot down some more. The Ju 87s turned away before letting go their bombs.

Monday, 13 May

The fate of the Stukas the day before suggests what might have happened to the relays of Stukas that were, more than any other factor, the key to Guderian's crossing of the Meuse on that Monday afternoon.

Granted the infinite wisdom that only hindsight provides, it is easy now to see that the Allied air forces threw away their chance of hitting the Schwerpunkt at the moment when it was most vulnerable. Certainly military experts then had some reason to believe that Guderian would wait three or four days for his heavy artillery and take this chance to rearrange his units for the assault. Allied bombing units had taken a terrible beating, and their commanders believed that they would need every available aircraft when that river crossing took place in a few days' time. From London the Chief of Air Staff displayed the Air Ministry's usual perspicacity by signaling, "If we expend all our efforts in the early stages of the battle we shall not be able to operate effectively when the really critical phase comes."

The confusing French air force command system, which put the planes under the orders of both the Air Cooperation Forces and of the group commander, was also clogging the communications. Local army units as well got through directly to the squadrons, pleading for immediate aid. The same air force that had not appreciated how much damage light flak could inflict, nor the necessity of close fighter escort for its bombers, now failed to understand the importance of concentration.

A typical day's demands upon the French First Army's air force units went: 5 per cent to the Seventh Army, 5 per cent to the Ninth Army, 60 per cent to General Touchon's detachment, and 50 per cent to the Second Army. The absurdity of ordering up air efforts like linoleum for an unmeasured room was compounded by the way in which this particular command was followed by another from the Air Cooperation Commander, who wanted 50 per cent for Mézières, 30 per cent for Sedan, and 20 per cent for Dinant. In addition, there were the usual constant calls from army units that were under attack.

After this sort of muddle had been sorted out and French air formations finally reached the battle area, as often as not they found themselves engulfed in skies filled with German aircraft, while elsewhere French fighters were returning home without finding a target. Worse than the duplication of command was the absence of any at all. Guderian's river crossing on 13 May took place with little or no interference from Allied air forces. By the following morning German flak was already in position on the south side of the river and while the French Second Army was being attacked by the Luftwaffe, its fighter group waited on the ground without receiving any orders at all.

As a measure of the concern felt about the speed of the German advance, two squadrons of RAF Armstrong-Whitworth Whitley bombers were dispatched to France by Bomber Command. Briefed by an officer of the air component of the British Expeditionary Force, these heavy bombers were sent to destroy the Meuse bridges. They too failed.*

Tuesday, 14 May

At Sedan the same flak regiment which had used its 8.8 cm guns to fire across the Meuse during the previous day's attacks now swung them into high elevation as British and French bombers tried des-

---

* The story of the Whitley bombers operating from French airfields is not in Bomber Command records. The information was given by Sir Victor Goddard, who was SASO there, and he arranged details with Bomber Command (Saundby). "A wing of two squadrons certainly came. They received my orders and I saw them on the way to making their attack," wrote Sir Victor in a letter to the author.

perately to destroy the pontoon bridge at Glaire. The gunners claimed 112 aircraft destroyed and the flak commander was awarded the Knight's Cross.

Yet the war diary of the Luftwaffe's II Air Corps named this "the day of the fighters." The French air force had put every available bomber into the sky against the Sedan bridges. The aircraft were organized in small formations, which gave the flak gunners a better chance against them. As the raids continued, the German fighter force met in battle the Allied fighters that provided the escort for this continuous attack. The RAF suffered the highest losses ever recorded for a raid of comparable size. The French air force suffered casualties so severe that they called off the operations.

The Germans had knocked out the Dutch and the Belgians and given the French a blow from which they stood no chance of recovering. Blitzkrieg was quite different from anything ever experienced in previous wars. In 1918 Germany had been starving and exhausted; pressed back toward the Rhine, its armies had had to ask the Allies for terms. But in 1940 the French Army was not being pushed back; it had been by-passed. Already the whole of northern France was occupied by a highly motivated, methodical, and ruthless enemy. Over the Whitsun holiday weekend Europe had been changed forever.

The Freiburg Incident

A description of the great battle of Whitsun weekend 1940 would not be complete without a mention of the bizarre and tragic bombing of Freiburg.

At teatime on Friday afternoon, three aircraft came out of the clouds to bomb the fighter airfield on the outskirts of the pretty little town of Freiburg-im-Breisgau in western Germany. The aiming was poor and most of the bombs exploded in the town. Eleven of them hit the railway station, and two fell on a children's playground. Twenty-two children died, as well as thirteen women and eleven male civilians. There were only eleven military casualties.

The Germans were shocked, and their official news agency report of the raid included a warning that any more such bombing of "illegal" targets would be answered by fivefold retaliation against French and British towns.

Knowing that Bomber Command had not bombed Freiburg and believing the denials of the French air force, it was tempting for the British leaders to suppose that the German propaganda service had invented the story. It was a view that gained many converts when, just four days later, Rotterdam was bombed. It seemed as if it might have been the sort of preparation Dr. Goebbels might make for such an attack, the details of which were now being exaggerated beyond recognition and used energetically by propagandists on the Allied side.

The RAF had given up all its prewar dreams of daylight bombing in formation. Until the time of the German thrust westward, Bomber Command had been scattering only leaflets across Germany. One RAF expert at this time estimated that scarcely 35 per cent of its bombers were finding their way to the targets assigned to them. It was to prove a remarkably accurate guess.

Accurate or not, RAF Bomber Command was, on the day following the Rotterdam raid, authorized to bomb the densely populated Ruhr area of Germany. It was the beginning of a bombing policy in which all belligerent powers shared the same ruthless indifference to the destruction of town centers. By December 1940 RAF crews were being told "to concentrate the maximum amount of damage in the centre of town" and were being helped to find it by a "fire-raising force" of aircraft flown by the best crews.

Long before that, however, the police president of Freiburg-im-Breisgau had carefully collected bomb fragments and pieced enough together to read the serial numbers on the casings. He proved beyond doubt that his town had been struck by German bombs. He traced them from the factory where they were made to the Luftwaffe armory at Lechfeld, near Munich. The attack had been carried out by three Heinkel He 111s which had lost their way on a bombing mission to Dijon airfield in France.

The affair was an accident, but by this time the Goebbels propaganda machine had made such capital of it that there was no chance that the Germans would publish the truth. By this time, too, the men who planned strategic bombing had long since forgotten the incident at Freiburg.

PART FIVE

The Flawed Victory

47. Guderian in his armored half-track command vehicle. Notice the Enigma coding machine, bottom left.

48. INSET: General Huntziger, commander of the French 2nd Army.

49. The artillery was the pride of France's army. Here a heavy howitzer of the 2nd Army is in action in 1940.

50. One of Rommel's 8.8 cm. anti-aircraft guns in action against British tanks in May 1940.

51. Rommel's photograph of a knocked-out German tank. Notice the turret rings on the ground.

52. Churchill at the War Ministry in Paris with General Sir John Dill, Clement Attlee, and the French Premier, Paul Reynaud, May 1940.

53. The commander of the BEF, Lord Gort (right) with General Georges, General Gamelin's adjutant.

54. General Weygand, who succeeded Gamelin.

55. Lieutenant General Brooke. 56. General Gamelin. 57. Vice Admiral Sir Bertra Ramsay.

58. German infantry cover a crewman from a French Char B1.

59. British infantry aboard an evacuation ship at Dunkirk, June 1940.

60. Dunkirk. A pier improvised from vehicles provided a chance for the infantry to get to the boats.

61. The Germans dictate terms to the French; Hitler is seated second from the right.

62. Marshal Pétain (left) with Pierre Laval.

"I received a postcard at my address, found on the body of an officer of Corap's army, who had just committed suicide at Le Mans station. He wrote, 'I am killing myself, Mr President, to let you know that all my men were brave, but one cannot send men to fight tanks with rifles.'"

—PAUL REYNAUD

On 17 May 1940 the world heard the news that Brussels had fallen to the Germans. The next day Paul Reynaud, the French Premier, changed his Cabinet. The sixty-eight-year-old General Maurice Gamelin was replaced as Commander in Chief of the French Army by the seventy-three-year-old General Maxime Weygand. Marshal Henri Philippe Pétain, a hero of the previous war, was appointed Vice Premier. Pétain was eighty-four years old.

Weygand was a weary, desiccated little man, described by one acquaintance as looking like a retired jockey, an impression fortified by his riding breeches and perfectly polished high boots. Weygand's undisguised dislike of the British and his contempt for all politicians made him a most unsuitable choice as Gamelin's replacement. Weygand was in Beirut, in Lebanon, on 17 May, when summoned to Paris; meanwhile, Gamelin's plan for a counterattack south of Sedan was shelved at the moment that he was relieved of his command.

General Weygand Takes Command

It took Weygand two days to get to Paris. Even after arrival he would not accept the appointment before consulting both Generals Gamelin and Georges, the commander of the Western Front, which took until evening. Reynaud then suggested a briefing, but Weygand said, "No. Tomorrow."

On 20 May, while the German panzer forces sped toward Abbeville and the sea, Weygand visited and consulted. At the end of the day he announced that he must go and judge the situation on the spot. He sent his car to Abbeville, intending to go there himself by train

The city was, of course, in German hands by that time. So instead Weygand took a plane to Béthune to see General Billotte, senior general on the northeastern front, but the airfield had been abandoned. Weygand flew on to Calais and arranged meetings with the Belgian King, Leopold III, and other commanders. General Lord Gort, commander of the BEF, did not receive any summons until the discussion came round to using British troops for a counterattack. Weygand then left for Paris before Gort arrived. Although aircraft were still flying between Calais and Paris, Weygand took a ship to Cherbourg. He got there the following morning and traveled on by train to Paris. By the time Weygand arrived in Paris, the Germans had reached the Channel coast, had turned north, and were beginning the attack on Boulogne.

Having made his on-the-spot judgment, Weygand now outlined a totally nonsensical plan of battle, adding some mythical French successes (the French armies were progressing toward Amiens, he said) in an effort to make it sound convincing.

This was not an isolated example of Weygand's careless utilization of false reports. At a meeting of the French Cabinet later in Tours, on 13 June, Weygand reported with a measure of satisfaction that the Communists had set up a government in Paris and that the Communist leader was installed in the Elysée Palace. When a phone call revealed this to be without any foundation, Weygand became very angry and stamped out of the room, shouting threats about arresting the whole Cabinet.

The Battle at Arras: 21 May

When the German offensive began in the North, the British Expeditionary Force had, together with the French armies on either side of it, moved forward across the Belgian border. They were not surprised that there were no German air attacks to delay their movement, since Lord Gort's staff explained that the Luftwaffe could not be everywhere at once. In fact, the German air offensive had been planned so that the Allied armies could advance into Belgium without hindrance. This emptied the rear areas through which the German armored columns raced to the sea.

The German armored forces moved along the northern side of the river Somme. The river provided protection against any French counterattacks from the South and denied the river as a defense line for the Allied armies to the north.

Soon Gort began to realize that the absence of German air attacks was not just a matter of good luck. He realized, too, that what the

French leaders, and Winston Churchill, were calling "a bulge" was a German thrust toward the sea that had severed the Allied armies from their supplies and communications.

This did not only apply to the supplies of the French armies. Showing extreme caution, British planners had since 1939 routed their soldiers through Cherbourg and Le Havre, and the vehicles through Brest and St. Nazaire. Using an area between Le Mans and Laval as an assembly area, the BEF was, like the French, supplied from the southwest. The Germans had cut through these supply lines, and now the British had to improvise other more direct supplies. Big dumps were started near Hazebrouck. Without this outstanding achievement the BEF would not have been able to move, let alone fight. In this respect, the supply services saved the BEF from destruction.

While an alternative supply route was being set up, Gort organized the sort of counterattack that the German commanders most feared: a thrust southward to sever the strung-out German advance.

Using Arras, traditional hub of the British Army in France, as a rallying point, Gort put together a miscellany of garrison troops, field artillery, two territorial infantry battalions, and a tank brigade. There was also a depleted French light mechanized division with about sixty Somua tanks. None of its H35 tanks had survived. Facing them on the German side was Rommel's 7.Pz.Div, the 8.Pz.Div, and the motorized SS-Totenkopf Division.

If the German force was representative of the best of the German Army of that time, the Allied force was a demonstration of Anglo-French weaknesses. The infantry arrived late at their allotted positions. Artillery support was also delayed. Because of inadequate netting and bad atmospherics, there was no proper radio contact between units. The promised air support did not arrive.

The British tanks had traveled 120 miles to the battle, on their own tracks, an achievement that surprised some of the crews. Only one tank in eight had been supplied with appropriate (1:100,000 scale) maps as required. Most tank commanders had journeyed across France depending upon 1:250,000 scale maps. Maps of any sort were so scarce that the commanding officer of one British unit had been "beseeched" to give up his map to the accompanying tank squadron commander, who did not have any at all. The officer re-counting this story had used a Michelin map bought privately.

German control of the air provided a much better, albeit still con-fused, picture of troop dispositions. The British commander, on the other hand, had no idea whether his force would meet entrenched infantry, tanks, antitank guns, or merely soft transport. Ordered to attack without delays for reconnaissance, the British commander compromised by deploying two mixed columns of armor, antitank units, and infantry, with little contact between them.

At 2:30 P.M. on 21 May, having given up all hope that the two promised French infantry divisions would ever arrive, the mixed British force began moving south in two columns on roads about 3 miles apart. The British tank component consisted of sixteen Mk. II Matildas with 2-pounder guns and fifty-eight Mk. Is armed only with machine guns.

By coincidence, the Germans had chosen 3 P.M. to move forward, one panzer division each side of Arras. Infantry of 7.Pz.Div were the first to make contact with the British force. German 3.7 cm antitank shells tore chunks from the thick metal of the British tanks but could not penetrate them. One British Matilda had fourteen gouges made by shells that failed to penetrate the steel. Although some of the British tanks were set on fire by tracer or suffered broken tracks, the rest of them overran the German gun batteries. But with command of the air, German dive-bombing attacks on the advancing tanks began to cause some casualties. In the late afternoon both British tank battalion commanders were killed, yet with commendable skill the units continued with little interruption.

German tanks artfully crossed the fighting to attack the British armor from the flank. The failure of German antitank guns made it necessary for the German tanks to engage British armor, something usually avoided by the Germans. In the fighting that began about 7 P.M. the Germans lost six of their PzKw IIIs and three of the PzKw IVs, as well as some PzKw IIs. The British lost seven Mk. Is. It was at this point of the battle when infantry of SS-Totenkopf Division saw their tanks knocked out and burning. It was a shock. The SS infantry panicked and withdrew quickly.

French Somua tank crews also saw the burning German tanks and were equally surprised. Unable to believe that at long last the Germans were suffering setbacks, the French crews concluded that the antitank guns were German and so opened fire on them. British gunners responded to what they thought was another flank attack and knocked out four of the French Somua tanks before the tragic error was discovered.

Convinced that hundreds of tanks were attacking, Rommel took personal command of his guns. He hurried from battery to battery giving them targets and urging them to faster action. When the antitank guns failed, he brought into play the guns of his artillery regiment, but it was the 8.8 cm antiaircraft guns that finally penetrated the heavy British tank armor. The Allied counterattack was halted by the versatility of German arms and their coordination effected by the personal energy of the divisional commander. It was the same story everywhere on the Allied fighting front.

SS-Totenkopf Division had panicked, but this motorized division (mostly consisting of concentration camp guards) had been considered too inexperienced for the spearhead of the assault. It had been kept in reserve until 16 May and was only now committed to the battle. But if the SS-Totenkopf men came out of the battle with their reputation damaged, Rommel emerged with even greater glory. Legends abounded wherever Rommel went. They were assisted by his flair for publicity—and his photographs. Soon after the fighting at Arras, a story circulated that Rommel had saved the day by using 8.8 cm antiaircraft guns in the antitank role for the first time ever. How this story gained currency is hard to imagine, for obviously the guns would have been virtually useless against armor unless they had already been supplied with *Panzergranate* (armor-piercing shells).

In fact, many of the German guns were supplied with ammunition suitable for both air and armor targets. In 1938 Hitler expressed special interest in the use of 8.8 cm guns against ground targets. As early as the 1938–1939 Catalonian offensive in Spain's civil war, the 8.8 cm guns had been towed into action behind the tanks, and it was estimated that over 90 per cent of their rounds were used against ground targets. At Ilza in Poland, Flakregiment 22, separated from their range finders and communications equipment, had been pressed into action as artillery. As well as the Luftwaffe's 8.8 cm guns, the army's 20 mm flak joined in the Ilza battle. The Luftwaffe suffered 195 ground staff casualties in the Polish campaign; 129 of these were among flak crews fighting in the artillery role.

The British counterattack at Arras came to a standstill. There could be no breakthrough of the long overextended German columns. After forty-eight hours, the British withdrew. It was during the Arras fighting that German columns reached the Channel. German victory was more or less inevitable. The attack westward to the sea was decisive because it severed the Allied armies from their lines of communication and required them to turn to face southward. To pass fighting components back along routes occupied by the ganglia of supply, while keeping command communications open, is virtually impossible, especially if the army is already engaged in battle. A modern army attacked from the rear is as good as defeated. It simply seizes up into a traffic jam of monumental confusion. Thus the greatest ambition of a strategist is to attack an enemy's rear and then sever the enemy from his supplies. The Manstein plan had achieved both these ambitions.

The Arras fighting had been the most significant counterattack made against the German thrust. Guderian agrees that the German infantry panicked, and Rundstedt admits that for a short time he feared that his armor would be separated from the advancing infantry. It probably disconcerted the OKH more than the forward units, but it is doubtful whether it affected them to the extent that has been claimed for it.

The importance of the Arras battle was in the two and a half days' delay it caused to the German armor. It enabled four British divisions and a large part of the French First Army to withdraw in relatively good order toward the Channel coast.

Subsequent to the fighting at Arras, Rommel's 7.Pz.Div was halted for rest and repairs. The necessity for this pause is worth remembering in the light of the controversy about the later halt before Dunkirk. By the time the division was moving again, on 26 May, Rommel had got official sanction to add two tank regiments of the neighboring armored division (5.Pz.Div) to his own command. This reinforcement—specifically given for the attack on Lille—made Rommel's division one of the strongest in the German army and enraged General von Hartlieb, the commander of the depleted division, who was still angry about the loss of his bridging equipment at the Meuse on 13 May.

Rommel, the newest and most junior of the panzer division commanders, now gained a new distinction. After a conference on 27 May, attended by the commanders of his enlarged tank force, Rommel's aide, Karl Hanke, had a surprise. Hanke, a fervent Nazi and onetime official of the Propaganda Ministry, was one of several Nazi officials who had followed Rommel to 7.Pz.Div.*

"On the Führer's orders," announced Karl Hanke, "I herewith bestow upon the general the Knight's Cross." Rommel was the first divisional commander to receive this award in France. Soon afterward, Rommel was able to do the same thing for Hanke. He not only recommended his aide for this coveted medal but, ignoring the regular procedure, sent his recommendation directly to Hitler for approval. Hanke foolishly chose this moment to point out to Rommel that his position in the Nazi hierarchy was senior to Rommel's rank in the army. Immediately Rommel sent a messenger to Hitler's headquarters so that the award could be canceled.

---

* Another Nazi was Karl Holz, chief editor of the hysterical and obscene anti-Jewish *Der Stürmer*. Holz and Hanke later became Gauleiters.

Dunkirk: The Beginning

In London all eyes were turned to the French and Belgian Channel ports. Historically, these constituted England's front line. Optimists were concerned to keep the British Expeditionary Force supplied and reinforced; pessimists were already calculating the chances of rescue through those ports. Meanwhile, a brigade of infantry and a battalion of tanks were hurried aboard ships at Southampton and sent over to Calais. The 20th Guards Brigade was similarly ordered to bolster the defenses of Boulogne.

Guderian also had his eyes on the Channel ports and allotted to his three panzer divisions assaults upon Boulogne, Calais, and Dunkirk. Rundstedt's caution, resulting to some extent from the fighting at Arras, made him change this order and put one of the armored divisions into reserve. By the time this command was rescinded, Guderian's men were encountering stiff resistance at Boulogne. When Boulogne fell, on Friday morning, 24 May, Guderian decided to bypass Calais and put all his available force into a thrust to Dunkirk. Once again he was overruled. Rundstedt ordered that the tank forces should remain where they were. The controversial "halt order," which did so much to preserve the BEF for a sea evacuation, had arrived.

The Belgian Army

Belgium's war began as a fiasco and ended as a tragedy. The complete lack of cooperation between the military forces of neutral Belgium and their French and British counterparts up to the very day of the German invasion produced endless muddles as the armies tried to form a line of defense against the invaders.

A unit of the British 3rd Division, led by General Bernard Montgomery, was denied admittance to Belgium on 10 May, the first day of the German attack, when a frontier guard said that it would need proper documentation. A British army truck then crashed the barrier and the soldiers moved onward. At its allotted position, in the defenses of Brussels, this same division found its way blocked by Belgian units whose commander objected to the British presence. As negotiations about this were beginning, firing started as Belgian soldiers misidentified the British, thinking that they were German parachutists.

The original plan to defend the line of the river Dyle had been abandoned when the Germans proved unstoppable. A general withdrawal was delayed while the Belgian King insisted that his army must remain in position to cover Brussels. Eventually he agreed. On the night of 16/17 May the Allies retreated.

Although King Leopold was eventually to find himself blamed for the failures of his army, Belgian soldiers fought well for seventeen days until almost the whole country was overrun by the Germans. It was not until Monday, 27 May, that messages from the French liaison officer at Belgian GHQ reported that they had "abandoned the struggle."

The King sent an envoy to the Germans to propose that a cease-fire should commence at midnight that same night.

Operation Dynamo

As early as the evening of 14 May, following the BBC's nine o'clock news, an Admiralty message requested owners of self-propelled boats between 30 and 100 feet in length to send details of them to the navy within fourteen days. It is convenient to begin the story of the evacuation of Dunkirk with this fact and many accounts do so, but it is also important to see the announcements as part of a series of actions now established as arising from the German use of magnetic mines. For at this time wooden minesweepers so occupied the resources of boat yards as to cause a shortage of other small craft. In no way can that announcement be said to provide, as prejudiced observers have tried to claim for it, proof that the British were getting ready to flee the continent of Europe when the German assault was only four days old.

In fact the Dunkirk evacuation was born out of the BEF's urgent need for a new supply route across the Channel. On 19 May both the British and French navies were instructed to prepare sea transport for the besieged armies. Since the BEF, organized on the expectation of a rapid expansion, had an unusually large proportion of nonfighting soldiers, it was decided to bring what the army calls "useless mouths" back to England.

The Ministry of Shipping in London worked valiantly to cut through the red tape and release ships that could ply between the two best French ports: Calais and Boulogne. At Dover, Vice Admiral Bertram Ramsay was given command of these seaborne operations. One of the underground rooms used by Ramsay's staff had once housed an electricity generator, and from this came the code word for the actual evacuation—OPERATION DYNAMO. From Ramsay's office window it was possible on a clear day to see France. On 23 May the visibility was good enough to see the explosions as 2.Pz.Div shelled

Boulogne. Even before OPERATION DYNAMO had started, one of Ramsay's ports had been lost to him.

It was common sense to use cross-Channel ferry boats for personnel carriers, but in war one must not take common sense for granted. The ships were suited to the task, and many of them were manned by the same peacetime crews who knew the waters so well. At the start these ships were supplying the BEF and bringing back nonfighting soldiers and the wounded from the base hospitals.

On Saturday, 25 May, Boulogne fell to the Germans. In London, Churchill decided that the rifle brigade and the tank battalion which had been landed in France less than a week before must hold out in Calais for as long as possible. The message sent to their commander, Brigadier Claude Nicholson, said, "Every hour you continue to exist is of the greatest help to the BEF. Government has therefore decided you must continue to fight. Have greatest possible admiration for your splendid stand. Evacuation will not (repeat not) take place, and craft required for above purpose are to return to Dover . . ."

With Anthony Eden, Secretary of State for War, and Sir Edmund Ironside, Chief of the Imperial General Staff, Churchill ordered the destroyers earmarked for the evacuation back to England. "It involved Eden's own regiment in which he had long served and fought in the previous struggle," wrote Churchill later. "One has to eat and drink in war, but I could not help feeling physically sick as we afterwards sat silent at the table."*

It is doubtful whether many of the British soldiers fighting in the streets of Calais ever heard the stirring words sent to Nicholson, but they carried on fighting anyway until, in the early evening of Sunday, 26 May, resistance petered out.

On that same Sunday evening the Admiralty in London signaled that OPERATION DYNAMO should commence, although Ramsay had already sent the personnel ships out on his own responsibility. By 10:30 that evening, the first homecoming fighting troops were disembarking at Dover. At this time there was only hope of rescuing a small proportion of Gort's men. Late on Sunday night, an urgent signal from the Admiralty urged Ramsay to use the greatest vigor in getting up to 45,000 soldiers away, as it was thought that the Germans would have occupied the coast within two days.

The port facilities of Dunkirk were soon out of commission, and Ramsay realized that he would have to find some way of bringing men directly off the beaches. Captain E. F. Wharton, deputy chief

* Winston Churchill, *The Second World War*, vol. II.

of the Small Vessels Pool, had already been preparing for this eventuality. Entirely on his own authority, he had started requisitioning every small boat he could find and was somewhat relieved to find that this unlawful seizure of private property was to be made official. Now he began to search out men who could sail these boats.

Lord Gort

For the commander of the British Expeditionary Force, the situation toward the end of May 1940 was becoming more and more desperate. There were French protests about the way in which he had withdrawn from Arras, and there were more confused promises about a big new Anglo-French counteroffensive.

John Vereker, 6th Viscount Gort of Limerick, had been a staff officer for most of the First World War. When, in 1917, he took command of 4th Grenadier Guards, he rapidly earned a fighting reputation that has few equals. He won the Distinguished Service Order three times, as well as the Military Cross. In September 1918, guiding tanks into action despite his wounds, he was hit again and continued to command from a stretcher. For this he was awarded the Victoria Cross.

After a spell as commandant of the Staff College, Gort finally got the job of Chief of the Imperial General Staff. This appointment was made over the heads of several senior generals, as was Gort's subsequent command of the British Expeditionary Force in 1939. Gort was a man with many enemies, and not all of them were German.

On Saturday, 25 May 1940, news reached Gort near Lille that the Germans had captured Calais as well as Boulogne. Reports were arriving at his room in the chateau at Prémesques that the Belgian Army was about to capitulate. The Germans had split the Belgian force and left it isolated from the British, who they must have heard had been evacuating men by sea for several days. For Gort, the Belgian capitulation would mean a 20-mile gap opening up on his left flank.

Now came the most important moment in Gort's career. At about six o'clock in the evening of 25 May, after sitting alone for a long time, he went next door to the office of his chief of staff, General Henry Pownall. Without preliminary discussion, he ordered him to move two British divisions from the south and "send them over to Brookie [General Alan Brooke] on the left."

There is no doubt that this decision, which went against his orders from the French, and from London, too, had come after much heart-searching. One of the men who knew him, Major General Sir Edward Spears, described Gort as "a simple, straightforward, but not very clever man" and went on to say he was an "overdisciplined soldier who felt above all else that orders must be obeyed."*

What Gort called a "hunch" had come within an hour of a gap opening in the Belgian front line. Now it would be a matter of waiting to see whether the Germans could race through it before Gort's two divisions could get there to plug the hole.

For the French, Gort's decision meant the end of any last hope for a counterattack southward. For the BEF, it meant a chance of a fighting withdrawal. For Gort, it meant the end of his military aspirations—he would never again command an army in the field. Yet if one contemplates what the British government might have been forced by public pressure to do, in coming to terms with a Hitler holding captive a quarter of a million British soldiers, then Gort's decision was a turning point in the war.

One of Gort's most vociferous critics was Lieutenant General Alan Brooke, a corps commander. "Brookie" was one of the generals whom Gort had overtaken in his military career. Writing of his chief's great charm, Brooke felt bound to add that he had no confidence in Gort's handling of a large force because Gort could not see the wood for the trees. It is an observation difficult to reconcile with Brooke's suggestion that the BEF should withdraw to the Belgian ports of Ostend and Zeebrugge, which would have proved disastrous when the Belgians capitulated.

Anyone reading the diaries that Brooke published could easily form the impression that the skills, courage, and success of the withdrawal and of the Dunkirk evacuation were solely those of General Brooke. Indeed, Brooke's own account clearly made a deep impression on the historian Sir Arthur Bryant. In his commentary accompanying Brooke's record of events as it appears in his book, *The Turn of the Tide*, Bryant draws the conclusion that the escape of the BEF was due mainly to one man (Brooke) who "by his speed and foresight anticipated the attacker's every move . . ." While Gort was at his headquarters near the coast, without any means of knowing whether his orders were reaching the battle line, Alan Brooke was "achieving one of the great feats of British military history."

Closer study of the facts, however, provides material with which to resist this suggestion. Not only was Brooke's headquarters nearer to the coast than Gort's, Brooke's "foresight" was owed largely to a

* Major General Sir Edward Spears, *Assignment to Catastrophe*, vol. I.

captured briefcase containing the German Order of Battle, and Gort's communications with the BEF were in good order, as Brooke well knew from his daily visits to him.

It is also worth noting that Brooke's fully motorized force was facing horse-drawn infantry divisions of Bock's Army Group B. Brooke did not encounter any of the German armored divisions. It was the limitations of Bock's transport that frustrated all the German efforts to get through the gap created by the surrendering Belgians before the British divisions got there. There is no doubt that the almost prescient decision of Gort to move the two divisions saved the British Expeditionary Force from destruction.

Dunkirk: The End

On 27 May the Senior Naval Officer Ashore at Dunkirk decided that only some drastic action would speed up the evacuation, now already stalling because of German air attack, the lack of port facilities, and a shortage of small craft to ferry men from the beaches to ships. As an experiment, he ordered a ship to come alongside the flimsy structure of the East Mole, a wooden pier, 5 feet wide, stretching about 1,400 yards out to sea. The decision to use it in this way was to prove a vital contribution to the evacuation. More than 230,000 men were to embark from the Mole as against less than 100,000 from the beaches.

From now on, the pace of the evacuation accelerated as Royal Navy destroyers went one after the other to the East Mole, weaving between the wrecks visible above water and returning so heavily laden with men that they heeled over dangerously.

German air raids tried to make good Göring's claim that his air force could crush the defenders of Dunkirk without the army's help. It is sad to relate that the Luftwaffe's determination was such that more than one pilot repeatedly pressed home attacks against shipping clearly marked with red crosses. Others went for tempting targets on the beaches, but here the sand absorbed the shock of the explosions and casualties were surprisingly few. Bombs that hit destroyers and personnel ships swelled the carnage. These larger ships were jammed tight with men. It became common practice to leave watertight doors open to increase the space available, and top-heavy craft rolled over very quickly. The surf was soon bobbing with the dead men; through these floating corpses the living pressed their way.

Soldiers on the shore rolled vehicles down into the sea to make long causeways over which the men could clamber to the boats. The problem of beached boats—which stuck more tightly when loaded

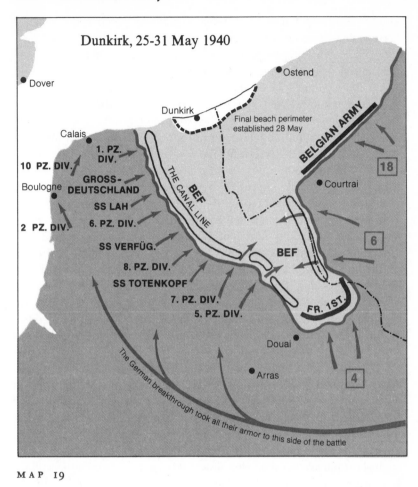

Dunkirk, 25-31 May 1940

Dover

Ostend

Dunkirk

Final beach perimeter
established 28 May

BELGIAN ARMY

Calais

10 PZ. DIV.

1. PZ.
DIV.

GROSS-
DEUTSCHLAND

THE CANAL LINE

BEF

18

Courtrai

Boulogne

SS LAH

2 PZ. DIV.

6. PZ. DIV.

SS VERFÜG.

8. PZ. DIV.

SS TOTENKOPF

7. PZ. DIV.

5. PZ. DIV.

BEF

6

FR. 1ST.

Douai

Arras

The German breakthrough took all their armor to this side of the battle

4

MAP 19

with men—was never really solved. At one time there were small craft taking men out to larger ones, which in turn went out to the ships in deeper water. It was cumbersome, but it worked.

It was the appearance of small craft along the water's edge that produced the spectacle that every survivor remembers. Many of the small boats were manned by civilians and had been towed across the Channel. They now provided the only means by which the soldiers, after standing for hours waist-deep in water, could get out to the rescue ships. In spite of the chaos and destruction, as the Germans bombed and machine-gunned the waiting lines of men, eyewitnesses testify to the calm confidence of the Royal Navy personnel. "At last we found people who knew exactly what they were doing" is a constantly recurring memory. But by 1 June the naval losses were so serious that it was decided to evacuate only under cover of darkness.

The Royal Navy's contribution to the evacuation was unstinted; destroyers—of which the navy was desperately short—were sent in again and again in spite of appalling losses. Ships' captains risked their vessels, sometimes even beaching them to get soldiers aboard, and were sent signals of approval by the Admiralty.

The soldiers had unqualified praise for the Royal Navy, but there were few good words spoken for the contribution the Royal Air Force made to the evacuation. For months afterward, men wearing air force blue were physically assaulted by Dunkirk survivors. Even today, Dunkirk is not remembered by the RAF with great pride. And yet it is hard to see what greater contribution the airmen could have made. To have kept standing patrols of fighters over the beaches would have sorely tested Fighter Command's resources, and even those sorties of British fighters that went there usually suffered heavy losses. It was soon decided that the fighter sweeps had to be of three- or four-squadron strength, and this meant long-time intervals between the sweeps. It was during these periods that German bombers and fighters could concentrate on destroying the big ships and strafing the men lined up along the beaches.

Although it is often said that the Messerschmitt Bf 109 single-seat fighter had a very short range, the truth is that neither the Hawker Hurricane nor the Supermarine Spitfire had better endurance. By the time British fighters were across the Channel they had only a few minutes in which to operate before turning back toward their own airfields. Since in the final three days of the evacuation less than four such short patrols per day were flown, it is easy to see why the soldiers felt neglected by the RAF. The Air Ministry's wild claims of the number of German aircraft destroyed (390 compared with an actual German loss of 156 aircraft on all parts of the front for the same period) did nothing to help the RAF's reputation with men who had seen with their own eyes German command of the air.

During the evacuation it had been the policy of the British ships to take French or British troops as they came. By 11:30 on the night of Sunday, 2 June, the navy was able to make the signal "BEF evacuated," but the ships continued to sail. The French Navy—and French merchant ships—played a vital part in the evacuation and faced the same appalling casualties as the British. It was the French Army which was given the task of holding off the Germans for the final hours.

The last British soldiers withdrew through the French-held perimeter, and French estimates said that by Monday there would be about 30,000 French soldiers still there. On Sunday night ships were returning to England half empty, with space enough for some 10,000 men more.

Admiral Ramsay prepared for one last hazardous attempt to lift off the French rearguard on Monday night and planned space for about 30,000 men. Skillfully the weary front-line infantry disengaged from the fighting line and moved quietly back to where the ships were waiting for them. It was then that a final tragedy marred the triumph. As if from nowhere, a huge army of French soldiers appeared along the beaches and the Mole. Unknown to the French command and undetected by the French military police, an estimated 40,000 soldiers came out of the cellars and ruins of Dunkirk where they had been hiding from the fighting. That night 26,175 soldiers were taken off by sea, but few of them were from the fighting rear guard for whom the ships were intended. The French historian Jacques Mordal described this as the most heartbreaking episode in the whole story of Dunkirk.

Dunkirk: The German Halt Order

The motive behind the decision to halt the German armor at Dunkirk, instead of letting the panzers race on to the beaches, is one of the most widely argued events of the campaign. Rundstedt even described it as leading to a turning point in the war.

Originally it had been the German intention that the armor on the west side should be the hammer that struck the Allies against the anvil of the stationary armies of Bock. But Rundstedt ordered a pause while the motorized infantry closed up to the armor to prepare for the attack. Hitler turned the pause into a longer halt. During this delay—and partly due to an understandable desire to preserve the armor for the coming battles in central France—Bock's armies became the hammer and the stationary armored divisions the anvil.

It has been said that a handkerchief floating in the air is like an army: striking it with a hammer will move it but do nothing more unless an anvil is brought into position behind it. This handkerchief analogy is popular with military lecturers because with it they are able also to illustrate another military principle. They point out that a bullet will penetrate a handkerchief even while it floats on air. This is because the velocity of the bullet is great enough to permit the anvil to be dispensed with.

So it was that the penetration of the French front line in May 1940 was achieved by high-velocity attack which shattered the defending armies instead of merely pushing them back. But as the Allied armies retreated to the sea, the German velocity was lost. Now it became a more orthodox sort of war, and the armies of Bock were suffering air attacks by the RAF as the Dunkirk fighting grew more desperate.

These air attacks were not made by the heavy bombers of RAF Bomber Command. Although the French government and Army High Command appealed for "the strongest possible air support in the coming battle," the British Air Ministry gave minimal air support to the land fighting. They preferred to continue with their strategic plan to bomb German oil targets and aircraft factories while the BEF fought for survival at Dunkirk. That the conquest of France would bring Germany war materials in abundance seems not to have occurred to them.

Manstein provides three possible reasons for Hitler's decision to halt the tanks. First, he wanted to keep his armor intact for the coming battle in central France. Second, Göring deserved the chance to gain a victory for his airmen. There was an element of politics in this idea, since the Luftwaffe was considered to be a Nazi Party arm because of Göring's political status and also because it was created by the Third Reich. Once Göring got permission from Hitler to destroy the enemy in the Dunkirk perimeter by air bombardment, the German Army commanders kept their front-line forces well back from the beaches lest they became victims of their own bombers. Third, says Manstein—far less credibly—Hitler believed that a compromise peace with the British would not be possible if he destroyed their army.

After the event, Hitler himself gave many different reasons for his decision. One of them was that the sudden heavy rain of 26 and 27 May made the "Flanders marshes" difficult for tank action. Some historians scoff at this excuse, but J. F. C. Fuller, one of the foremost tank experts, agreed and added that the network of drainage dikes to the south of Dunkirk was impassable by tanks.

By 28 May Guderian agreed too. Although a severe critic of the halt order, he found that the heavy rain of the previous two days made the terrain difficult for him. The XIX Corps diary quotes him advising Kleist's chief of staff that a tank attack would be pointless in such marshy ground. He said that infantry was more suited for that sort of country and his tanks were suffering unnecessary casualties. Ultimately the German armor was withdrawn from the fighting to refit for the coming battles in the south.

Hitler was concerned about the casualty returns from his tank units. By this time, half of the tanks of Kleist's panzer group were out of action and so were one third of the tanks of Hoth's XV Panzerkorps. Tank men, among them General Nehring, say Hitler could not understand that such statistics included tanks disabled for small faults that could be rectified within a few hours. That was small comfort for Hitler and his more nervous high commanders, who could scarcely believe that they had defeated what was considered the best army in Europe and so every moment waited for the massive counteroffensive that they felt must come sooner or later from the French armies in the south.

It is difficult to believe that Hitler had evolved any strategic reason for sparing the BEF. As recently as 24 May, Hitler's Directive No. 13 had begun to be put into effect. "Next goal of operations is the annihilation of the French, British and Belgian forces . . . During this operation the task of the Luftwaffe is to break all enemy resistance in the encircled parts and to prevent the escape of the British forces across the Channel."

The halt order is more easily understood if the coastline is seen as the German and French High Commands saw it. They had no staff experience, historical tradition, or equipment for amphibious operations. They saw the coastline as the end of the European land mass —the edge of their world. The Germans did not even consider the possibility of a sea evacuation. Gort himself had not envisaged it, and neither had Churchill. Even the men who were organizing OPERATION DYNAMO had only limited hopes for its success. The Dunkirk evacuation was a miracle of improvisation and desperation. As far as the records reveal, no one anywhere even began to guess what would be done at Dunkirk until it happened.

The halt order was originally a sensible precaution, a logical military procedure, whether the next stage of the campaign was to be a move north or a move south to central France. There were cities to be taken, and any built-up areas were mincing machines for the panzer divisions. The Germans were right to be nervous. Whichever way this great concentration of armor turned they would be exposing their supply lines and rear echelon to an active enemy. These same German armies had just proved how suicidal that could be.

Only after the BEF had been "miraculously" rescued by sea was the halt debated. Even then, the German High Command had no idea that well over 300,000 had escaped them. "Even 100,000 would have struck us as greatly exaggerated," said Luftwaffe General Albert Kesselring afterward.

The British Expeditionary Force included virtually the whole of Britain's regular peacetime army. Had that been lost, there would have been very few first-class professional soldiers left to set about training a new army. Besides, the escape of so many brave young men was a great morale booster. Although the survivors were chastened by the fierce German attack and impressed by German fighting skills, equipment, and organization, this mood changed quickly to one of indignant belligerence. The British began reminding each other of the theory that Britain lost every battle except the last one. Had the BEF been captured, as the greater part of France's army eventually was, then Hitler undoubtedly would have used those men to bargain for an end to the war. Could such overtures have been curtly brushed aside by a government which needed a population unified in its determination to continue the war?

The Battles in Central and Southern France

There was much fighting still to come. The Germans had to battle their way south, but few had any doubt of the final outcome. Already sixty-one Allied divisions, the greater part of them made up of the best troops that could be found, had been beaten.

Forty-nine divisions, very few of which included young, fit, first-rate troops, confronted the new onslaught. The French had less than 200 tanks to throw into the battle. At some places civilians tried to prevent their soldiers fighting so that their homes would not be destroyed. At Vienne, near Lyon, the mayor mustered the women of the town to stop French Army engineers from destroying the bridge. Reluctant to hurt their own people, the French soldiers let the bridge remain intact and the Germans advanced over it. At other places the French troops were not so concerned with their fellow countrymen. Soldiers routed on the battlefield became violent, drunken gangs, pillaging houses and churches and stealing from other refugees. At Royan the anxious townspeople welcomed the German invaders and drank their health, knowing that the presence of the Germans would restore law and order.

By 10 June the Germans had crossed the river Somme in a campaign which had little to distinguish it from the German military methods of the nineteenth century. There were no armored thrusts or breakthrough battles. Guderian might have proved his theories in the north, but now the army command was determined to show that foot soldiers and horse-drawn artillery could win wars too.

On 10 June Mussolini, anxious for a seat at the peace conference and a share in the spoils, declared war upon a prostrate France. Italian troops moved across the southern frontier.

Over the radio Premier Reynaud said to his people, "Signor Mussolini has chosen this time to declare war on us. How can this be judged? France has nothing to say. The world will judge." But

Reynaud's cable to President Roosevelt of the United States was less restrained: "What really distinguished, noble, admirable people the Italians are to stab us in the back at this time."

The American State Department strongly advised the President not to condemn Italy in the speech he was about to deliver at the University of Virginia. Disregarding these warnings about the effect it might have on international relations and without regard to the influence that voters of Italian extraction might exert upon his own political career, Roosevelt told the world what he thought of Mussolini's decision. "On this tenth day of June, 1940," he told his audience, "the hand that held the dagger struck it into the back of his neighbor."

The American ambassadors in Paris and London had been providing Washington with inaccurate and often hysterical accounts of what was happening in Europe, but despite these reports Roosevelt clearly saw the predatory nature of the totalitarians and in this speech gave warning that America would oppose them.

As Italian troops moved across the border into southern France, Paris was declared an open city and the government moved out, first to Tours and then to Bordeaux. Reynaud even considered taking the government to North Africa and continuing the war from there.

In Bordeaux, Reynaud's mistress, Hélène de Portes, put all her amazing energies into promoting an immediate peace with the Germans. What the senile Marshal Pétain described as the "moral rottenness of French political life" made him and the elderly General Weygand look with some perverse satisfaction at the triumph of the disciplined German armies. Neither man supported in any way Reynaud's desire to fight on. Yet when French air force cadets at Mérignac airfield near Bordeaux were issued automatic weapons, in what was probably the first step in a military takeover from Reynaud, they were told an entirely different story. The cadets heard that it was Pétain and Weygand who wished to continue the war and the civilians who wanted to capitulate. The plot was discovered and quashed.

On 17 June Guderian reported that he was at Pontarlier, and Hitler wired back, "You probably mean Pontailler-sur-Saône."

"No mistake," said Guderian. "I am myself on the Swiss border."

Now he was able to move northeast and penetrate the Maginot Line fortifications from the rear, using the panzer group which since 28 May had been his new command. This great line of fortifications, which had cost France an immense amount of money and into which were shut so many thousands of her soldiers, was virtually useless against an attack from the rear. "The Maginot Line was a formidable barrier," wrote one military commentator, "not so much against the German Army as against French understanding of modern war."

From the French ambassador in London there came a dramatic idea for a political union between Britain and France. Churchill approved, and the British Cabinet was enthusiastic. The proposed union would provide for joint organs of defense, foreign, financial, and economic policies. British subjects would enjoy immediate citizenship of France and French citizens would become citizens of Great Britain. "M. Reynaud might by tonight be Prime Minister of France and Britain," said de Gaulle on the telephone from London to Bordeaux.*

But Reynaud's hopes that this would stiffen his Cabinet's determination to continue the war were dashed when his mistress leaked the news to the defeatists. "It would be like fusion to a corpse," said Pétain, and another member of the Cabinet said he would rather see France as a Nazi province than as a British dominion. With well over half his Cabinet against him, Reynaud resigned. President Lebrun asked Pétain to form a government.

Churchill's offer was generous and sincere, but the future of the French fleet was always in his mind (just as later in 1940, during the Battle of Britain, the idea of Britain's fleet being captured by the Germans was a constant worry to the President of the United States). Churchill's conversation with the newly appointed Premier Pétain has never been revealed, but one who overheard it, General Leslie Hollis, Military Secretary to the British War Cabinet, described it as the most violent conversation he had heard from Churchill.

If Churchill was asking Pétain to continue the war, he was too late. Pétain had already summoned the Spanish ambassador, who phoned two of his attachés waiting at St-Jean-de-Luz. They walked across the Franco-Spanish frontier and from Irun passed on Pétain's plea for armistice terms to the Germans in Madrid. If only the French generals had waged war as smoothly as they sought peace.

Churchill's fear that the French fleet would be combined with the Italian Navy, and perhaps ultimately with that of Japan, led him to what he came to call "a hateful decision, the most unnatural and painful in which I have ever been concerned." The Royal Navy was given the unenviable task of disabling, by consent or gunfire, the major French warships. At Oran the British bombardment lasted for ten minutes and was followed by air attacks. Relations between France and Britain sank to an all-time low, but friends and foes throughout

* Noel Barber, *The Week France Fell.*

the world realized that, in Churchill's words, "the British War Cabinet feared nothing and would stop at nothing."† This was true.

The Missing French Aircraft

In a confusion not unlike that of infantrymen running from non-existent tanks, many French historians rationalized their terrible defeat with stories about German tank armies faced by nothing better than riflemen and swarms of Stukas without opponents. One by one, these long-standing myths have collapsed under scrutiny. Just as France had tanks as good, and as numerous, as those of the invading forces, so was the French air force at least numerically equal to the Luftwaffe.

General Kesselring said that the two Air Fleets of the German invasion force in France had a total of 2,670 aircraft. Of these about 1,000 were fighters, including the twin-engined Messerschmitt Bf 110 fighters.

The French air force, according to Guy La Chambre, the French Air Minister from 1938 to 1940, had 3,289 modern aircraft available. Of these 2,122 were fighters. He went on to explain that only a third of these planes were at the front; the others were in the interior of France. It is a strange remark, especially for an Air Minister. France measures only 620 miles from Brest to Menton, and even the most antiquated French bomber—the Bloch MB 200—could cross the country in four hours.

"Our air force ran into an enemy that outnumbered it by five to one," wrote General Joseph Vuillemin, Chief of the Air Force. That is untrue and made the more absurd by the fact that, during the fighting, more and more new aircraft were sent to the French units. Between 10 May and 12 June 1,131 new aircraft were received, of which 668 were fighters. Vuillemin admitted that more aircraft were delivered during this period than were lost by enemy action. Thus French air power actually *increased* during the battle.

None of the foregoing takes into account the RAF contribution, from units based in France and from those that fought there from bases in the British Isles. Indeed, the RAF's combat losses exceeded those of the French air force.

So where were the aircraft? French commanders have given evidence of the lack of air support. Infantrymen under bombardment by the slow, unarmored, and ill-armed Stukas wondered why the French fighter arm did not knock them from the sky. General d'Astier de la Vigerie, air commander of 1st French Army Group, said he had only 432 fighters, and 72 of those were RAF planes. General Gamelin himself asked, "Why, out of 2,000 modern fighters on hand at the beginning of May 1940, were fewer than 500 used on the northeast front?" Perhaps the answer to that question is contained in the fact that the Commander in Chief was asking it. "We have a right to be astonished," added Gamelin. *We* have that right perhaps, but did Gamelin have it?

So what really happened to all those missing aircraft? The German attacks upon the French airfields—the very first step of any blitzkrieg —had unexpected results. Undamaged aircraft were hastily flown out of the immediate danger zone and parked at training fields, civil airports, and rear-echelon strips. No proper records were made of what was happening. Deliveries from the factories were diverted from front-line units and also parked in safe places.

While the front-line soldiers watched the German bombers wheel lazily through undefended skies, eyewitnesses counted 200 aircraft parked on Tours airfield, 150 of them fighters. After the armistice, in the unoccupied zone of France there were 4,200 French aircraft, of which 1,700 were suitable for front-line use. The Italian Control Commission, which reported on North Africa in 1940, found 2,648 modern French aircraft there. Over 700 of these were fighters, many brand-new.

Capitulation

Blitzkrieg evolved naturally as a method by which a highly trained and newly equipped German Wehrmacht could invade its neighbors. To avoid detection by air reconnaissance, the invasion force was best deployed under peacetime conditions. Enemy air forces were to be knocked out with little or no warning. The juxtaposition of muddled and politically divided prewar democracies with Hitler's expansionist dictatorship gave rise to the blitzkrieg, just as surely as did General Guderian. The geography of France, its lack of natural frontier obstacles and the converging valleys that offer the invader a route to Paris, made her the most perfect of targets for German armored divisions.

Yet the rashness of the German plan must not be eclipsed by its success. The most precious part of Germany's military resources was to be overextended in a way that ignored every lesson of history. It would have needed little expertise, very little boldness, and no more than the available Allied forces to cut Panzergruppe Kleist off from its support (there was no air supply in this campaign) and force Germany to a humiliating defeat. The Germans gambled everything on the slowness and incompetence of the Allies and were proved right: France capitulated.

Few people in the Western world were left untouched by the news that France had fallen. It was a second homeland for millions who had never been there. They read its literature, sang its songs, admired its paintings, watched its films, and ate its food. For many such people— not a few of them German—the news brought a shock that bordered on physical pain. France had long been considered the ultimate sanctuary, not only for Russian Tsarists, German Jews, Italian Communists, American writers, and Spanish Republicans, but also for men who, harassed at home or work or school, cherished a secret comfort that France would give them a home, if only in the Foreign Legion.

Now the Third Republic, born of the battle of Sedan in 1870, was dead. The slogan *Liberté, Egalité, Fraternité* was officially discarded in favor of *Travail, Famille, Patrie*, and upon the reverse of France's lightweight alloy coins *Etat Français* replaced *République Française*. This "French State" was a curious parcel of land, deprived of coastline and abounding in regulations. No comfort there for anyone.

The defeat of the Allies on the Continent in 1940 was a failure of communication and command. Time was the most vital factor, but it was squandered, not by sluggish production of aircraft or by slow tanks, but by slow decisions and a paralysis of command. The German drive to the sea had continued virtually without opposition, while thousands of French aircraft stood on safe airfields, antitank guns remained at storage depots, and whole armored divisions were spread out in a *defensive* formation.

The fall of France was a turning point in European history, but no aspect of it was more far-reaching than the tragic turnabout it brought in Anglo-French relations. It came at a time when these two nations, their interests so close, were about to embark on a new and far more intimate pooling of military, industrial, and economic resources. There is nothing new about acrimony between allies in defeat, but the special circumstances of 1940 were to fan the sadness, recrimination, and shame in France into a bitter Anglophobia.

It was to be expected that those most responsible for France's agony should devote the most energy to finding excuses and scapegoats. It was more comforting to describe the Dunkirk evacuation as the British running away than as the result of the French Army's failure. It was convenient to believe that if the whole RAF fighter

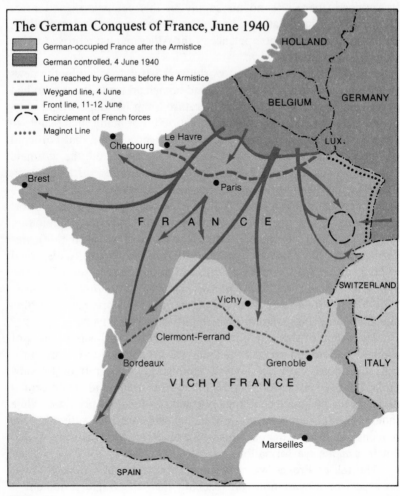

The German Conquest of France, June 1940

German-occupied France after the Armistice

German controlled, 4 June 1940

- - - - - Line reached by Germans before the Armistice

——— Weygand line, 4 June

▬ ▬ ▬ Front line, 11-12 June

⌒ Encirclement of French forces

• • • • Maginot Line

HOLLAND

BELGIUM   GERMANY

LUX.

Cherbourg   Le Havre

Brest

Paris

F R A N C E

SWITZERLAND

Vichy

Clermont-Ferrand

Bordeaux   Grenoble   ITALY

VICHY FRANCE

Marseilles

SPAIN

M A P   20

force had been thrown into the battle, France would not have been defeated.

That all British decisions contained a measure of self-interest was undeniable—"vous autres Anglais, vous êtes de grands politiques," Pétain told one British officer. The British brigade that landed at Calais with orders to fight to the last man could hardly be included. Besides, Churchill was sending RAF fighter planes to France at a rate that threatened Britain's survival. Yet neither should anyone ever forget that, at the Dunkirk perimeter, it was the French infantry, fighting to the end, who made the whole evacuation possible.

The men who rose to prominence in defeated France, aided by a German propaganda machine and provided with the Riom show trial to inquire into the defeat, were able to fabricate a totally distorted history and provide themselves creditable roles in it. Displaying an amazing talent for self-preservation, France's inept military leaders, whose shortsightedness had brought on the catastrophe, showed a new-found prescience as they planned their political futures.

Weygand perversely refused to order a cease-fire when Reynaud wanted it. Eventually it emerged that he wanted the politicians, rather than the soldiers of the High Command, to bear the stigma of defeat. Other devious calculations concerned the fears that Britain would use her empire and fleet—and the army evacuated from Dunkirk—to gain better peace terms than France might be able to get. The possibility that Britain might not capitulate immediately was nowhere discussed in France.

Armistice

In a gesture that at once revealed his inadequacies as a statesman and the spite that motivated him, Adolf Hitler staged an elaborate and theatrical humiliation for the French leaders. Instead of effecting a reconciliation with them and attempting to exploit France's new Anglophobia, he made the Frenchmen sign their capitulation in the same railway carriage that had been used to dictate the armistice to the German plenipotentiaries at the end of the First World War.

An enraptured Hitler was filmed at the event. He smiled broadly and stamped his foot. The British propaganda film service looped the sequence to make it look as though a demented Hitler were dancing a jig. It was small compensation for a desperate reverse.

De Gaulle: One Lonely Voice

The German armistice terms were moderate only if compared with those that other conquered nations signed. France was to be governed by Frenchmen, but only by Frenchmen who would do as Hitler wished. French prisoners of war were to remain in German prison camps with no promise of release.

General Charles de Gaulle, who went to London and proclaimed a "Free France" that would continue to fight, provided the only voice of protest. In Britain there were three other French generals and two

French admirals, as well as thousands of soldiers and sailors, either en route from Norway or brought from Dunkirk. Virtually all of these men denounced de Gaulle and demanded to be sent back to conquered France. Nor did any notable French civilian join him. "Not a single public figure raised his voice to condemn the armistice," wrote de Gaulle in his memoirs. It was a personal defeat and one that was later to embitter de Gaulle at a time when he was able to influence Europe.

In July 1940 a curious figure emerged in France from the shadows of the interwar years. An ex-Premier, Pierre Laval, brought a shaky unity to France's political life. He had been a left-wing Socialist and now found accord with the German totalitarians. He used Anglophobia, anti-Semitism, and the almost religious veneration in which all Frenchmen held Marshal Pétain, hero of Verdun.

Laval attached himself to Pétain. Using the threat of German disfavor, a fictitious coup d'état by Weygand, the marshal's benediction or political favors, and the coveted ambassadorships, Laval persuaded the French Parliament to vote itself into extinction. No pressure was put upon the members, neither did the Germans regard the move as beneficial to them. Rather the reverse: if they were to have men do their bidding, they felt, then let them wear the trappings of a republic.

France's military leaders, having lost the war, took over the defeated land. As well as the old marshal himself, Pétain's government gave employment to three generals and an admiral. One ex-minister remarked, "The Republic has often feared the dictatorship of conquering generals—it never dreamed of that of defeated ones."

Congratulations

But it was not entirely a right-wing government. There were two Socialists sitting alongside the marshal. The French Communists, their party outlawed since war began, openly supported the Germans. L'Humanité, a clandestine Communist paper, so pleased the German military commander that he gave it permission to publish openly.

In Soviet Russia, the Communists had been similarly cooperative with the Nazis. On 31 October 1939, Vyacheslav Molotov, the Russian Foreign Minister, showing an uncharacteristic respect for both democracy and Nazism, proclaimed, "It is criminal to take part in a war which, disguised as a war for the preservation of democracy, is nothing but a war for the destruction of National Socialism." Communist parties everywhere were ordered by Moscow to condemn the war as an imperialist war. German propaganda units had been delighted to translate this speech into French and English. In leaflets it had been dropped by the thousands over the French front lines.

Now that France was crushed, the Russians did not hide their pleasure. The German ambassador in Moscow wired Berlin to tell them, "Molotov summoned me this evening to his office and expressed the warmest congratulations of the Soviet government on the splendid success of the German armed forces."

The French Communists, who had done so much to undermine France in its opposition to Nazi Germany, who during the German attack were circulating a tract, *L'Humanité du soldat*, which claimed that it was a war on behalf of Anglo-French financiers, now began to blame the collapse of France on the same people who had done so much to avoid the war. Thus emerged the Communist slogan, "The traitors of Munich opened France to invasion."

One Fatal Flaw

In France, Belgium, and Holland the Germans found military supplies and factories enough to transform their war potential. In Germany, war production was actually cut back. France's motor vehicle industry—to say nothing of vehicles abandoned by the British or taken from the other Allied armies—alleviated the German Army's desperate shortages in the motorized infantry and motorized supply units. And Germany's stockpiled fuel oil, deeply drained by ten months of fighting, was replenished with enough to keep the war machine going for another two years.

German soldiers were provided with occupation marks. The French and Belgian francs and the Dutch florin were pegged artificially low—the French currency about 20 per cent below its true value—and issue banks were forbidden to devalue.

This not only had the effect of draining everything—from champagne to real estate—into German hands at bargain prices, but it prevented German goods leaving Germany, except at bonanza prices. It was a subtle form of plunder, and it took a long time before the citizens of the conquered countries were anything but delighted at the generous prices they were being paid for their goods and services.

In addition, each defeated country was made to pay for the maintenance of the German occupation forces. In the summer of 1940 France began paying 400 million francs per day as a "contribution to her defense against Britain."

The battle of France ended, not as it had begun, with the dramatic blitzkrieg that Manstein and Guderian had designed, but with plodding infantry and horse-drawn artillery that had reverted to the Kessel-schlacht techniques. The blitzkrieg method was never again success-fully used. The scale and the shape of northern France had provided the perfect board for this exciting game. From now on there would be mountains and empty deserts and the vast space of the Russian landscape—no convenient road networks and sophisticated armies that could be unbalanced by a pinprick where they least expected it. The Germans would strike eastward and find a cruder enemy with simpler supply problems, men and women who laughed at pinpricks and kept fighting without food, water, and communications.

Tanks were never again to inspire the same widespread brain-numbing terror they caused France in May 1940. Bigger and better antitank guns were already on their way and soon would come exotic tapered bore weapons and curious discarding and composite missiles. The infantry would be issued with lightweight weapons with which one determined man could destroy a tank, and trained soldiers would realize how vulnerable armored vehicles could be.

And yet before we declare PLAN YELLOW to be the only success-ful blitzkrieg, it is worth looking at the declared objectives of that offensive. One stated aim was to engage and defeat the strongest possible part of the Allied armies. Hitler had specifically ordered the annihilation of the BEF and that it should be prevented from escaping across the Channel. The Germans had failed in that endeavor. It was to prove a fatal flaw.

Sources and Bibliography

DOCUMENTS *(All documents are courtesy of the Imperial War Museum, London.)*

English, Major I. R. Untitled Lecture at an Official Army Battlefield Tour.

Notes on 5th Division, Exercise Acrospire (Battlefield Tour of N.W. France & Belgium 1940). 2 vols. (cyclostyled). British Army, 1970.

Reinhardt, General G.-H. XXXI Panzerkorps: General Reinhardt's Comments on the Meuse Crossing, 13–15 May 1940. (AL1400).

Rommel, Erwin. History of the 7th Panzer Division, 19 May–25 September 1940. (AL596).

Schroeder, Hans-Ulrich. Untitled, text of a lecture on the battle.

BOOKS AND PAPERS

Addington, Larry H. *The Blitzkrieg Era and the German General Staff, 1865–1941.* New Brunswick, N.J.: Rutgers University Press, 1971.

Alquier, François Fonvielle-. *The French and the Phoney War, 1939–40.* Translated from the French by E. Ashcroft. London: Stacey, 1973.

Bacon, Sir Reginald, J. F. C. Fuller, and Sir Patrick Playfair, eds. *Warfare Today.* London: Odhams, 1944.

Barber, Noel. *The Week France Fell.* London: Macmillan, 1976.

Barker, Arthur J. *Dunkirk: The Great Escape.* London: Dent, 1977.

Beaufré, General André. *1940: The Fall of France.* London: Dent, 1977.

Bekker, Cajus. *The Luftwaffe War Diaries.* Translated from the German by F. Ziegler. London: Macdonald, 1967.

Bender, Roger James. *Air Organisations of the Third Reich: Luftwaffe.* Calif.: R. James Bender Publishing, 1967.

———, and Hugh Page. *Uniforms, Organisation and History of the Waffen SS,* vol. I. Calif.: R. James Bender Publishing, 1969.

Bennett, Geoffrey. *Naval Battles of World War II.* London: Batsford, 1975.

Benoist-Mechin, J. *Sixty Days That Shook the West: The Fall of France, 1940.* Edited by Cyril Falls; translated from the French by P. Wiles. London: Jonathan Cape, 1963.

Bidwell, Shelford. *Gunners at War: A Tactical Stndy of the Royal Artillery in the Twentieth Century.* London: Arms & Armour Press, 1970.

Bingham, Major James. *Chars Hotchkiss, H35, H39 and Somua S35* (AFV Weapons 36). Windsor, Berks.: Profile Publications, 1971.

————. *French Infantry Tanks: Part I (Chars 2C, D, and B)* (AFV Weapons 58); *Part II (including R35 and FCM 36)* (AFV Weapons 59). Windsor, Berks.: Profile Publications, 1973.

Blaxland, G. *Destination Dunkirk: The Story of Gort's Army.* London: Kimber, 1973.

Blumentritt, Guenther. *Von Rundstedt: The Soldier and the Man, by his Chief of Staff.* London: Odhams, 1952.

Boelcke, Willi A. *Deutschlands Rüstung im Zweiten Weltkrieg: Hitler's Konferenzen mit Albert Speer, 1942–45.* Frankfurt am Main: Akademische Verlag Athenaion, 1969.

Bryant, Sir Arthur. *The Turn of the Tide, 1939–1943: A Study Based on the Diaries and Autobiographical Notes of Field Marshal The Viscount Alanbrooke, K.G., O.M.* London: Collins, 1957.

Bullock, Alan L. C. *Hitler: A Study in Tyranny.* London: Odhams, 1952.

Burne, Alfred Higgins. *Strategy as Exemplified in the Second World War.* The Lees Knowles Lecture for 1946. Cambridge: University Press, 1946.

Butler, E., and J. S. Bradford. *The Story of Dunkirk.* London: Hutchinson, 1955.

Calvocoressi, Peter, and Guy Wint. *Total War: Causes and Courses of the Second World War.* London: Allen Lane, 1972.

Chamberlain, Peter, and Hilary L. Doyle. *Weapons on German Built Fully-tracked Chassis* (Bellona Handbook no. 1, part 1). *Weapons on Foreign Built Fullytracked Chassis* (Bellona Handbook no. 1, part 2). *Prime Movers and Self-propelled Carriages* (Bellona Handbook no. 2, part 1). *Light Armoured Personnel Carriers* (Bellona Handbook no. 2, part 2). Bracknell, Berks.: Bellona, 1967, 1968, 1968, and 1970.

————. *Schützenpanzerwagen SdKfz 251 and SdKfz 250.* Windsor, Berks.: Profile Publications, 1973.

Chapman, Guy. *Why France Collapsed.* London: Cassell, 1968.

Churchill, Winston S. *The World Crisis 1911–18.* Abridged. London: Butterworth, 1931.

————. *The Second World War.* 6 vols., rev. ed. London: Cassell, 1949.

Ciano, Galeazzo. *Ciano's Diaries: 1939–1943.* London: Heinemann, 1947.

Cooper, Matthew. *The German Army 1933–1945.* London: Macdonald & Jane's, 1978.

Craig, Gordon A. *Germany, 1866–1945.* London: Oxford University Press, 1978.

Davis, Brian Leigh. *German Army Uniforms and Insignia, 1933–1945.* London: Arms & Armour Press, 1971.

De Gaulle, Charles. *France and Her Army.* London: Hutchinson, 1948.

De Guingand, Major General Sir Francis. *Operation Victory.* London: Hodder & Stoughton, 1947.

Department of the Army (U.S.). *German Tank Maintenance in World War II* (Pamphlet 20-202). Washington, D.C.: Govt. Printing Office, 1954.

Department of the Army (U.S.). *Airborne Operations: A German Appraisal* (Pamphlet 20-230). Washington, D.C.: Govt. Printing Office, 1951.

Deutsch, Harold C. *Hitler and His Generals: The Hidden Crisis, January–June 1938*. Minneapolis: University of Minnesota Press, 1974.

Divine, David. *The Nine Days of Dunkirk*. London: Faber, 1959.

Duncan, Major General N. W. *Panzerkampfwagen I & II* (AFV Weapons 15). *German Armoured Cars* (AFV Weapons 33). Windsor, Berks.: Profile Publications, 1970 and 1971.

Dupuy, R. Ernest, and Trevor N. Dupuy. *The Encyclopedia of Military History*. New York: Harper & Row, 1970.

Ellis, Major L. F. *The War in France and Flanders, 1939–1940*. London: HMSO, 1953.

Fest, Joachim C. *Hitler*. Translated from the German by Richard and Clara Winston. London: Weidenfeld & Nicolson, 1974.

Friedrich, Otto. *Before the Deluge: A Portrait of Berlin in the 1920s*. London: Michael Joseph, 1974.

Fuller, Major General J. F. C. *Watchwords*. London: Skeffington, 1944.

————. *Armament and History from the Dawn of Classical Warfare to the Second World War*. London: Eyre & Spottiswoode, 1946.

————. *The Decisive Battles of the Western World and Their Influence Upon History*, vol. 3: *From the American Civil War to the End of the Second World War*. London: Eyre & Spottiswoode, 1948.

————. *The Second World War, 1939–45: A Strategical and Tactical History*. London: Eyre & Spottiswoode, 1948.

————. *The Conduct of War 1789–1961*. London: Methuen, 1972.

Gallicus. *General de Gaulle: The Hope of France*. London: Collins, 1941.

Gardner, Charles. *A.A.S.F.* London: Hutchinson, 1940.

Gilbert, Felix. *Hitler Directs His War: The Secret Records of His Daily Military Conferences*. Annotated from the ms. in the University of Pennsylvania Library. New York: Oxford University Press, 1950.

Gilbert, Martin. *First World War Atlas*. London: Weidenfeld & Nicolson, 1970.

Gisevius, Hans Bernd. *To the Bitter End*. Translated from the German by Richard and Clara Winston. London: Jonathan Cape, 1948.

Goerlitz, Walter. *The German General Staff: Its History and Structure, 1657–1945*. Translated from the German by Brian Battershaw. London: Hollis & Carter, 1953.

Goodspeed, D. J. *Ludendorff: Soldier, Dictator, Revolutionary*. London: Hart-Davis, 1966.

Goutard, A. *The Battle of France, 1940*. Translated from the French by Captain A.R.P. Burgess. London: Muller, 1958.

Grunberger, Richard. *Hitler's SS*. London: Weidenfeld & Nicolson, 1970.

Grunfeld, Frederic V. *The Hitler File: A Social History of Germany and the Nazis 1918–45*. London: Weidenfeld & Nicolson, 1974.

Guderian, General Heinz. *Panzer Leader*. Translated from the German by Constantine Fitzgibbon. London: Michael Joseph, 1952.

Hart, W. E. *Landmarks of Modern Strategy*. London: Methuen, 1942.

Hartmann, T. *Wehrmacht Division Signs, 1938–1945*. London: Almark, 1970.

Hay, Ian. *The Battle of Flanders, 1940*. London: HMSO, 1941.

Heiss, F. *Der Sieg Im Westen: Ein Bericht vom Kampf des deutschen Volks-heeres in Holland, Belgien und Frankreich.* Prague: Volk und Reich Verlag, 1943.

Hitler, Adolf. *Hitler's Secret Conversations, 1941–1944.* Introductory essay, "The Mind of Adolf Hitler," by H. R. Trevor-Roper. New York: Farrar, Straus, 1953.

———. *Mein Kampf.* Translated from the German by R. Manheim. London: Hutchinson, 1972.

———. *Letters and Notes.* Compiled by Werner Maser; translated by A. Pomerans. London: Heinemann, 1974.

Hogg, O. F. G. *Artillery: Its Origin, Heyday and Decline.* London: C. Hurst, 1970.

Höhne, Heinz. *The Order of the Death's Head: The Story of Hitler's SS.* Translated from the German by R. Barry. London: Secker & Warburg, 1969.

Horne, Alistair. *To Lose a Battle: France 1940.* London: Macmillan, 1969.

Humble, Richard. *Hitler's Generals.* London: Barker, 1973.

International Military Tribunal. *Trial of the Major War Criminals: Nuremburg 14 November 1945–1 October 1946.* Nuremburg: 1945–6.

Irving, David. *Breach of Security: The German Secret Intelligence File on Events Leading to the Second World War.* London: Kimber, 1968.

———. *Trail of the Fox: The Life of Field Marshal Erwin Rommel.* London: Weidenfeld & Nicolson, 1977.

———. *The War Path.* London: Michael Joseph, 1978.

Jackson, Robert. *Air War Over France, 1939–40.* London: Ian Allen, 1975.

Jacobsen, Dr. H.-A., and Dr. J. Rohwer. *Decisive Battles of World War Two: The German View.* Translated from the German by E. Fitzgerald. London: Deutsch, 1965.

Kedward, Harry Roderick. *Resistance in Vichy France: A Study of Ideas & Motivation in the Southern Zone, 1940–42.* London: Oxford University Press, 1978.

Keitel, Wilhelm B. J. G. *The Memoirs of Field-Marshal Keitel.* Edited by W. Goerlitz; translated from the German by David Irving. London: Kimber, 1965.

Kennedy, Major Robert M. *The German Campaign in Poland, 1939* (Department of the Army Pamphlet 20-255). Washington, D.C.: Govt. Printing Office, 1956.

Kersten, Felix. *The Kersten Memoirs, 1940–45.* London: Hutchinson, 1956.

Kloss, Erhard, compiler. *Der Luftkrieg über Deutschland 1939–1945.* Munich: Deutscher Taschenbuch Verlag, 1963.

Krausnick, Helmut, and Martin Broszat. *Anatomy of the SS State.* Translated from the German by Dorothy Long and Martin Jackson. London: Granada, 1970.

Laval, Pierre. *The Unpublished Diary of Pierre Laval.* London: Falcon, 1948.

Leverkuehn, Paul. *German Military Intelligence.* Translated from the German by R. H. Stevens and C. Fitzgibbon. London: Weidenfeld & Nicolson, 1954.

Lewin, Ronald. *Rommel as Military Commander.* London: Batsford, 1968.

Liddell Hart, B. H. *The British Way in Warfare.* London: Faber, 1932.

———. *The Defence of Britain.* New York: Random House, 1939.

————. *The Strategy of Indirect Approach.* London: Faber, 1941.

————. *The Other Side of the Hill: Germany's Generals, Their Rise and Fall, With Their Own Account of Military Events, 1939–1945.* London: Cassell, 1948.

————, et al., ed. *The Rommel Papers.* Translated from the German by Paul Findley. London: Collins, 1953.

————. *The Memoirs of Captain Liddell Hart,* vol. I. London: Cassell, 1970.

————. *The History of the Second World War.* London: Cassell, 1970.

Linklater, Eric. *The Defence of Calais, May 22–27, 1940.* London: HMSO, 1941.

Maassen, Heinz. *Über die Maas: Die Erzwingung des Übergangs bis Monthermé.* Düsseldorf: Völkischer Verlag, 1942.

Macintyre, Donald. *The Battle of the Atlantic.* London: Batsford, 1960.

————. *Wings of Neptune: The Story of Naval Aviation.* London: Peter Davies, 1963.

Macksey, Kenneth J. *The Shadow of Vimy Ridge.* London: Kimber, 1965.

————. *Tank Warfare: A History of Tanks in Battle.* London: Hart-Davis, 1971.

————. *Guderian: Panzer General.* London: Macdonald & Jane's, 1975.

————, and John H. Batchelor. *Tank: A History of the Armoured Fighting Vehicle.* London: Macdonald, 1970.

McLean, D. B. *German Infantry Weapons* (Military Intelligence Service Special Series no. 14). Washington, D.C.: Govt. Printing Office, 1966.

Mallory, Keith, and Arvid Ottar. *Architecture of Aggression: A History of Military Architecture in North West Europe, 1900–1945.* London: Architectural Press, 1973.

Manstein, Field Marshal Erich von. *Lost Victories.* Edited and translated from the German by Anthony G. Powell. London: Methuen, 1958.

Mason, Jr., Herbert M. *The Rise of the Luftwaffe.* London: Cassell, 1975.

Mellenthin, Major-General F. W. von. *Panzer Battles, 1939–1945.* Edited by L. C. F. Turner; translated from the German by H. Betzler. London: Cassell, 1955.

————. *German Generals of World War II.* Norman: University of Oklahoma Press, 1977.

Messenger, Charles. *The Art of Blitzkrieg.* London: Ian Allan, 1976.

Miksche, Ferdinand Otto. *Blitzkrieg.* London: Faber, 1941.

Military Academy (U.S.), Dept. of Military Art. *The West Point Atlas of American Wars,* vol. II, *1900–1953.* New York: Praeger, 1959.

Milsom, John. *Panzerkampfwagen 38(t) & 35(t)* (AFV Weapons 22). Windsor, Berks.: Profile Publications, 1970.

————. *Armoured Fighting Vehicles.* Feltham, Middlesex: Hamlyn, 1973.

Mollo. A. *Uniforms of the SS,* vol. I, *Allgemeine-SS 1923–1945.* London: HMSO, 1968.

Montgomery, Field Marshal The Viscount. *Memoirs.* London: Collins, 1958.

————. *A History of Warfare.* London: Collins, 1968.

Montross, Lynn. *War Through the Ages.* 3rd ed., rev. New York: Harper & Row, 1960.

Mordal, Jacques. *La Bataille de Dunkerque.* Paris: Self, 1948.

Morgan, Brigadier General J. H. *Assize of Arms: Being the Story of the Disarmament of Germany and Her Rearmament (1919–1939).* London: Methuen, 1945.

Mrazek, James E. *The Fall of Eben Emael.* London: Hale, 1970.

Necker, Wilhelm. *The German Army of Today.* London: Lindsay Drummond, 1943.

Nehring, Walther. *Die Geschichte der deutschen Panzerwaffe, 1916–1945.* Berlin: Propyläen Verlag, 1969; Stuttgart: Motorbuch-Verlag, 1974.

The Netherlands. Generale Staf. *De Strijd op Nederlands grongebied tijdens de Wereldoorlog II.*, vol. 4, part 3, *De Strijd om Rotterdam.* 1952.

Office of the Chief of Counsel for Prosecutor of Axis Criminality. *Nazi Conspiracy and Aggression.* Washington, D.C.: Govt. Printing Office, 1946.

Ogorkiewicz, Richard M. *Design and Development of Fighting Vehicles.* London: Macdonald, 1967.

————. *Armoured Forces: A History of Armoured Forces and Their Vehicles.* London: Arms & Armour Press, 1970.

O'Neill, Robert J. *The German Army and the Nazi Party.* London: Cassell, 1966.

Orgill, Douglas. *The Tank: Studies in the Development and Use of a Weapon.* London: Heinemann, 1970.

Paget, R. T. *Manstein: His Campaigns and His Trial.* London: Collins, 1951.

Postan, M. M., et al. *Design and Development of Weapons. Studies in Government and Industrial Organization.* London: HMSO, 1964.

Pownall, Lieutenant General Sir Henry. *Chief of Staff: The Diaries of Lieut.-General Sir Henry Pownall.* 2 vols. London: Leo Cooper, 1974.

Preston, R. A., S. F. Wise, and H. O. Werner. *Men in Arms: A History of Warfare and Its Interrelationships with Western Society.* London: Thames and Hudson, 1962.

Reitlinger, Gerald. *The SS: Alibi of a Nation, 1922–1945.* London: Heinemann, 1956.

Renz, Otto Wilhelm von. *Deutsche Flug-Abwehr: im 20. Jahrhundert.* Frankfurt am Main: Verlag Mittler und Sohn, 1960.

Richards, Denis, and Hilary Aidan St George Saunders. *Royal Air Force 1939–1945*, vol. I, *The Fight at Odds*, by Denis Richards. London: HMSO, 1953–4.

Richardson, William, and Seymour Freiden, eds. *The Fatal Decisions.* Translated from the German by Constantine Fitzgibbon. London: Michael Joseph, 1956.

Rogers, Colonel H. C. B. *Tanks in Battle.* London: Sphere Books, 1972.

Roskill, Captain S. W. *The Navy at War 1939–1945.* London: Collins, 1960.

Scott, J. D. *Vickers: A History.* London: Weidenfeld & Nicolson, 1963.

Shaw, Lieutenant Colonel G. C. *Supply in Modern War.* London: Faber, 1938.

Shirer, William L. *The Rise and Fall of the Third Reich: A History of Nazi Germany.* London: Secker & Warburg, 1961.

————. *The Collapse of the Third Republic: An Inquiry into the Fall of France in 1940.* London: Heinemann, 1970.

Snyder, Louis L. *Encyclopedia of the Third Reich.* London: Hale, 1976.

Spears, Major General Sir Edward. *Assignment to Catastrophe.* 2 vols. London: Heinemann, 1954.

Spielberger, Walter J. *Panzerkampfwagen III* (AFV Weapons 2). *Panzer-kampfwagen IV* (AFV Weapons 43). *Schützenpanzerwagen SdKfz 241* (AFV Weapons 57). Windsor, Berks.: Profile Publications, 1970, 1972, and 1974.

———, and Uwe Feist. *Militärfahrzeuge.* Fallbrook, Calif.: Aero, 1970.

———, and Friedrich Weiner. *Die deutschen Panzerkampfwagen II und IV mit ihren Abarten 1935–1945.* Munich: J. F. Lehmanns Verlag, 1968.

Stein, George H. *The Waffen SS: Hitler's Elite Guard at War 1939–1945.* London: Oxford University Press, 1966.

Stembridge, Jasper H. *The Oxford War Atlas,* vol. I, *The First Two Years (Sept. 1939–Sept. 1941).* London: Oxford University Press, 1941.

Stoves, R. O. G. *1. Panzer Division 1935–1945: Chronik einer der drei Stamm-Divisionen der deutschen Panzerwaffe.* Bad Nauheim: Podzum Verlag, 1961.

Strawson, John. *Hitler as Military Commander.* London: Batsford, 1971.

Taylor, A. J. P. *The Origins of the Second World War.* London: Hamish Hamilton, 1961.

———. *English History 1914–1945.* London: Oxford University Press, 1965.

———. *The Second World War: An Illustrated History.* London: Hamish Hamilton, 1975.

Taylor, Telford. *The Sword and Swastika.* London: Gollancz, 1953.

———. *The March of Conquest.* London: Hulton, 1958.

———. *The Breaking Wave.* London: Weidenfeld & Nicolson, 1967.

Thompson, Lieutenant Colonel Paul W. *Modern Battle.* Washington, D.C.: Infantry Journal, Inc., 1941.

———. *Engineers in Battle.* Harrisburg, Pa.: Military Service Publishing, 1942.

Tissier, Lieutenant Colonel Pierre. *The Riom Trial.* London: Harrap, 1942.

Toland, John. *Adolf Hitler.* New York: Doubleday, 1976.

Trevor-Roper, H. R. *Hitler's War Directives: 1939–1945.* London: Sidgwick & Jackson, 1964.

Turner, Ernest S. *The Phoney War on the Home Front.* London: Michael Joseph, 1961.

Unser Kampf in Frankreich. Munich: Bruckmann Verlag, 1941.

War Department (U.S.). *Handbook on German Military Forces* (Technical Manual TM-E 30-450). Washington, D.C.: Govt. Printing Office, 1942.

War Office (G. B.). *The German Forces in the Field.* London: HMSO, 1940.

———. *Periodical Notes on the German Army* (irregular). London: HMSO, 1942-5.

Wavell, General Sir Archibald. *Generals and Generalship.* The Lees Knowles Lecture for 1939. London: Times Publishing, 1941.

Webster, Sir Charles, and Noble Frankland. *The Strategic Air Offensive Against Germany,* vol. I, *Preparation Sept. 1939–January 1943.* London: HMSO, 1961.

Weller, J. A. C. *Weapons and Tactics: Hastings to Berlin.* London: Nicholas Vane, 1966.

Westphal, General Siegfried. *The German Army in the West.* London: Cassell, 1951.

Weygand, General L. M. *L'Histoire de l'armée française*. Paris: Flammarion, 1953.

Wheeler-Bennett, J. W. *The Nemesis of Power: The German Army in Politics 1918–1945*. London: Macmillan, 1967.

Wheldon, John. *Machine Age Armies*. London: Abelard-Schulman, 1968.

Who's Who in Nazi Germany. 3rd ed. War Office: restricted, 1942.

Williams, John. *The Ides of May: The Defeat of France, May–June 1940*. London: Constable, 1968.

Wintringham, Tom. *Weapons and Tactics*. London: Faber, 1943.

Ziemke, Earl F. *The German Northern Theatre of Operations*. (Dept. of the Army Pamphlet 20-271). Washington, D.C.: Govt. Printing Office, 1959.

Index

The text of this book was set on the linotype in a face called Times Roman, designed by Stanley Morison for *The Times* (London) and first introduced by that newspaper in 1932.

Among typographers and designers of the twentieth century, Stanley Morison has been a strong forming influence, as typographical advisor to the English Monotype Corporation, as a director of two distinguished English publishing houses, and as a writer of sensibility, erudition, and keen practical sense.

Composed by Maryland Lintotype Composition Company, Inc., Baltimore, Maryland.
Maps by Jean Paul Tremblay

Typography and binding based on designs by Camilla Filancia